"In this book you will discover wonderful things about your sisters, past and present. You will learn beautiful things about yourself and others. Now read on, relax, and enjoy the journey!"

—Gail M. Hayes, PhD

Do you . . .

Wear your hair:
    a. demurely?
    b. flowing?
    c. elaborately?

Perhaps you are strong like Hannah, loving like Esther, or sensuous like Abishag.

Have a working style that is:
    a. organized?
    b. independent?
    c. structured?

Perhaps you are capable like Naomi, compassionate like Phoebe, or dedicated like Hulda.

Prefer a home that is:
    a. elegant?
    b. cozy?
    c. traditional?

Perhaps you are dedicated like Priscilla, steadfast like Miriam, or generous like Dorcas.

"At the heart of Gail Hayes's message is a passionate desire to end the divisions and judgments that keep women apart. What drives her is a clarion call to unity for all women regardless of their ethnicity, color, or style. It is a timely message that flows from the sincere heart of a Daughter of the King."

—Sharon Ewell Foster, author of *Passing by Samaria*
and *Ain't No Mountain*

"This is simply a great book!"

—Glenn R. Plummer, chairman of the
National Religious Broadcasters

Daughters
of the King

FINDING VICTORY
THROUGH YOUR
GOD-GIVEN PERSONAL STYLE

GAIL M. HAYES, PhD

West Bloomfield, Michigan

WARNER BOOKS

NEW YORK   BOSTON

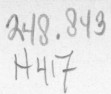
All scripture taken from *The Open Bible,* Expanded Edition, New King James Version. Copright © 1983 by Thomas Nelson Publishers.

Published by Warner Books with Walk Worthy Press™

Warner Books
Time Warner Book Group
1271 Avenue of the Americas
New York, NY 10020

Walk Worthy Press
33290 West Fourteen Mile Road, #482
West Bloomfield, MI 48322

Visit our Web sites at www.twbookmark.com and www.walkworthypress.net.

Printed in the United States of America

First Edition: May 2005
10 9 8 7 6 5 4 3

Library of Congress Cataloging-in-Publication Data
Hayes, Gail M.
  Daughters of the King : finding victory in your God-given personal style / Gail M. Hayes.
    p. cm.
  Includes bibliographical references.
  ISBN 0-446-69464-9
  1. African American women—Religious life. 2. Christian women—Religious life—United States. 3. Typology (Psychology)—Religious aspects—Christianity. I. Title.
  BR563.N4.H379 2005
  248.8'43'08996073—dc22

                                                          2004019670

Book design and text composition by Stratford Publishing Services
Cover illustration: Hierography Productions

To my Lord and Savior Jesus Christ, who sent to us His precious Holy Spirit to serve as a Comforter and Confirmer of His will. Because of His love and the work done on Calvary's cross, I know that I truly am a Daughter of the King.

To Gabrielle Christina, who shows me daily the true beauty and power of the Daughters of the King message.

And to R. Douglas Hayes Jr., my precious husband, who advised me to write the message of Daughters of the King. With him, I dared to take risks that I had, until this time, only dreamed of. He is my friend and the father of my two precious children. Without him, this book would have been words lost in the air.

Contents

Daughters
of the King

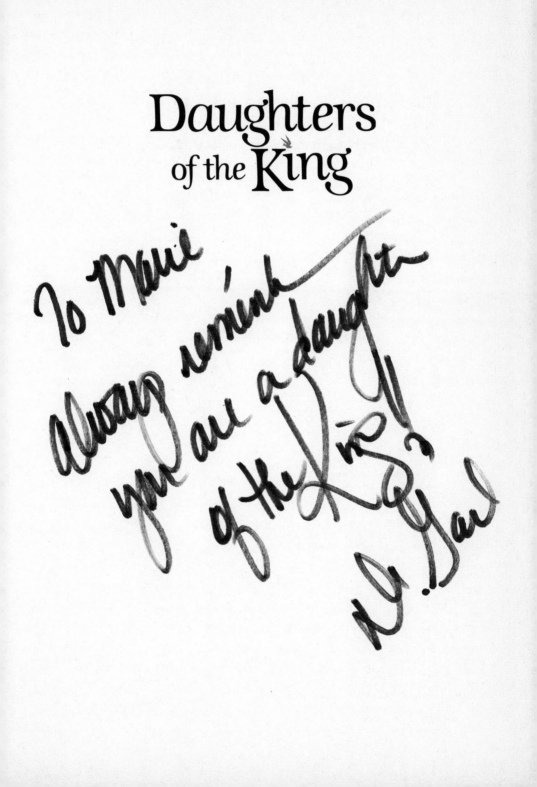

To Marie
always remind
you are a daughter
of the King!

The royal daughter is all glorious within the palace.
Her clothing is woven with gold.
She shall be brought to the King in robes of many colors.

PSALMS 45:13–14

1. Discovering Your Image Type

A man's [woman's] heart plans his [her] way, but the Lord directs his [her] steps.

PROVERBS 16:9

*D*o you remember the first time you noticed that you had a unique sense of style? If you stop and think, it surfaced when you were just a child. Your sense of style comes with the package that is you. It is not only the way you dress, but also your way of doing things. It is your very essence. The Lord placed this sense of style in your spirit during the creation process.

Things as simple as the way you hold your fork, and as complex as the way you process information, are all facets of your sense of style. If you have children, you may have already noticed that they like certain clothing styles and have developed their own unique way of doing things. Their choices may be very different from yours. Even before they could speak, they let you know what they liked and who they were. As they matured, they became vocal about their preferences.

When I was a child, my mother dressed me in lace and ruffles. She put large, matching, satin ribbons on my hair and made me wear crinoline slips. At the time, I felt simply beautiful. Sometime later, around the age of nine, things changed. I developed my own sense of style. Mom and I then reached a point where we did not always agree on the size and color of those hair bows. I also realized that crinoline slips were hot and scratchy. This tug-of-war revealed that our style preferences were similar, but a difference was becoming obvious.

The difference was our image types. My mother preferred wispy fabrics with lace and ruffles. To me, they felt uncomfortable, cumbersome, and fluffy. I wanted straight lines with dashes of high drama. Those dashes of high drama started one of the age-old struggles between mother and daughter—my tastes over Mom's authority and pocketbook. Mom was almost a nervous wreck by the time I got through puberty. I remember getting off the school bus with my satin bows hanging down around my neck. During war games with the boys, I tore the delicate lace trim on my dress to "smithereens" (one of Mom's favorite sayings when it came to my lace dresses and me).

This struggle with my mother over image was a critical part of my journey to wholeness. Even as a child, I knew there was something missing. I needed something different from the lace and ruffles. I needed something more like me. I needed something elegant and flamboyant. Why did I feel so out of place in all those wisps of femininity? I decided to search for the answers.

For many years, I studied the differences in personal clothing choices. I discovered that women with distinctive personality traits preferred certain clothing lines. The styling or cut of a particular clothing line spoke their language. I also noticed that the main theme of the clothing choices did not change, even after they became Christians. Of course, in many cases, the women lowered hemlines and eliminated tightness, but the main theme of the clothing did not change. My studies culminated with the creation of the Image Indicator.

On the following pages, you will take the Image Indicator, an image inventory that gives information on six image types. When you've completed the Image Indicator and discovered your image type, you begin a fascinating journey toward identity, purpose, and destiny.

The Father created you for a wondrous purpose and a divine destiny as a daughter of the King. He created you with a specific image type with a specific purpose that only you can fulfill. Isn't that good to know that you are just that special to our heavenly Father?

Before you go any farther, I need a promise. I need for you to promise that you will allow the Lord to minister to you through this process. Promise that you will answer the questions honestly and from your heart. Your first answer will always be correct. No one has to see your answers. They are between you and the Lord. If anyone else sees them, it will be because you choose to share them.

While writing this book and speaking about image, the Lord did a great healing in my life. He taught me to accept myself just the way He created me. I learned to accept every bump, lump, hair, and inch. He created me as an intricate unity, and that excited me. After this acceptance, the Lord instructed me to share the information with you.

I often wondered why the Lord has so many names. A few examples of His names are Jehovah Jireh, my Provider; Jehovah Rapha, my Healer; Jehovah Shalom, my Peace; and Jehovah Nissi, my Banner. I asked the Lord for an answer regarding these labels. He told me that the labels were not for Him. He does not need anyone to remind Him who He is. He already knows His power, strength, and awesome majesty.

He does not operate with an identity crisis. He already knows who He is, even without us using those beautiful names. He created the names for us, His beautiful, finite creations. This is the reason the Image Indicator is so important. In this book, the Lord provides beautiful labels for His daughters to wear with honor.

I thank God daily for His sacrifice at Calvary. Without that precious sacrifice, I would not have received this message and learned just how much He loves me. The Father is so good and wise. His system works miracles of healing and brings wholeness to our lives.

Through the Image Indicator, He helped me gain a greater appreciation, understanding, and acceptance of other women. He now wants to do the same for you.

So sit back, relax, and work your way through the Image Indicator. Remember, this is a gift from our Lord, to you, His daughter.

THE IMAGE INDICATOR

Please record your answers in the spaces provided on page 10.

1. Which of the following words best describe your wardrobe choices?
   A. Comfortable and easy-care.
   B. Tailored and classic.
   C. Dramatic and stylish.
   D. Original and all yours.
   E. Flowing and feminine.
   F. Glittering and glamorous.

2. Which of the following best describes your work style statement?
   A. I want everyone to help get the job done . . . yesterday.
   B. I want everyone to plan their work and work my plan.
   C. I want to know who is in charge and who has the resources I need for my project.
   D. I want harmony and no arguing when I work, so that my creativity flows.
   E. I want everyone to be happy with each other and with their work.
   F. I want everyone to be comfortable while they work.

3. Which of the following best describes the hairstyle that most suits you?
   A. Carefree—wash-and-go or low-maintenance hair.
   B. The perfect cut with every hair in place.
   C. Elegant and sculptured.
   D. Lots and lots of curls, crimps, or braids.
   E. Long and flowing.
   F. Full and layered.

4. Without thinking about your figure, which of the following outfits best speaks your language?
   A. A sweater and jeans or sweatpants and a comfortable, unstructured top.
   B. A lined wool or silk suit with an elegant silk blouse and pearls or a gold signature chain.
   C. A tailored pant- or skirt suit with a dramatic shoulder-draped shawl, and an oversized brooch holding it in place.
   D. Pants with a vest and matching oversized jacket.
   E. A soft and flowing off-the-shoulder lace dress.
   F. A belted off-the-shoulder sweater and a leather skirt with a side-seam zipper.

5. Which of the following would you wear to a sporting event?
   A. Jeans with a cotton shirt, or sweats.
   B. Slacks with a matching jacket and a classic blouse or shirt.
   C. A studded or beaded denim outfit with matching shoes and hat.
   D. Knit pants and an oversized shirt and sweater.
   E. A cotton lace T-shirt and pearl button sweater with a skirt or jeans.
   F. An athletic suit with jewels and studs and a matching headband.

6. The perfect makeover for you would be:
   A. Au naturel—no makeup.
   B. Harmonically perfect.
   C. Deep, rich, and vibrant.
   D. Depends on my mood.
   E. Soft and natural.
   F. Electrifying and glamorous.

7. If you attended an evening event, what outfit would you choose to let everyone know you had arrived?
   A. An unstructured evening pant- or skirt suit with a silk T-top.
   B. The classic black dress with pearls or diamonds.
   C. A purple silk pantsuit with a dramatic beaded coat.
   D. A one-of-a-kind original creation of my own.
   E. A Victorian lace dream.
   F. A red sequined stunner with a side split.

8. Not thinking about money, which of the following would be known as your signature piece(s)?
   A. A simple gold chain with a small pendant or diamond dot earrings.
   B. A Rolex or Gucci watch or a string of hand-knotted pearls.
   C. A large hammered-gold or -silver bangle watch with large matching earrings.
   D. A pair of handcrafted earrings or a string of hand-strung semiprecious beads.
   E. An antique cameo brooch with matching earrings.
   F. An eighteen-karat-gold anklet, or gold and silver rings for all my fingers.

9. Which of the following best describes your perfect manicure?
   A. Short, clean, and clear.
   B. Perfect, natural-length and neutrally colored.
   C. Medium long and vibrantly colored.
   D. Whatever strikes my mood.
   E. Natural-length with soft, transparent color.
   F. Glamour-length with electrifying color and nail designs.

10. Not thinking about your figure, which clothing shapes or styles attract you the most?
A. Unstructured with natural fibers.
B. Tailored to fit me perfectly.
C. Straight lines with a dashes of high drama.
D. One-of-a-kind, layered originals.
E. Light and airy with lace and ruffles.
F. Body hugging and feminine.

11. Assuming your feet and lifestyle could stand it, what shoes would you wear over and over again?
A. Low-heeled casual or athletic shoes.
B. Medium-heeled designer pumps.
C. Suede and leather, jeweled, or studded pumps to match all my outfits.
D. Boots, boots, and more boots.
E. Medium-heeled sandals.
F. Stiletto heels with sparkling ankle straps.

12. Without thinking about what others have said, what words would you consider a compliment—and one that best describes the real you?
A. Down-to-earth and comfortable to be with.
B. Classic and orderly.
C. Sophisticated and stylish.
D. Artistic and creative.
E. Soft and feminine.
F. Sensual and exciting.

THE IMAGE INDICATOR ANSWER SHEET

1. _____   7. _____

2. _____   6. _____

3. _____   9. _____

4. _____   10. _____

5. _____   11. _____

6. _____   12. _____

Total A's _____   Total D's _____

Total B's _____   Total E's _____

Total C's _____   Total F's _____

Now go the next page to interpret the results of the inventory.

If you scored more A's, your image type is:

Jaunty Esprit

If you scored more B's, your image type is:

Harmonic Refined

If you scored more C's, your image type is:

Elegant Flamboyant

If you scored more D's, your image type is:

Creative Poetic

If you scored more E's, your image type is:

Chantilly Graceful

If you scored more F's, your image type is:

Sensual Exotic

If your score is evenly distributed among several letters—for example, three B's, four D's, and three C's—use the Rule of Combinations to determine your image type. If you are a combination of the three types, you will switch from one to the other depending on your mood or the occasion. Your dominant type may be Creative Poetic, for example, but you love clothing with the classic lines of the Harmonic Refined, and add Elegant Flamboyant accessories to achieve your look. With Creative Poetic creativity, you skillfully combine facets from the three image types to attain the look you want. This mixture of styles is what I call the Rule of Combinations.

Do not be alarmed if you discover that you have traits from several of the image types. This is the beauty of the Lord's system. It works equally well for those of us who fit into a distinctive type and for those of us who are more diverse. It simply means that you have traits from several of the types, but you need to look again at your answers to find your dominant type. You may also need to re-take the Indicator.

After presenting the Image Indicator to thousands of women over the last several years, I have discovered every woman has traits from all the image types, but each woman still has a domi-nant type. If your scores are distributed equally or there does not appear to be a dominant type, please go back and reread the ques-tions. In answering the questions, please remember, there is al-ways a first choice.

Here are a few pointers to consider when taking the Image In-dicator. If the Indicator does not mention your favorite piece of jewelry, what piece mentioned most closely resembles your fa-vorite? If the Indicator does not mention your ideal outfit, what outfit mentioned is most like you? Choose what comes closest to what you like. The answers do not have to match exactly.

For example, if comfort is your main goal in dressing, but the only choice on the Indicator is pants—and you never wear them, even for evening wear—your choice would still be A. Look at the goal of the question. All answers should match your heart choices, not your head choice or what others have told you. Just choose items that are as close to your true choices as possible.

If your results on the Indicator are unclear, or don't feel right to you, you can take the Indicator again—this time answering with your heart. Forget that your figure is less than what the world calls perfect. Forget that you may have gained a few pounds, or that your hair may not be the length or thickness you feel it should be. Put everything on cruise control. Put everything in the hands of the Holy Spirit. Remember, you are a lovely creation, and there is not another person on earth, or even in the universe, exactly like you. You are the Lord's original work of art, and He does not make any mistakes. If your answers are the same, then again, use the Rule of Combinations.

In the pages of this book, you will discover wonderful things about yourself and your sisters, both past and present. You will discover beautiful things about yourself and others. The Lord, in His infinite wisdom, knew when He created us that we would live in a world of visual people who would place great value on physical appearance. He also knew that when He created the human race, His enemy would try to pervert His precious first gift to us. He knew before we were born that there would be times when we would minimize His first gift. His first gift to the human race was that He loved us so much that He created us to look like Him. He created us in His beautiful image.

By truly accepting and believing that God created you in His image, you overcome the oppression of living with a negative self-image. You leave the enemy powerless. With God's Holy Word as the road map, and His Holy Spirit as the Guide, you can and will overcome any obstacle, including a negative self-image. Now read on, relax, and enjoy your journey!

> *S*o God created man [woman] in His own image; in the image of God He created him [her]; male and female He created them.
>
> GENESIS 1:27

2. Jaunty Esprit

Lively, sporty,
Casual and free;
You see the joy of the Lord
In Jaunty Esprit!

Do not sorrow, for the joy of the Lord is your strength.
—NEHEMIAH 8:10

The Beauty of Jaunty Esprit

Do you consider yourself down-to-earth and casual? Do you love the feel of your jeans, sweats, and comfortable clothing? Do you wear your hair in a carefree style that does not take a great deal of fuss or bother? If you wear it long, do you pull it back in a ponytail to hold it in place? Are almost all your shoes low-heeled or flats? In choosing clothes, do frills and details take a backseat to comfort and casualness? If you answered yes, then you are the Jaunty Esprit image type.

Webster's Dictionary defines *jaunty* as nonchalant or relaxed, and without a great deal of fuss. It also means sprightly—lively in manner or appearance. *Esprit* refers to cleverness and freedom of mind and spirit. What a beautiful word combination to describe you and your image type! You are a no-nonsense person who wants to feel uninhibited in your lifestyle and appearance. You refuse to accept anything less. Your Jaunty Esprit spirit perpetually screams for the fresh air of freedom.

The Inner You

Jaunty Esprit is a peacemaker and defender of justice. You hate to see injustice and quickly speak up to defend others. Nevertheless, it is hard for you to admit when you are wrong. When you find out or suspect that something you said or did hurt someone, you sometimes avoid the situation altogether. When this happens, everything in your life becomes unbalanced.

Go to the Lord and ask Him to reignite and redirect that Jaunty Esprit energy. Make the situation and the offended person your target. Do not give the enemy an opening. With the help of the Holy Spirit, go to whomever you've hurt and straighten things out. Once this is done, your life will be back in balance and ready for another Jaunty Esprit project.

You always support your chosen causes and beliefs and stand your ground. Once committed, there is no turning back. Whether it is finding a precedent for a court case or drafting a proposal for the new city youth center, you see it through to the end. You organize letter-writing campaigns to city hall about the homeless. You donate food and clothing to the local women's shelter. If a shelter does not exist, you organize a committee to start one. You are the one who takes off your new winter coat and places it around the shoulders of a homeless woman standing on the corner on a frosty morning. The Lord placed a special fire in your heart for the poor and suffering. You do not just talk the talk, but you also walk the walk and freely give of your comforts to help others. Like your biblical sister Abigail, you are quick to right an injustice.

Abigail

THE HONORABLE AND WISE JAUNTY ESPRIT

> The name of the man was Nabal, and the name of his wife Abigail. And she was a woman of good understanding and beautiful appearance.
>
> I SAMUEL 25:3

As David's men approached the large house, they smelled the meat roasting, and their salivary glands worked overtime. The smell was intoxicating. It had been days since they had eaten. Their pace quickened as the aroma grew stronger.

Entering the courtyard, they saw servants carrying platters piled high with roasted meats and large bowls of vegetables. The mountains of fig cakes and clusters of raisins nearly caused them to collapse. They fought the desire to bury themselves in the roasted grain. These were mighty men of valor, and they had to remain strong. They were on a mission to bring food to their comrades in arms. David had sent these men to ask for food. His request was not extravagant. He and his men had saved the shepherds of this house from danger many times while they watched their flocks. Since they were together in the wilderness (I Samuel 25:7), we can imagine that Nabal's shepherds had told David of the upcoming shearing feast planned by their master's household.

But Nabal scoffed at their request and sent them away empty-handed. When the men reported back without food, David became angry and started out for the home of Nabal. In I Samuel 25:13, he instructed each of his men to gird on his sword. He was determined to kill every man in sight. Nabal, because of his crude manners and drunkenness, had endangered the lives of his servants and family when he refused to give food to these hungry warriors.

It was going to take a miracle to save his household from destruction. It was going to take someone with wisdom, insight, and humility. There was only one person in Nabal's home who possessed these God-given qualities. There was only one person in Nabal's household who could stop certain destruction. The name of this miracle was Abigail.

In I Samuel 25:3, the Bible tells us that Abigail was a physically beautiful and wise woman. Your Jaunty Esprit sister is known as one of the earliest peacemakers. Her actions throughout this chapter of the Bible reinforce her biblical description. Her husband, Nabal, was a prosperous man. He owned many flocks and lands. The Bible tells us that Nabal was "harsh" and evil in his doings, and he drank so heavily that it affected his judgment.

On feasting day, we can imagine Abigail dressed in fine purple linen with a matching headdress and sash. Her headdress gently draped around her shoulders and encircled her waist. She wore leather sandals, golden earrings, bracelets, and a thin neck-lace, given to her by her husband as a birthday present. She was the perfect image of the mistress of a wealthy household. We can also imagine that she was a gracious hostess, taking care of the needs of her many guests with Jaunty Esprit style.

After overhearing the confrontation between his master and David's men, one of the servants went to Abigail and told her of Nabal's behavior. He also described how David and his men had been like a wall to them (verse 16) in the wilderness. The Bible tells us that Abigail, in her wisdom, made haste and prepared sup-plies for David and his men. She did not tell her husband. Be-cause of her God-given wisdom, Abigail knew Nabal was drunk with wine and had not used good judgment. She also knew David would be angry—and rightly so, since he and his men had been kind to the house of Nabal previously. As mistress of the house, Abigail felt it was her duty to protect her household, including her foolish and evil husband, from certain destruction.

Loaded with provisions, Abigail met David on the road to her home. Being led by the Holy Spirit, she humbled herself and fell on her face before him. She then asked him to forgive the house of Nabal. In verses 24–31, she further honored David by confirm-ing the word of the Lord that he was the future leader of Israel. We can imagine it was at this moment that David not only saw Abigail's outer beauty, but also discovered her inner strength and wisdom. Her brave actions kept him from shedding innocent blood and from avenging himself by violence. Her influence helped David to remember God's promises for his future.

The Bible says that when Abigail returned, Nabal was still feasting and was drunk. She did not tell him what had happened with David until morning. After learning how his attitude and words had nearly cost him his life, Nabal's heart died within him, and he became like a stone. After ten days, he died. When David heard of his death, he praised the Lord for taking vengeance for him. In the midst of his praising, David also remembered the beautiful and wise Abigail. He sent her a proposal of marriage, and she graciously accepted to become the wife of the future king.

The Lord knew David needed a wife who was modest, sober-minded, gracious, strong, and wise. She displayed this strength and wisdom when she saved her household from David's wrath. Her new husband had faith in her wise counsel. When he chose Abigail as his wife, it signaled the beginning of change for David, for his life did indeed change dramatically after their first meeting.

Her Jaunty Esprit spirit was a beautiful beacon of light. She humbled herself before a man who constantly sought to please the Lord and touch His heart. David had the heart of a shepherd and knew that his Shepherd had guided his path in meeting Abigail. Her light—and yours, her Jaunty Esprit sister—was, is, and always shall be the Lord your Shepherd, Jehovah Raah!

> She extends her hand to the poor, yes she reaches out her hand to the needy.
>
> PROVERBS 31:20

Because Jaunty Esprit is so energetic, you can easily become overextended. When this happens, other areas of your life suffer. Make sure the Lord approves each activity. After praying, discuss the activities with your family. They are the ones most directly affected by your flurries.

The Lord uses your family as confirming witnesses. Encourage them to speak freely when they feel neglected. The Holy Spirit will let you know by gently tugging at your heart. Listen to His voice and the voices of those who love you, in that order.

Before you became a Christian, you did some investigative work. You closely observed other Christians and their lifestyles. You were serious about all commitments and checked out all aspects of them. Once committed, you were sold out to your chosen cause. The Lord, being faithful and knowing your curious spirit, allowed you to be around those best able to minister to your spiritual needs. He wanted you sold out for Him. As a Jaunty Esprit, you would not have it any other way.

The Lord is so faithful and awesome that He knew exactly the perfect time, place, and person to send your way. He drew you to Him and made you His own. Because of your experience, you have no problem going an extra mile to witness or minister to someone. You allow the Lord to use you to draw others like you to Him. Your witness for Him is urgent yet gentle. You want others to know Him and experience His love. As a Jaunty Esprit, you know that the joy of the Lord is your strength, and you share that joy with everyone you meet!

Because you are committed, you do not compromise when it comes to spiritual things. There is no such thing as a "little lie" in your book. Either you do or you don't; you will or you won't. Everything is black or white. You are in sin or you are not. Jesus did not shed His precious blood out of compromise. He went the distance for you.

After you tell others about His love, you are also quick to point out the alternative if they choose not to accept His perfect sacrifice. Letting others know that they have a choice about where they will spend eternity suits you just fine. You believe the Lord wants you to truthfully explain His perfect plan.

Jaunty Esprit Strengths in the Body of Christ

Hospitality Chair
Outreach Coordinator
Bible Study Leader

Jaunty Esprit and Family Life

You shine at home social events. People talk about your parties for years after they happen because you give your all to make your guests feel special. You love themes and work extra hard to ensure that all details fall into place. A Western barbecue complete with cowboy hats for each guest is your idea of the perfect party. After all, how can you have a theme party without the props? You are only too happy to provide these props because you want everything done in perfect Jaunty Esprit style.

Each guest feels like the guest of honor in your home. Your lively spirit permeates every detail. The Lord blessed you, and you freely share His goodness with others through one of your strongest gifts—the gift of hospitality.

> Do not forget to entertain strangers, for by doing so some have unwittingly entertained angels.
>
> HEBREWS 13:2

Bringing out the best in your children is challenging, but you are up to the task. Children of the Jaunty Esprit receive the best of your world. To encourage them to explore their creative talents, you help them finger-paint a wondrous picture or put together their favorite puzzle. These activities help them flex their artistic muscles and inquisitive minds. If the day's activity is painting, you have a special roll of paper and a set of paints labeled and set aside.

They know to go to the activity closet and get ready for a wonderful afternoon. If puzzles are the theme, then on the puzzle shelf they are sure to find a brand-new puzzle that Mom picked up on one of her outings. You are always prepared for the unexpected and keep their activity closet full of surprises.

You do not mind your children getting things dirty while learning. Part of the experience is cleaning up after a fun session. You can make even cleaning a part of the learning process and an enjoyable and challenging event. You let them see that responsibilities come with fun activities. By showing them how to take care of small things, all activities become fun. With you guiding them, your children learn the balance of responsibility and fun all in the same activity!

All their recreational activities must meet with your complete approval. If you have the least bit of doubt about something, then it is put on hold until you seek the Lord and consult your spouse. All movies, books, and games have to meet your high standards. You are responsible for these precious souls, and their natural and spiritual welfare is critical. You do not hesitate to throw out things that you feel are inappropriate. Their rooms are cleaned out regularly so that the enemy will not find openings into your home.

You discuss your decisions and actions with your little ones and let them know your position. These discussions are essential to family harmony, because your children openly share their views with you. After things settle down, it may take a while for them to understand your decision. One thing is always clear: Their welfare is your top priority. The Lord established the home as a safe haven, and Mother Jaunty Esprit always seeks the Lord in protecting her children.

Schoolwork takes priority over creative activities. Academic achievement is important in your household because you believe it helps shape a successful future. If you have a child who needs extra help, you get a tutor to help with school assignments. When they do their best, you are satisfied. Even if the grades are not all A's and B's, you want them to pass. With your support, they will not fail. You encourage them to always do their best. If they have done their best, then C's are just fine. Being the smart mother you are, you always know when they are putting forth their best effort.
– You are not easily fooled, and your little ones know it. They

know to ask for help and not be ashamed for asking. You pray against oppression and pride in your children. They follow your example when they daily hear you ask your heavenly Father for help. Your humility is an example of a godly mother who loves her children. You want them to know that they can come to you for anything. Your relationship with them is a mirror reflection of your relationship with the Lord.

While helping them get ready for bed, you teach them to pray. You encourage them to talk to the Lord using their own words, knowing He understands all. There are many times when you turn your head to keep from smiling as they express their feelings in prayer. The things they ask of Him are sometimes humorous, yet so real and honest. Listening carefully, you hear requests and thanks most adult minds and hearts only think about expressing. In the innocence of their youth, your children openly and unashamedly talk to the Lord from their hearts. Nothing is too small or seems too unimportant to mention. They never forget to mention the one who taught them to pray, their prayerful Jaunty Esprit mother.

There are times when tears well up in your eyes as you hear their words of praise and thanks. You wonder if the Lord does the same when you pray, as you can only imagine how He sees you. Listening to your children pray is one of your life's most precious moments. These are moments you will not soon forget. As you watch and listen to them grow in the Lord, you know they are forming a solid foundation that they will use and appreciate in times to come.

At dinnertime, you allow your little ones to serve as your special kitchen helpers, getting them to set the table or serve the drinks. They each get the opportunity to prepare their favorite meal for the family and clean up after the fun event. You prepare them for the experience by explaining that each member of the family will have a turn as the on-duty cook for an evening meal, and you encourage them to enjoy the experience of trying new and different foods—even if some of them may be unrecognizable.

These times are great fun, and each one of your young ones learns a tremendous amount about him- or herself during the process. As you watch this youthful metamorphosis, your heart swells with maternal love.

Each cooking night teaches them to be more accepting of others and their differences. They also learn whether they like cooking and working in the kitchen. One important lesson they learn is not to take Mom for granted. That is one lesson you like teaching. You also prepare your sons to work in the home. It is your prayer that they will marry and respect their future mate. For the Jaunty Esprit, marriage and home management are fifty–fifty arrangements. You feel your children should know they are contributing members of the family and are responsible for all that goes on in the home, including housework.

You promote family spiritual time. Bible study and family fellowship are important events in your household. You feel these sessions are the glue that holds your family together. You encourage your children to bring spiritual questions to this forum. It is your heart's desire that they feel they can come to you with anything; like your biblical sister Deborah, you are fair and honest in your judgment. During these times, you also express your faith openly and honestly to show them that it is more than just okay to worship and praise the Lord in all that you do and say. You allow them to see your faith in action by teaching them to pray and to rely on the Lord for all things, great and small. These times are one of many jewels in the Jaunty Esprit household treasure chest.

> We will not hide them from their children, telling to the generation to come the praises of the Lord, and His strength and His wonderful works that He has done.
>
> PSALMS 78:4

Deborah

THE JUDGE

Now Deborah, a prophetess, the wife of Lapidoth, was judging Israel at that time. And she sat under the palm tree of Deborah between Ramah and Bethel in the mountains of Ephraim. And the children of Israel came up to her for judgment.

JUDGES 4:4

A woman made her way through the streets to the market, looking for the oil merchant. The heavy oil jar seemed light on her shoulders as she burned with anger. She could not forget last night. The merchant had promised her that his products were fresh and of the highest quality, but as soon as she had begun to dip into the jar, she'd known something was wrong. She'd been forced to borrow oil from her curious next-door neighbor and knew that she would never hear the last of it.

As she rounded the corner, she could hear the familiar voice. Yes, he was still selling his spoiled wares! A surge of strength pulsed through her as she made her way through the crowd. The large oil jar parted the crowd like the Red Sea before her.

As his eyes met the woman's, the merchant quickly looked away and engaged himself with another customer. She set down the jar and took off its cover. The foul smell filled the air. Prospective customers scattered like frightened mice. The merchant insisted that he'd sold her good oil, and that she must be trying to return the wrong jar. He refused to give her new oil or a refund. He dismissed her as if she were a fly that disturbed his meal.

She was not a rich woman who could make demands with authority. Since her husband was working in another town, she had no choice but to appeal to someone who would hear a woman's story. As she and her oil jar left the marketplace, the merchant smiled a smile of victory.

Walking through the streets, tears wet the front of her dress. Anger became her friend, and disgust guided her footsteps. She only wanted to take care of her family. She had purchased the oil in good faith and wanted what was rightfully hers. She knew tears would not help her. She stopped and set the jar down, wiped her face, and cleared her throat.

There was only one person who would understand her plight. She would take it to the highest authority in the land. She would take it to Israel's judge. She would state her case before another woman and sister. She would speak to Deborah, judge over Israel.

Deborah sat erect under her tree, named the Palm of Deborah, where she passed judgments, gave counsel, and told stories of days gone by and things to come. This great woman held a place of honor in the nation of Israel. Surrounded by young people who were caught up in the spirit of the moment, she told of God's awesome goodness and power. She told of how He delivered and saved His children and performed mighty miracles for His chosen ones. This was her witness for God, and she knew that with her position came great responsibility. She had the responsibility to give glory to the Lord and tell of His goodness and mercy.

As the people stood before her, each telling their story, she quietly listened. She heard each side fully before passing judgment. Nothing distracted her as she took in all the words, actions, and emotions of the case set before her. Her position was a gift from the Lord, and she treated it with honor. She was the first and only woman to hold such a position. Anointed and appointed by the highest Authority in the land, she judged Israel. No one dared question or rebuke her. Her appointment was from the Lord God of Hosts. Deborah committed all matters to prayer and waited on guidance from the Holy Spirit. This Jaunty Esprit of wisdom humbly sought His will before making decisions. She was wise enough to know that the Judge of all judges would aid her in leading His people.

After hearing the woman's story, Deborah instructed the merchant to restore her money and to give her two jars of oil for her trouble. Everyone knew that her decision was just. The woman thanked her and went on her way, knowing that the Lord had heard her petition.

We can imagine that Deborah was a woman of medium stature. She wore her dark brown hair pulled back with a comb. A soft coral-colored headdress covered her head to protect her from the sun. It beautifully matched her ankle-length dress. Leather sandals adorned her feet. Around her waist was a sash of braided linen. Her shining eyes resembled jewels that burned with the intensity of the sun. Her flawless olive skin blended with the deep green of the surrounding trees. She was natural Jaunty Esprit beauty at its best.

Deborah was an extremely busy woman and did not have an abundance of time to spend on her appearance. The two C's, Casualness and Comfort, had to be her beauty routine. Being casual and comfortable, Deborah was ready to judge, give counsel, and even go to war with the children of Israel. She did not worry about her nails being broken or having every hair in place. Just like you, her present-day Jaunty Esprit sister, her main concern was doing the will of the Lord.

We can imagine that as a judge, she walked with her head held high—and yet had a kind word for all. For the authority she held was a gift from the Lord of Hosts. She exercised this authority with wisdom, not ever wanting to abuse it. Her Jaunty Esprit spirit was a shining light of inspiration to all who saw her.

Deborah is remembered not only for being the first woman to sit in judgment over Israel, but for leading Israel in war as well. The people were afraid to go and fight against the enemy's nine hundred chariots of iron because at the time, Israel did not have a single chariot. Deborah was angry that her people were oppressed and knew that Jehovah Nissi, the Lord our Banner, would deliver them if they would honor Him and truly look upon Him as their leader.

She boldly sent for Barak, one of Israel's great military leaders, and helped him devise a war plan to defeat the enemy. She convinced Barak that the Lord would give Israel victory over Sisera and his chariots, just as He had given Moses and Joshua their victories. She was an exhorter and a woman of action who knew that the Lord God would do battle for them. Barak, knowing Deborah and her spiritual insight, believed and told Deborah that he would go if she would accompany him and the army (Judges 4:8). This is one of the most unusual requests in the Bible, made by a man of a woman.

Barak humbled himself and honored not only Deborah but also God by wanting His messenger to go to war with him. It did not matter to him that the Lord used a woman to speak His will for Israel and the battle. The Holy Spirit used Deborah as a holy example to show that the Lord will use any willing vessel, male or female, to speak His word and do His will. The Song of Deborah (Judges 5:2–31) reveals Deborah's devotion to the Lord. It also shows that she knew He and He alone must be exalted. He delivered her people by fighting the battle for Israel.

Just like you, her present-day Jaunty Esprit sister, she had an urgent witness for the Lord to His people. Like Deborah, you, too, can be used for the Lord and His glory. Remember that you, like Deborah, are alive, free, and a beautiful Jaunty Esprit!

The Jaunty Esprit Spouse

The husband reaps the benefits of the loving spirit of the Jaunty Esprit spouse. You enjoy making him feel special. That expression of love takes on many forms, and you freely express it in your home. If the children catch a brief glimpse of affection, such as a kiss or a hug, you willingly explain. You want them to know that Mom and Dad love each other and express that love with kisses and hugs. To you, it is important for your children to know about the love of our heavenly Father as expressed through marital love. You feel that it's good for your children to see love expressed between their parents; it helps promote a healthy view of marriage. It is also your wish that they learn by your example as you learn from the loving example of the Lord.

You enjoy quiet times with your husband. He helps you relax. You are prone to allowing interruptions, such as the telephone or the doorbell, to cut into your time. He gently lets you know that during his times, you belong to him and he wants all your attention. If he does not get you to himself, he may become a little impatient, especially if he misses you and you have consistently put other things before him.

Remember, you are his earthly companion and he has a deep need to spend time with you. The Lord created this need even before Eve was given to Adam in the garden. In Genesis 2:18, the Lord Himself said that it was not good for man to be alone. Which clearly means that your husband needs companionship— the companionship of his wife. You are his mate, and he has a God-created need to spend time with his mate to renew his love and commitment. Set aside a special time for your husband, and your marriage will prosper.

> *A*nd the Lord God said, "It is not good that man should be alone; I will make him a helper comparable to him."
>
> GENESIS 2:18

So put away your committee project for just a few minutes. Forget the doorbell and put on the answering machine. Put the children to bed early or have them work on special projects in their rooms for the evening. Better yet, allow them to stay overnight with friends. Your children understand when you take time to explain. You let them know that Dad and Mom need special time together. It shows that you love their father, and it sets up a living example that they will carry with them to their own marital relationships. The Lord loves a woman who uses wisdom with her family, and for you, wisdom is the only way to operate.

You do not worry about your husband playfully running his fingers through your hair or having your lipstick smeared from one of his impromptu kisses. Just the thought of him doing this thrills you. It is wonderful to know your man finds you desirable; you would not have it any other way! While cooking dinner or while just sitting and watching television, there is never a wrong time for one of his special touches. He always feels free to give you one of his hugs or an affectionate touch, even during one of your marathon working sessions. This is one area where your appearance being secondary is a definite asset to marital harmony.

You wear your slightly tussled hair like a badge of honor and your smeared lipstick as a memorial of love. Every time you look in the mirror and see that misplaced lock of hair or smeared lipstick, you get goose bumps. To you, they are symbols of love freely given by the man you love. You always want him to know that pleasing him is one of your top priorities and will never be out of season. You pass your Jaunty Esprit love of freedom on to your mate in loving style. Being the smart woman you are, you know what you sow, you will definitely reap, especially in the marriage department. You fully intend to reap the love you sow a hundredfold!

*A*nd let us not grow weary while doing good, for in due season we shall reap if we do not lose heart.

GALATIANS 6:9

Jaunty Esprit Working Style

As a Jaunty Esprit, you are goal-oriented and love the feeling of accomplishment. You enjoy seeing a project through to completion. People like having you around because your high energy and enthusiasm are contagious and set the tone for a project. Your attitude on the job is, *Pull up your sleeves and let's get things done.*

Once assigned a project, you quickly organize people and develop schedules before anyone has the chance to speak or breathe. While these are great skills, you need to keep in mind that, when working with a committee, it is good to include others in the decision-making process. Others may believe you are trying to take over and run things. They can easily misinterpret that wonderful *get-the-job-done* Jaunty Esprit attitude.

You are organized and have a knack for motivating others. After harnessing all available resources, your Jaunty Esprit energy kicks in and you become a heat-seeking missile attacking a target. Others have difficulty understanding your ability to focus. They do not understand how you are able to mentally drown out all noise and interruptions when working. For you, focus is as automatic as breathing. Once you set your mind to accomplish something, everything else fades into the background.

The thrill of coming full circle is important to you. Once you find a group of committed people to work with on a project, you stay until it's completed. During these times, you always find new friends. Your keen eyes seek out those who share your energetic fire.

Although you form friendships, remember that others do not always enjoy moving at the speed of light to finish a project. Make sure you do not offend anyone during one of your energetic flurries. Fearing your response, others may choose to strategize with someone else. Learn to watch and listen to what others may *not* be saying.

Pray and ask the Holy Spirit to lead you. You represent the

Lord, and with Him, you establish a reputation of honor. Representing Him, unity must be your priority. You want others to experience that unity in all you do.

> *T*he refining pot is for silver and the furnace for gold, and a man [woman] is valued by what others say of him [her].
>
> PROVERBS 27:21

While your fresh energy and contagious vitality are admirable traits, it may seem that you place these things before your appearance. There are times when your energetic attitude overflows and your casual appearance becomes borderline sloppy. When this happens, you could jeopardize your credibility.

Getting the job done is important, but so is how you look. This does not mean that you must be obsessed with your appearance. It simply means that it is important to remember whom you represent. You never know who may be watching you. Make sure you always keep your comb and a mirror handy for a touch-up job. All it takes is a minute to stay neat.

An unkempt appearance can give your superiors the impression that even though you work hard, you do not care about your image or the image of the company. They then may hesitate before considering you for a position where you will have extensive public contact.

Take a little extra time with your appearance and consider it an investment in your future. Be prepared to take advantage of all the Lord has for you. Remember, you always represent Him, even in your appearance.

Wisdom is the principal thing; therefore get wisdom. And in all your getting, get understanding. Exalt her, and she will promote you; She will bring you honor when you embrace her.

PROVERBS 4:7–8

While you enjoy working with others and thrive in group ventures, your energy can also be exhausting to others. You will work on a project for hours, expecting your colleagues to follow suit. This is especially true if you are committed to the cause behind the project.

Members of the project team may need to eat, sleep, or do any number of things other non–Jaunty Esprit humans need to do. Give them the chance to rest and take care of their personal needs. Offering others the opportunity to take a much-needed break gives them a new perspective; they come back refreshed and ready to work hard to finish the job. It also keeps them from locking you in a closet to take a break! You may not believe it, but you also need the rest. Do not be afraid to stop and recharge so you can continue at your usual fast pace.

You like being in a decision-making position. This does not mean you like being in control of all aspects of a project. You are content with a smaller portion of a larger project if you're given freedom to complete it. For you, it is not important to see the big picture until after you have finished the work and see where it fits. Just tell you what needs to be done and when it needs to be completed and let you go. Jaunty Esprit sprightliness prepares you to climb any mountain!

Jaunty Esprit and *energy* are both terms synonymous with *freedom*. You motivate others to success. The Lord uses your energy to stimulate the body of Christ into action. In your church group, you are the one who will do the legwork for a project, make phone calls, and make sure everyone has a ride to an event. Sometimes it appears others take your energy and commitment for granted. One of your biggest irritations is that you seem to hear more complaints than compliments. This only happens when things are unbalanced and you become overworked. This also affects your positive attitude if you are not careful to stay in prayer and read your Bible.

Remember, the Lord never sleeps or slumbers, and He knows what you have accomplished. Stop and take a good look at things with the help of the Holy Spirit. Who are you working for? Is it for your glory or for the Lord? Remember, He gets the glory. Give Him the praise and honor and you will not need the compliments of others to survive. If that were the case, we would all starve. In due season, as you give Him glory, others will take notice and the Lord will make sure you are rewarded. Like your biblical sister Martha, you often need to remember for whom you are working.

Martha

WOMAN OF GREAT FAITH

> Now it happened as they went that He entered a certain village; and a certain woman named Martha welcomed Him into her house. And she had a sister called Mary, who also sat at Jesus' feet and heard His word. But Martha was distracted with much serving, and she approached Him and said, "Lord, do You not care that my sister has left me alone to serve? Therefore tell her to help me."
>
> LUKE 10:38–40

What was this thing that ravaged her brother's body? He was not an old man, so this was not an illness of age. Lazarus had

never been so sick before. What would they do if something happened to him? Martha and her sister began to worry. They'd all
been born in this house, and now it seemed their brother was
going to die here. As Martha looked around, she saw all the
housework left undone. Guilt welled up in her heart as she fed her
brother his evening soup. How could she even begin to think
about the condition of her home when Lazarus was so ill? As he
sipped his last spoonful, she sighed with relief.

It seemed as if housework was the only thing that gave her
joy these days. It kept her mind off the sickness that surrounded
her. Maybe if she had kept things cleaner, or worked harder, he
would not have become ill. Maybe if she had prepared better,
more nutritious meals, he would still be sitting up laughing
and enjoying the evening with them. Maybe if she had paid more
attention to the little household details that seemed to laugh at
her from the shadows, he would now be reading by the evening
light.

It was hard for her to picture him smiling with satisfaction
after one of her meals, as he had done so often in the past. As she
looked into his discolored face, she knew what had to be done.
She had to send for the Master Healer. Your Jaunty Esprit sister
Martha was prepared to take action and send for Jesus.

Martha was the sister of Mary and Lazarus. She and her family
were people of means, and Jesus stayed with them when He visited Bethany. When He heard that Lazarus had died, Martha and
Mary witnessed the Lord's open expression of grief. This display
of emotion showed that Jesus had a close relationship with
Martha and her family. She was known for her excellence in
housekeeping. Her home was a lovely, pleasant, orderly place
where the smell of delicious food always filled the air.

Since she was a woman of means, we can picture Martha
dressed in linen. Soft teal and lavender were her daytime colors
because they kept her cool in the heat. In the evening, she looked
beautiful in deep shades of sapphire and purple, with soft-colored

headdresses that circled her head then draped gently around her waist. Being a woman who was more concerned with her home and the comfort of her family than her appearance, she wore little jewelry. A golden bracelet and some small earrings, perhaps given to her as a gift by her brother Lazarus, would have been her first choice. Martha was Jaunty Esprit at its best: an unadorned, natural beauty.

It appears that she was older than her sister Mary, for she supervised the home-front operations. This is evident in Luke 10:38, where the Bible tells us that Martha was busy with cooking and cleaning. She wanted Mary to help with the household chores. Mary chose instead to sit at the feet of Jesus and listen to His word. Martha wanted Jesus to tell Mary to help her. Jesus gently told her, in verses 41–42, that she was worried and troubled over many things, but Mary had chosen the good part, which would not be taken from her. Mary chose to sit at the feet of the Master Teacher and receive His word.

These words changed the course of Martha's life. She'd wanted to honor Him by serving a lavish meal for His natural body. Jesus, instead, wanted to serve a lavish meal for her soul. By showing her life's true priorities, Jesus showed Martha how to live more fully by being filled with His word. From that day forward, Martha's life took on a different meaning. She learned how to set new and more meaningful priorities from the Master of priorities, the Lord Jesus.

Martha also witnessed and was personally touched by one of Jesus' most dramatic miracles: the raising of her brother Lazarus from the dead. Lazarus had been dead for four days when someone spotted Jesus on the road approaching Bethany. When Martha heard He was coming, she went to meet Him. When she stood before the Lord Jesus, she knew all her words had to be spoken in faith. She told Jesus, in John 11:21, that if He had been there, Lazarus would not have died. She also knew God the Father would grant any request from the Lord Jesus.

In verse 23, Jesus told Martha that her brother would rise. Martha replied that she knew Lazarus would rise in the resurrection—but also knew in her heart, through faith, that if Jesus wanted it so, Lazarus would rise that day and hour. The Lord Jesus wanted to hear Martha speak the words hidden in her heart. In verses 25–26, He tells Martha that He is the resurrection, the truth, and the life. Anyone who believes in Him, though he dies will live, and whoever lives and believes in Him shall never die.

Jesus then asked Martha if she believed Him. Martha's answer was to become one of the most powerful confessions of faith in the New Testament.

She responded in verse 27 by telling Jesus that He was the Christ, the Son of God, who is to come into the world. In this statement, we can see the full impact Jesus had on Martha's life. Even during her time of obvious grief, she still recognized, honored, and worshiped the Lord. It was also following this statement, in verse 35, that Jesus openly expressed His grief for the death of Lazarus by weeping.

Martha's faith was the spiritual catalyst for the working of this miracle. This miracle revealed Jesus' identity to all, letting the world know that He indeed was the Christ, the Son of the Living God. Her Jaunty Esprit spirit put godly faith into action. She stood in the presence of the Lord and believed, confessed, and received her place as a great woman of faith. She witnessed the wonder-working power of the Lord Jesus and stands as a model of faith to all who seek Him. Like you, her Jaunty Esprit sister, she was touched by the Master's hand, and from that point on her life was never the same.

> *F*or You O Lord are a shield for me.
> My glory and the One who lifts up my head.
> PSALMS 3:3

Great Career Choices for the Jaunty Esprit

Journalist
Freelance Writer
Photographer
Entrepreneur
Publisher
Advertising Director

The Outer You

Jaunty Esprit Clothing Choices

For you, the two C's, Comfort and Casualness, are the true ingredients of beauty. While you prefer casual dress, it sometimes seems that your appearance is not one of your top priorities. Let no one be fooled: You are a woman who does care about appearance, but frills and fuss take a backseat to comfort. You do not want clothing that fights with you. It must meet your strict requirements of quality, comfort, and cleanliness. Even when wearing your favorite jeans, you have on your clean, cool cotton shirt and cardigan. A great alternate is a T-shirt with your favorite message, letting all the world know where you stand. Your shoes are either athletic, slip-on, or lace-up flats.

You enjoy wearing natural fibers and clothes that breathe and move with you. You have few things that are tight or binding in your wardrobe. Just the thought of being uncomfortable in clothing makes you cringe. You often wonder how other image types wear those high-heeled shoes, straight skirts, tailored suits, and jackets all day long. Your body and feet must be ready to meet the challenges of your busy lifestyle. Soft, relaxed, unstructured clothing is the nucleus of the Jaunty Esprit wardrobe.

A typical Jaunty Esprit outfit is jeans, a cotton shirt, and athletic shoes. You also love sweats and may own several sweatshirts, if not entire sweat suits. When you go out to a sporting event, you need room to stand up and cheer, and your clothing must stand up and cheer with you. If you wear a skirt, it will be unstructured and made of denim, cotton, or corduroy. You wear your flats without hose if you can get away with it depending on the weather. If the weather is cold, you wear your favorite socks or winter hosiery. Everything has to be loose and unstructured and no-nonsense for it to be Jaunty Esprit, or you are not comfortable.

While this is good, your dressing tends to be predictable. You fall into a routine with your appearance. You may wear only about 25 percent of your clothes because you are not sure how to make proper use of them all. Your favorite pieces wear out quickly because you wear them so often.

Take a look through your closet and do an assessment. If you have not worn something in more than a year, take it out and decide if it meshes with your present lifestyle and wardrobe needs. Also inspect each piece. Decide whether or not you need to have it repaired and if it still fits. If not, give it away. It never pays to hold on to something that may benefit someone else. Donate the things to the local homeless shelter, where they will be put to good use. There are many needy people who will appreciate your generosity. The Lord will also be pleased with your gifts. If you are not wearing them, you will not miss them. Ensure that the remaining items are clean and in good shape. Then you are ready to do some coordinating.

> *H*e [She] who has pity on the poor lends to the Lord, and He will pay back what he [she] has given.
>
> PROVERBS 19:17

If you work outside the home, you have quite a few separates. One of your favorite suits is a matching skirt and cardigan with a soft textured blouse or oxford shirt. There are times when you need a more structured image. At those times, choose an unconstructed jacket in your favorite color instead of your usual cardigan. You can replace your flared skirt with a straight sweater or knit skirt. This will give you a relaxed elegance that easily transitions from day to evening.

You look best in a soft crew-neck or turtleneck sweater. You own quite a few in many different colors. Because you like order, even in your dress, your sweaters are never bulky or too oversized. You also buy quality because it saves time. Your investment pays off by allowing you to spend more time on interesting Jaunty Esprit projects.

Sometimes you have a tendency to underdress. You believe that you have exerted enough energy into the few "uniforms" you do wear and do not especially feel the need to upgrade your image. Try taking an objective look at your wardrobe and appearance. This can be a difficult task for some, but—armed with Jaunty Esprit energy and commitment—it is easily accomplished. If this is done on a regular basis, the results are life changing.

Ask yourself these questions. Do the pieces fit in with your present lifestyle? When it is time for a special event, such as a night out or a special meeting, do you need to go out and find something presentable to wear? Do you feel stressed preparing for a special dress-up function? Do your present clothes still fit properly? Are they up-to-date? Depending on your answers to these questions, it may be time to revamp your closet and go shopping. This is the time to buy clothing that fits your Jaunty Esprit image type. Now that you have discovered that the Lord created you Jaunty Esprit, go shopping and take Him with you!

Being prepared for special events before they happen is a great stress reliever. Your entire attitude will change if you take the time to regularly look for outfits and have them in your closet when the time comes. You will feel more relaxed and confident. Make an investment in your appearance and it will make an impression that will last a lifetime. If you follow the Lord and His shining light of wisdom, you will stay ready for any event life has to offer.

*T*he path of the just is a shining light, that shines more and more unto the perfect day.

PROVERBS 4:18

JAUNTY ESPRIT FULL-FIGURED CLOTHING CHOICES

If you are a full-figured Jaunty Esprit, today's clothing choices certainly are more numerous. There are many catalogs that cater to your size and image type. Specialty boutiques also carry many fashionable outfits and accessories. Thank the Lord for the fashion industry finally realizing that full-figured women need and want comfortable clothing, too! Elastic-waisted skirts with soft knit pullovers and matching jackets are comfortable and easy-care. These unstructured pieces are transitional and easily take you from day into evening.

Beautifully colored sweat suits with matching headbands add fun to your wardrobe. Matching cardigan-sweater-and-skirt sets give you an added boost in the office setting. They are comfortable, stylish, and in tune with your image type's love of comfort and order. They meet the criteria for the two C's, and that is a top priority that pleases you. Make sure the items you choose give you room to move freely. You will mirror the joy of the Lord in all your Jaunty Esprit glory!

If the buttons pull or the blouse opens while you're trying it on, get the next larger size. If there is not a larger size available, get another blouse style. A great alternative is a pullover blouse with a back keyhole closing. A slipover sweater or a loosely fitting knit top is also a great choice. Take note of the sleeves and under the arms. How do they feel? Is there extra stress on the seams? Remember, the extra stress means your blouse will not look good for long and may rip under the arms.

If your hips are the fullest part of your body, use the Fingertip Rule for the fit of your jackets or cardigans. This simple technique enables you to wear just about any type of skirt. It works as long as the skirt fits properly. Stand with your arms relaxed at your sides. Notice where your fingertips fall. This is the perfect length for your jackets. If your arms are short, add two inches. Your jacket should fall approximately a hand length below the fullest part of your hips. This length will enable you to wear straight skirts if you choose. Those sweater dresses you love are no longer off-limits because of your hip size. Your new jacket length will enable you to wear them all in Jaunty Esprit style.

Being full-figured does not change your image type. You wear the same clothing styles as a smaller woman. The only difference is the size. Different clothing lines may mean you will wear one size in one line and another size in different line. Size is unimportant as long as the garment fits. There is never an excuse for looking bad, especially now when so many clothing options are readily available and cut properly. Your main concern should be how you look and feel in a particular piece. If you follow these simple rules, you glorify the Lord and stay alive, free, and a beautiful Jaunty Esprit!

> *A*rise, shine for the light has come! And the glory of the Lord is risen upon you. . . .
>
> ISAIAH 60:1

KEY WORDS FOR THE JAUNTY ESPRIT DRESS CODE

Relaxed
Casual
Sporty
Wash-and-Wear

JAUNTY ESPRIT COLOR SCHEMES

Colors that illuminate your lively spirit should dominate your wardrobe. You like bright colors and patterns, but sometimes like to play it safe by choosing solids and small prints. If you choose safe colors, it may be because you feel uncomfortable with adventurous dressing. It is now time to experiment!

Look for your core colors. Your core colors are the ones you have the most of in your wardrobe. Begin to observe what colors attract your attention when you shop. You will probably find that you already have these colors in your closet. Look closely and you will see a pattern. Most of your clothing is probably in the same color family. If you have been color-analyzed, use your seasonal palette as your main wardrobe theme and play around with colors from the other seasons as accents. After discovering your core colors, begin to experiment to see what other colors blend. If you do not feel comfortable, go to your local bookstore and ask for a book on working with colors, or visit a color consultant. An even better solution is to look in the mirror and ask the Holy Spirit to act as your Consultant. After all, who created color anyway? I do believe He played a big part in its creation.

When choosing your wardrobe favorites, you choose comfort and cleanliness over coordination. Since comfort is key, try mixing and matching patterns of the same base colors. Once started, it will not be unusual to wear a pair of blue slacks with a blue polka-dot top. A striped blue unstructured cotton knit jacket completes your new outfit. Of course, your favorite denim skirt coordinates with any blouse or sweater color combination. It is easy to see that you will not have to do a great deal of work in that department. Whatever you choose to wear, it will be fun, free, and Jaunty Esprit.

Go to the Color Expert and He will show you wondrous color creations. Remember, He created you in His image, and He wants only the best for His daughter. If you stop and think, you will realize that He has passed on some of His color knowledge to you. Go on, try it. The only thing standing in your way is fear, and you know what He says about that.

> *F*or God has not given us a spirit of fear, but of power and of love and of a sound mind.
>
> II TIMOTHY 1:7

The Lord created you lively and free, so glorify Him and go for it! Your safety net is the Holy Spirit. If you are not feeling sure about something, ask for help. Your first thought and feeling will usually be correct. If something attracts your attention, it is probably what your heart longs to wear. Do not be influenced by others unless they confirm what the Lord has already spoken to your heart. If you do feel the need for additional assistance, ask the Lord for guidance in finding a professional who can share new color options.

Jaunty Esprit and color are both gifts from above. You share the same beauty of freedom and gentle excitement. Relax, enjoy, and feel free to experiment. With your beautiful spirit and style, you can wear color combinations that other, more conservative image types would never try. Your love of freedom and energy dazzle with color enhancement.

When God said, "Let there be light," He simultaneously created color. Without light there is no color. Can you imagine the world without color? Of course not. The Lord cannot imagine His world without color or His wondrous creation—you! God is the Lord of variety. He beautifully stimulates our lives, emotions, and senses with color, His perfect creation. Just like color, you are a perfect creation. You and color dance with Jaunty Esprit freedom. So trust Him and use your ally in dressing Jaunty Esprit perfect: the Lord's beautiful gift of color.

> *T*hen God said, "Let there be light," and there was light. And God saw the light, that it was good; and God divided the light from the darkness.
>
> GENESIS 1:3–4

JAUNTY ESPRIT JEWELRY

Jaunty Esprit jewelry is usually small and understated. You choose good-quality jewelry that is not ornate. Your wedding ring, a small watch, and your favorite pair of dot earrings are just enough to complete your usual look. You have always wanted to wear something larger and different, but felt uncomfortable. You have a need to feel safe and not attract attention. While shopping, you see larger shapes and colors, but often do not take the risk and buy them. Lively shapes and colors attract you for a reason. They are naturally Jaunty Esprit!

It is now time to experiment. Try making subtle changes by wearing earrings a little larger than usual, with soft rounded edges. Take your time and try them on before leaving the store. If you feel a little unsure, take an Elegant Flamboyant friend with you. She will be honest and gentle. She also has an eye for fashion and style. Watch the style she chooses and then select something similar but smaller. This way, you are sure to be on target. Elegant Flamboyant styling will most likely be too dramatic for you, but using her styling as a foundation, your new bolder, brighter look will give you a fashionable change of pace.

Geometrically shaped earrings and matching brooches are other options for a change of pace. Add matching bangle brace-lets and you have changed your entire look. Select something you think is just a "little bit much" for you. Instead of your usual small half-inch bangle, for instance, try a wider bracelet accented with small faux stones.

Romantic styling also works well for your image type. If you do not like faux stones, look for jewelry with small floral designs. These work well for dressing up and even carry over well for ca-sual wear. There are many beautiful porcelain floral designs on the market that are more dramatic than your usual styling. They are softly feminine but still beautifully Jaunty Esprit.

Exchange your delicate gold chain and pendant for a heavier version without the pendant. The change is subtle yet noticeable. Exchange your small dot earrings for larger, more noticeable dots of bright color. Choose matching pendants and brooches to pull them into view. They speak a gentle whisper of change. Lively theme jewelry is also great for your image type. In the warmer months, for example, you can find jewelry in fun summer shapes. Lively sunflowers and juicy watermelons dance in the jewelry section. Some are definitely not your image type, but you will quickly see the Jaunty Esprit pieces that make your heart sing!

A wonderful array of colorful jewelry comes out usually in spring and summer, and usually in sets complete with earrings, necklace, and bracelet. It may be made of fun, high-quality plas-tic as opposed to precious metals. Okay, okay, work with me now on this one. This may not sound like the usual jewelry you wear, but trust me: It will look great with your colorful new outfits and Jaunty Esprit styling!

Pick up a few bright brooches to add dashes of color and fun to your outfits. If you do not feel comfortable in the matching ear-rings, then buy just the bracelet instead. Still, the wise choice would be to buy the entire ensemble so that you can interchange pieces according to your mood and the occasion. Being prepared will take the guesswork out of dressing. Remember, your goal is to make dressing less stressful.

A little wardrobe adventure will look and feel great, especially when led by the Holy Spirit! Once you try a little pizzazz, you will see and feel the difference. You are a beautiful Jaunty Esprit creation who is filled with the joy of your Lord while you feast on His word.

> *Y*our words were found, and I ate them, and Your word was to me the joy and rejoicing of my heart; For I am called by Your name, O Lord God of hosts.
>
> JEREMIAH 15:16

JAUNTY ESPRIT HAIR

Your hair is your crowning glory and must always complement your face. You like no-nonsense hairstyling. Easy care and maintenance are Jaunty Esprit priorities. If your hair is short, a casual, easily managed style is your first preference. Any style that requires a great deal of maintenance is not for you. You like the *wash, blow-dry, and comb* theory. That is the end of your hair story. If you wear your hair longer, you own plenty of ponytail or banana clips to hold it in place. You like your long hair because you can wash, comb, and pull it back with one your famous clips. Clean, under control, and presentable, your hair looks great.

> *B*ut if a woman has long hair, it is a glory to her; for her hair is given to her for a covering.
>
> I CORINTHIANS 11:15

For a different look and feel, try a permanent to add curl, or have your hair straightened. This really depends on your hair. Consider your personal preferences and face shape. Before making a change, check hairstyle guides for ideas. A good hairstylist can also assist you.

If you want to color your hair, make sure the shade complements your natural coloring. Do not make the mistake of going to the extreme and dramatically changing your hair color in one sitting. If you are a brunette on Friday, coming out with blond hair on Saturday is one sure way to attract unwanted attention. If you do decide to go blond, do it gradually. First, make a subtle change and highlight your hair. Then, after a few months, lighten again. This way, you have more control and can make sure that the color is really what you want. It also gives you time to change your mind and control the color. Coloring your hair is one way to have fun with a new look.

Jaunty Esprit women of color have little problem with hair color. You like neutral shades and know that a deep, rich auburn, cocoa, or chestnut brown will look wonderful. There are some wonderful burgundies on the market that give your hair brilliance and luster in any lighting. They also look great with any skin tone. Choose your coloring wisely to complement your honey-gold, caramel-brown, walnut, cocoa-brown, and ebony skin coloring. Remember, the Lord presented you with the natural gift of awesome coloring, so do not distort it with an uncomplimentary hair color.

This word goes out also for women of Latina, Asian, and Native American descent. Your magnificent hair is beautiful the way it is. Nothing man has created can compare with your deep, rich tresses. If you feel you need to experiment, try some of the burgundies described above. They will add spirited highlights without detracting from your God-given beauty. Burgundy will also blend with your natural skin coloring and give you that wonderful Jaunty Esprit glow.

Another hairstyling consideration is lifestyle. Whether you're a busy mother or career woman, your style should be one of great ease with little fuss. If you have a busy social calendar, attending day and evening events regularly, you need a transitional style— one that will take you from day to evening and still look great. If your hair is short, try a permanent to add a little more curl or to straighten your regular style. If your hair is long, wear it pulled away from your face and use hair clips that are more ornate than your usual banana clips. Use curlers to create wisps of curls to frame your face. Try a little adventure. Go on, you can do it! Remember, you are lively, sporty, casual, and free. Best of all, you are a beautiful Jaunty Esprit!

JAUNTY ESPRIT MAKEUP

Many Jaunty Esprit women choose not to wear makeup. The main reason is that you feel it is troublesome and takes up too much of your time. You also notice other women heavily made up and find the look unappealing. You may have a desire to try makeup, but since you do not know how to wear it, you leave it alone. If these reasons sound familiar, then these obstacles are easily overcome.

The first step is investigation. Try starting with makeup artists. They can be found at a good cosmetics counter in a department store. These professionals will help you find your perfect look. Do not let someone talk you into wearing and buying something you will not use after you leave the consultation. It is your job to tell your consultant how you want to look at the end of the session. If you want a natural look for daytime wear, say so. You look best in minimal makeup, applied skillfully to enhance your natural features. This small amount of enhancement will just brighten your already glowing and healthy appearance and keep you from looking tired, even when you are.

If you choose not to wear makeup during the day but you want a special look for evening, say so. Whatever you try, make sure it is on evenly for a fresh and natural look. Evening will be heavier than your daytime look, with just a touch of glamour. The best evening look will gently highlight your facial features and give you a glow, even under artificial lighting.

When choosing your cosmetics, look for natural colors that blend easily with your skin tone. Nothing garish or vibrant works for you. Leave those to the other image types who can wear them. Instead, look for colors that remind you of spring and summer. Soft peach, subtle coral, turquoise whisper, and golden plum speak the Jaunty Esprit language. Look for soft blushers that give you just a hint of color on your cheeks. Colors like rose-petal pink and gentle fuchsia add to your soft, natural coloring when lightly brushed on cheeks.

Contrary to what you may have heard, your eye shadow need not match your clothing. In fact, it is probably not a good idea to match your clothing. This way you can wear the same makeup with all your outfits. If you make sure your makeup blends with and enhances your natural coloring, you will look great. Even if you choose to wear soft blue, your soft brown eye shadow will look great, as long as it blends with your skin tone.

If you are medium- to dark-skinned, your skin is a natural canvas for your preferred style. You use the soft plums and gentle pinks to enhance your radiant dark beauty. Expertly highlighting your ebony, bronze, or olive skin with low-key, subdued coloring is one of your natural trademarks. Your lips, cheeks, and eyes will be gently kissed by color because you like a natural look. You use a little deep navy for eye defining. Gentle purples and delicate blues sing your sweetest Jaunty Esprit song.

Lively teal dances throughout your palette, and the beauty of your countenance from café au lait to deepest ebony shines for all the world to see. You are as beautiful as Abigail during the shearing feast when she went to meet the future King David in all her Jaunty Esprit beauty. Whatever your ethnic heritage, you are the Lord's creation and beautiful to behold. You are ready to speak the Jaunty Esprit language without saying a word. Your glowing appearance says it all for you.

If you are not sure about coloring, please consult a professional. It will be an investment well spent because it will save you time. A good makeup artist, cosmetologist, or professional color analyst can assist you in determining the undertone of your skin and the foundation that will blend with that undertone. You'll learn how to apply a natural look for daytime and a glowing look for evening. Once you learn the basics, you can work until you get exactly what you want.

Whether your ethnic heritage is that of the European queen, the Asian empress, the Latina *condesa,* or the Native American or Nubian princess, you shine and give God glory with your glowing Jaunty Esprit countenance!

> *A* merry heart makes a cheerful countenance.
> PROVERBS 15:13

3. *Harmonic Refined*

All things together, all things in line.
Like our Lord, she loves order,
The Harmonic Refined.

Let all things be done decently and in order.
I CORINTHIANS 14:40

The Beauty of Harmonic Refined

Are order and organization the main themes in your life? Do others often tell you that you seem to be dressed up even for a casual event? Are you loyal to wardrobe classics that never go out of style? Do you prefer quality to quantity in your wardrobe and lifestyle choices? If you answered yes, then you are the Harmonic Refined image type.

As a Harmonic Refined woman, you embrace the classic look in every facet of your life. Structured balance is the essence of your image type. Your choices in clothing, home decor, and even career are your style signatures. You are the epitome of class and refinement. While these things are a part of who you are as a person, they are not the center of your life. You still believe in balance, and you know the Source of all your blessings is the Lord.

The Inner You

You have the presence of aristocracy. You love quality and excellence in all things. One look and you know if something is an original or an imitation. That includes the people you meet. You are an excellent judge of character, and those close to you seek your advice before making decisions, especially decisions involving other people. Your strength in this area is a gift from your heavenly Father. You have the innate ability to quickly see beyond the emotions and into the core or the spirit of people. If they are genuine, then you know it. If they are masquerading, then your Harmonic Refined radar picks up the facade. To keep this gift sharp, you keep in touch with the Father. Doing this, as with all things in your life, decently and in order, you keep a healthy balance in your relationship with the Lord.

You change the atmosphere when you enter a room. Your re-fined spirit is so evident that everyone feels your presence. This change is like a breeze that soothes, relaxes, and gently trans-forms others. You seem to make everyone in the room walk taller, choose their words more carefully, and watch their manners more closely. This does not mean that you are stuffy or snobbish. It sim-ply means that you are a class act and others can see it, feel it, and often try to emulate it.

To you, class and refinement are natural gifts from your heav-enly Father, just as a beautiful voice is to a gifted vocalist or flight is to the eagle. You have what is called soft authority. This soft au-thority is the core of the Harmonic Refined spirit. You walk with the authority that comes straight from the throne of the Lord. You know who you are and have no problem accepting and using your gifts. Conflict comes when others do not understand or ac-cept this part of you. Everything in your life must have order, and you use your soft authority to make it happen. This is your pur-pose in the body of Christ. You are the perfect administrator with standing orders to keep things together, in line, and in order.

When others imitate your actions, you take it as a compli-ment. You take on the responsibility of being a role model with style and grace. This role can weigh heavily on you if you do not keep in touch with the Lord. Balance keeps all things in perspec-tive. You see the positive impact your actions have on the lives of others—but if you are not careful, you can start to take credit for the results.

The Lord must be your first priority; all other things will then fall into place. It is a true relief to know that for any pressure or temptation you experience, He has already provided the way of escape and will take the load from your shoulders.

*N*o temptation has overtaken man [woman]; but God is faithful, who will not allow you to be tempted beyond what you are able, but with the temptation will also make the way of escape that you may be able to bear it.

I CORINTHIANS 10:13

You are direct and usually tell others how you feel about a situation and the people involved without being unkind. Others often have difficulty with your direct honesty. You do not believe in hurting others but believe in truth. Before giving counsel, you let those coming to you know that you will be truthful, even if it hurts their feelings. You will do all within your power to dig out the truth in any given situation. You pray for guidance and always seek the guidance of the Holy Spirit in problem solving. Your lifestyle leaves no room for gossip, and you are quick to let others know it.

You are very frank and are sometimes described as being brutally honest by others. Because you love order and control, God uses you to see discord and its source so there is no time wasted, especially yours. You are a good steward of everything the Father has entrusted to you, and you pass that advice on to others, who usually listen.

Because of your classic presence, it may appear that you have an air about you. To others who do not know you, this air may resemble arrogance or judgment. Although it is not your intent to appear judgmental, your very spirit is so fine-tuned to see disorder that you may not be aware of its impact on others. Even a look from you can leave a great impression. Remember, you can see into the spirit of people, and this is sometimes unnerving to them, especially if they are hiding something. Try as you may, you cannot change this God-given part of your spirit—and you really do not want to change it. This gift has kept you from trouble many times.

The Lord continuously fine-tunes your Harmonic Refined beauty. He also uses others as instruments to refine His Harmonic Refined vessel—which, like all useful vessels, needs cleaning and refinishing on a continuous basis. That includes you, my Harmonic Refined sister. The process is not always pleasant. Cleansing and refining require rubbing, scrubbing, and the digging out of dirt. As He rubs, scrubs, and scrapes, He simultaneously applies His healing balm to make you ready for His purpose.

As a Harmonic Refined, you know He is faithful and just. You want Him to test, refine, and make you ready for every situation He places before you. Without the Lord, you know you could not do things in the classic Harmonic Refined way. Your way is the way of your Lord, decent and in order.

You believe in studying your Bible; in fact, you feel it is important for everyone to schedule private time with the Lord. You also believe that if everyone took their private time, there would be less conflict in the world. Wisdom is the key for you, and in keeping with this lifelong theme, you know the Lord cuts through conflict, if we all just regularly turn to Him. You cannot imagine why others cannot see this, because it is so apparent to you.

Just by observing people, you can tell if they have been spending time with the Lord. Their words, actions, and mannerisms send out clear messages of being bathed in God's Holy Spirit—or a lack thereof. You pray that they will learn the art of prioritizing, and you share this message with those who listen.

Being the wise woman you are, you know to hold fast to your times with the Lord because they keep you in balance. You always want to be a sharp instrument ready for the Master's use. During your quiet time, you renew your spirit and receive insight and wisdom from your Creator to ensure you stay ready for His call. Like your biblical sister Anna, you are open to His calling.

*B*e diligent to present yourself approved to God,
a worker who does not need to be ashamed,
rightly dividing the word of truth.

II Timothy 2:15

Anna

The First to Acclaim Jesus as the Christ

Now there was one, Anna, a prophetess, the daughter of
Phanuel, of the tribe of Asher. She was of a great age,
and had lived with a husband seven years from her
virginity.

Luke 2:36–37

Whenever there was sickness or family difficulty, the people
called on Anna to pray. She stayed in touch with her heavenly
Father, regularly interceding for those in need. One particular
morning, she arose with great joy in her heart. She did not yet
know the reason; only that this would be a day of great rejoicing
and praise. Not knowing exactly what to expect was not important to her. She was simply sure that today would be a day she
would long remember; that it would change not only her life, but
the lives of many others as well. Today the Holy Spirit had told
her she would see His glory. The Lord had let her know to expect
a miracle. She stood prepared for whatever He had planned.

As Anna watched the people coming and going from the
Temple, she saw birds flying about in cages and small calves being
led by ropes. She saw all the usual sights and sounds you would
expect at this time of the year, when the priests offered sacrifices

to the Lord for the sins of the people. Things looked as they did every year, but she sensed something unusual in the air.

What was it that so stirred Anna's spirit that she could barely contain her joy? There was a burning in her heart that caused her to pace back and forth on the Temple grounds and not stay in her usual seat near the entrance. The Holy Spirit had let her know to be on the lookout for something special, so she continued to watch and pray. She asked the Lord not to let her old eyes miss His special blessing. As she continued to walk and move through the crowd, Anna saw a young couple with an infant on the Temple grounds. They had come to the Temple to offer a sacrifice according to the law of the Lord. As she watched them, a giant Power Surge hit her body. All of a sudden, her feet went into motion, and she ran toward the young couple. Her heartbeat raced as she made her approach. She gathered the hem of her dress to keep from tripping although, in her heart, she knew her Lord would not let her fall. With newfound strength, she kept up with her running feet and maintained her balance.

Anna knew this young couple had something to do with the spiritual stirring in the air. What was it about this family that was so special? As she touched the young woman on her shoulder, she caught a glimpse of the face of the Child in her arms.

The young woman turned, and Anna's eyes filled with tears. She could hardly speak. Could it be true? Was this the One whose coming the prophets of old foretold? Before another question could enter her mind, the Holy Spirit confirmed what she already knew. For as she gazed into the tiny Face, she knew in that moment she was looking into the Face of Holiness. This Face belonged to the King of kings and the Lord of lords. This small Child was the One who had come to save the world. The Messiah was here, and she had seen Him! Your Harmonic Refined sister Anna, the prophetess, had beheld Jesus Christ, the Son of the Living God.

We can imagine Anna was an elderly woman who, despite her age, walked briskly through Temple grounds and corridors.

Empowered by the Holy Spirit, with fire in her voice and an energy level that would rival a more youthful woman's, she taught, counseled, and prayed for those entering the holy dwelling. Her dark dress flowed gently around her ankles. A bright purple shawl served as a headdress. It softly flowed around her shoulders and draped to encircle her waist. She kept her silver hair swept back to reveal eyes that had seen most of the city's people come into the Temple from youth through old age. Her bright eyes never missed anything that went on around her, including the comings and goings of the Temple priests. She constantly prayed for her people and for the fulfillment of the prophecy of the coming Christ.

Anna has a special place in biblical history. Although she was mentioned in only three verses of Scripture, her actions were of great significance. She was the first person to acclaim Jesus as the Christ. Luke 2:37 describes Anna as a woman who did not depart from the Temple but served God with fasting and praying night and day. She was a familiar sight at the Temple. It is easy to imagine that the devout Anna was a teacher and an encouragement to many.

As she went about the Temple, she talked and prayed with the people. Anna was also a prophetess, and the people had great respect for her. She had lived at the Temple for many years and was knowledgeable in the things of the Lord. They knew the wise Anna would answer any questions concerning the things of God because she was a woman of prayer who continuously served the Lord. She was a stately Harmonic Refined who was not given to emotional outbursts. It is for this reason that her overt gestures of praise attracted so much attention.

That day, Anna praised the Lord like a young woman in her twenties. The Holy Spirit had given her the strength she needed to do the will of the Father; the strength to proclaim that His beloved Son had come to save the world. Your Harmonic Refined sister had been faithful. Through her fasting and prayer, Anna found favor with the Lord. Because of this favor, He allowed her to live long enough to see His precious Son. He honored her by allowing her to be the first to acclaim Jesus as the Christ. She saw the Holy One sent from God, the blessed Messiah.

Her rejoicing caused a giant ripple, for she began to tell everyone she saw that the Messiah had come. Once they heard the story, did they believe? It is safe to say that many did, indeed, believe Anna. They knew that something had so stirred the elderly prophetess that it made her leap for joy and run wildly through the streets.

Anna's story can best be described as having the same effect as dropping a pebble into a pond. The incident may have only lasted an instant, but it started a spiritual tremor that reverberates even today. The Messiah had indeed come into the world, and your Harmonic Refined sister Anna was the first to publicly acclaim His coming.

> *B*ut He knows the way that I take; He has tested me, I shall come forth as gold.
>
> JOB 23:10

Goal setting is a Harmonic Refined key to success. You plan everything, and everything has a plan. This attribute shines through even in the management of your chosen relationships. You plan your letter writing, phone calls, and visits to friends and family. Spontaneity is not the norm for you. Others admire your networking skills, because you follow up meetings with notes to almost everyone you meet. People do not realize this takes planning and organization—the very traits that make you so successful. Because of these traits, you are on the guest list for many events, both personal and professional. Although you cannot accept all the invitations you receive, you are an expert at graciously bowing out without offending the prospective host or hostess. This is one of the qualities that make you beautifully Harmonic Refined.

Harmonic Refined Strengths in the Body of Christ

Teacher
Prayer Chair
Church Administrator

Harmonic Refined and Family Life

As a parent, you ensure that your children have the best you can afford. You make excellent use of your time and resources and do everything in your power to make sure they learn to use their talents wisely. They take piano, ballet, voice, and private lessons in all their areas of interest. You take special notice of these talents and encourage your young ones to strive for excellence. You want them well prepared to take advantage of any opportunity the Lord presents in their lives. You believe in a well-rounded educational base in many subjects, especially the Scriptures. You know that all things were made through Him, and without Him nothing was made. Exposing your children to the Lord is wisdom. Walking with Him, you know they will make the best choices for a prosperous future.

> *A*ll things were made through Him, and without Him nothing was made that was made.
>
> JOHN 1:3

Your children learn early in life about the consequences of their actions. You believe in making them ready to face the outside world as soon as possible. In your home, you design schedules for activities and household responsibilities. You discuss these schedules along with the consequences of not completing the assigned tasks. You give your children the opportunity to give input for appropriate consequences if the tasks are not completed. They also discuss the rewards if all is done as agreed.

When your little ones do not live up to the terms of the family agreements, they must bear the outcome. There is no discussion. Before the process started, you also discussed the importance of planning. If they experience problems with their assigned task, then it is their responsibility to come to you before they reach the deadline for the task. This does not mean you lack compassion. It simply means you are a realist and believe in planning for everything. You teach your children to plan for success. In your view, children should learn at an early age how to set goals and experience the good feeling of accomplishment that comes with reaching goals. They should also learn about the consequences of not following through with a promise or a responsibility. You will not always be there to take care of them. You want them to be ready to face life's challenges.

When your children have important projects coming up, you encourage them to start early with the research. You instruct them on how to do things in stages. They learn to divide the project into smaller pieces, so it is not so overwhelming. After they have prepared each stage, you show them the simplicity of putting together the entire project to make it complete. You let them know that they can eat a whole cow a steak at a time if they choose to do so. Organization is the key. Only you could be so organized, and only you could teach such a brilliant lesson and make it look so simple.

You screen all recreational activities. Any movie or book that you feel is inappropriate does not stay in your home. You openly discuss your decisions with your children and let them know your position. It is critical that you educate them not only in natural, but also in spiritual things. You let them know the house rules and also warn them that you will clean out their rooms regularly.

Your Harmonic Refined spirit and ungodliness cannot coexist in the same dwelling. You will not allow any openings for the enemy of their souls into your home. You let your children know they can come to you about any questionable items. The Lord established your home as a safe haven, and Mother Harmonic Refined works His plan in keeping it that way.

Your children know they can depend on Mom to help them find the best way to do just about anything. With Harmonic Refined style, you make assessments in an instant and come up with organized plans. This is one of your strongest gifts. You also know that all your children have different talents. You teach them to exercise their gifts, to spread their wings, and fly to success. They love you for it!

You know that if they prepare for success, then you will not have to worry about them later in life. Your motto for successful parenting is, "Lessons learned are lessons retained." With you as their earthly guide, your children learn that planning and timing equal success. Groomed for success by the Master of all plans and His earthly vessel, their beautiful Harmonic Refined mother, they are ready to face the world.

> *B*ehold, children are a heritage from the Lord, the fruit of the womb is His reward. . . .
>
> PSALMS 127:3

The Harmonic Refined Spouse

Your husband depends on your eye for detail to help him keep things in order. He respects your intellect and your keen sense of organization, and he never takes you for granted.

These qualities have saved your family from hardship and disaster many times in the past. Your spouse feels he can go on a business trip and remain worry-free because you have everything on the home front under control. He knows that all will run smoothly while he is away. Let there be no misunderstanding, however: You do not like being without him, and you tell him this on a regular basis.

You present him with a written schedule of your planned activities, so he will know where to reach you in case of an emergency. He knows when to expect your call and when to call you to check on the family. He is able to relax, for his wife is a woman of substance who handles anything that happens. When he returns home, you give him a report of everything that went on in his absence. You keep him up-to-date on the children and any activity he needs to attend. He knows that the source of your orderliness is the Lord. Your man praises Him every day for the wonderful gift of his beautiful Harmonic Refined wife.

He looks forward to your times together. He loves your ability to ensure that these cherished times go uninterrupted. He knows you have taken care of all details beforehand. You delight in these times because you can focus all your energy on him, forgetting everything else. Candlelight, a delicious dinner, soft music, and the two of you are all the ingredients needed for an unforgettable evening. As you bask in the love light of your mate, all sights and sounds fade into the background of the night. Harmonic Refined planning has again paved the way for success.

During these times, he is the center of your attention, and there is no place he would rather be. You sit back, relax, and enjoy these special times and each other. Talking about the past and making future plans, you quietly and sweetly love into the night.

You and your mate emerge newly refreshed and ready to tackle any- and everything together. These times of renewal and revival are Harmonic Refined necessities for a successful marriage. You renew your love for one another and revive the passion that you never want to leave your marriage. Revived and renewed, you are a better wife and friend to your husband. These times help you and your mate maintain a healthy balance. This balance is a critical facet of doing "the marriage thing" decently and in order. You realize that even in marriage, planning is critical to harmony. Balance, planning, and order, combined with your Harmonic Refined beauty, create a marital event worth writing about.

Your heart is full of praise for the Lord. He has given you the insight to manage all details so you and your spouse can relax and focus on one another to rejuvenate your love. Only your heavenly Father could bless you so abundantly. To Him, you give all glory and praise for your blessings. There could be no better threesome than you, your husband, and the Lord, making precious memories destined to last a lifetime. Everything is in order. Everything is in line. Like your biblical sister Hulda, you are steadfast and strong. You remain loyal to your spouse, knowing he was chosen for you, and he in turn admires your virtue. He relies on your guidance and wisdom, for he knows you seek God with all your heart.

Hulda

PROPHETESS OF THE LORD

> So Hilkiah the priest, Ahikam, Achbor, Shaphan, and
> Asaiah went to Hulda the prophetess, wife of Shallum
> the son of Tikvah, the son of Harhas, keeper of the

wardrobe. She dwelt in Jerusalem in the Second Quarter.
And they spoke with her. . . .

II KINGS 22:14

Fasting and praying was the only way Hulda survived. She
was surrounded by all sorts of idolatry and other things that she
was sure offended her Lord. After all He had brought them
through, the children of Israel had now fallen into worshiping
false gods. The thought of it all disgusted her. She had to keep her
mind on the Lord or she could not continue. Hulda knew that He
and He alone would give her strength to stay faithful. Someone
had to pray for her people. She knew beyond the shadow of a
doubt that the Lord would answer her prayer and would send a
ruler who would honor and worship Him. She waited in faith for
the answer. Jehovah had not failed her yet and she knew if anyone was faithful, it was the Lord.

As the morning sunlight peeked through her window, she felt
a stirring in her spirit. Today the Lord was going to do something
wonderful. He was, after all, an extraordinary God, so nothing He
planned would surprise her. She did not have any idea what He
was going to do, but she was ready and available to do His will.
She quietly prayed and waited for the Holy Spirit to move her.

King Josiah had ruled Israel for eighteen years. During this
particular time of his reign, the Temple of the Lord was being repaired. During the remodeling, Hilkiah, the high priest of the
Lord, discovered the Book of the Law. After dusting off the book
and thumbing through the pages, Hilkiah gave it to his scribe.
The scribe then went before the king and read the contents.
Upon hearing the reading, King Josiah tore his clothes and repented. In II Kings 22:12, he gave strict instructions to the high
priest, his scribe, and his group of advisers. They were to go and
inquire of the Lord for him and all the people regarding the contents of the book. The king needed an expert to authenticate the
book, and he demanded confirmation from one of God's true mes-

sengers. The group of advisers did not have to go far—they knew exactly who could tell them the word of the Lord.

As the men approached her door, Hulda could sense the urgency in their footsteps. When she opened the door and saw the king's messengers, she knew her answer had finally arrived. They entered and, at first, did not speak. As they laid the Book of the Law before her, she began to look through its pages. Yes, it was indeed authentic. The Lord God had answered her prayers and had sent a king who would seek His will and way. The advisers knew the Lord had led them to His chosen messenger. As they watched this godly woman read the Book of the Law, they saw tears of joy well up in her eyes and her hands involuntarily being raised in praise to the Only Wise God. This holy woman who was to authenticate God's Holy Word was your anointed Harmonic Refined sister Hulda, the prophetess.

We can imagine Hulda was a stately woman with silver hair. She dressed in dark wool dresses that kept her cool during the day and warm at night. She wore a shorter overcoat in a lighter color. Her headdress was a light gray that blended beautifully with her silver crowning glory. Her sash was the same dark color as her dress. Hulda's eyes had not been dimmed by her age. Her countenance had a healthy glow that continued to amaze all who saw her. Hulda was a woman who sought God and stayed in His presence. His Holy Spirit kept her youthful and vigilant to do His will.

The Bible tells us, in II Kings 22:14, that she lived in the Second Quarter of Jerusalem, where she could teach and stay near the dwelling place of her heavenly Father. When the group brought the Book of the Law to Hulda, the Holy Spirit empowered her and she began to speak the word of the Lord, thus giving the group an immediate confirmation of its authenticity. Hulda prophesied that the Lord was angry; calamity would befall the people because they had turned their backs on Him. With His wrath, the Lord would bring great destruction—but to King

Josiah, the Lord sent a different message. Because he had humbled himself and repented, the Lord would spare him. He would allow Josiah to be at peace and rest with his fathers before the disaster took place.

Evidently King Josiah had known a strong, godly, feminine influence earlier in his life or he certainly would not have entrusted the Book of the Law to a woman. We can imagine that the Lord placed a godly mother in his life to ready him for his royal position. This mother or feminine guardian also prepared him to accept Hulda as God's messenger. The Lord used Hulda's Harmonic Refined spirit as a standard for a king to follow, and she was known for her guidance and wisdom.

Even in a time when men ruled the earth, she was summoned to verify and confirm the will of the Lord. The Lord used her to open the eyes of royalty. She authenticated the Lord's Holy Word that had been lost to an entire generation. Hulda was a true example of a godly woman doing all things decently and in order. Like you, her Harmonic Refined sister, she modeled her life after the Master of order, the Lord God Almighty!

> The heart of her husband safely trusts her; so he will have no lack of gain.
>
> PROVERBS 31:11

Harmonic Refined Working Style

You like working in a highly structured, organized environment. Because of these traits, the more authority you are given, the more you thrive. Ideal positions for you include management or administration. You are the person always asked to head up the committee to write new policies and procedures for your organization. With your keen eye for detail, you address every issue. Nothing is left to chance. Your Harmonic Refined signature is on every piece of work. Everyone knows that if you signed it, then things are in order.

Your preferred style of dress, as well as your spirit, make the corporate environment the ideal place for you to work. Your image type has the corporate image well in hand. Because you like tailored, classic lines, you look the part of the efficient executive and relate well to management. You are a corporate trailblazer; other image types take cues from you in order to climb the corporate ladder. Dressing for the position you want, and not the one you hold, is an unspoken rule of career progression for Harmonic Refined.

A Harmonic Refined might develop and distribute questionnaires to gather data used in decision making. If there are any concerns after the finished product, you simply inform every person involved that you considered their comments before arriving at a final decision, and you make sure everyone understands the process for future reference. For you, every organization should have clear, logical, and orderly policies and procedures in place. If not, you are just the person to develop and implement them. For you and other Harmonic Refineds, this process is clear-cut.

The Harmonic Refined woman needs to be a bit more patient with other image types who need time to process such a system, since they may not fully understand the impact of the results of a questionnaire. Less detail-oriented types simply will not take the time to fill it out—or they may feel that their opinions do not matter, and so not bother. Give them a second opportunity to voice concerns and buy into the process. There will be less future conflict if you and your team take the time to address as many human factors as possible. This action also shows that you care. People respect an understanding leader who respects their opinions. By accepting and working with the differences of others, you help create harmony and calmness in the workplace, and add to your reputation as a truthful and just leader.

> *H*e [She] who has knowledge spares his [her] words, and a man [woman] of understanding is of a calm spirit.
>
> PROVERBS 17:27

You are a genius at planning large events. Only one other image type, the Elegant Flamboyant, is truly suited to put together these events with the same finesse and flair as you. When planning such events, seek out your sister Elegant Flamboyant for assistance. She is great at public relations and very skilled in dealing with people. She can also gain access to people easily because of her savvy. All your sisters can help with such a project—just learn where they best fit in before asking them to join your committee. You are the woman with the plan and the one chosen by the Lord to do all things decently and in order. Have their assignments ready so there will be no conflict.

You strive for stability in your life. Inconsistency in anything is unsettling for you. Being an entrepreneur and starting a business may not be on your list of priorities. If you do desire to go into business, you buy into an existing franchise that has already proved to be successful. The up-and-down swings of a new, untried venture are not appealing to you. One moment things are going well, the next the ceiling is falling in—this type of environment is more suited to image types who love the thrill of uncertainty.

Your need for balance outweighs the rewards of a business venture. For you, it would be a struggle. Your conservative nature allows you to take only calculated risks. You would rather manage the business for the risk taker and receive a handsome salary because the "sure thing" is your usual way of operation. This does not mean you would never take such a risk, but it would only be after extensive investigation and having the necessary capital. With a business plan in hand (remember, Harmonic Refined, you plan your work and work your plan), and your safety net, the Holy Spirit, you feel equipped for success.

When you serve in an executive position, you strive to keep management controls. You and inefficiency cannot survive in the same environment. When this situation arises, you immediately set about repairing what you see as a broken system. You are like a skilled surgeon going after a cancerous tumor: Something will have to go and it is not going to be you, especially if the Lord has placed you in your position. You must have balance, structure, and order. Armed with, and standing on, God's Holy Word, you are a warrior ready for battle.

This goes equally for policies and people. To alleviate any misunderstandings, you revise and rewrite policies with a keen eye until all things are crystal clear. With personnel, you have no problem documenting and counseling until the problem no longer exists. You deal fairly and consider all sides of the issue before making a final decision.

You excel in career fields that call for diplomacy. You do not mind making fair-minded, tough decisions. This attitude does not help you win any popularity contests, but you feel it is more important to be fair than play favorites. You disconnect your personal feelings for the good of the organization. You know from experience that any other way of thinking is counterproductive. With the Lord acting as your Guiding Light, you know He will direct your footsteps and help you make wise decisions.

*D*irect my steps by Your word, and let no iniquity have dominion over me.

PSALMS 119:133

It may appear that you ignore the human factor when dealing with a task. To prevent this, make sure a member of your management team has strong people skills. This member is responsible for keeping you abreast of how your decisions affect personnel. This also helps you keep your Harmonic Refined balance and ensures that people issues are addressed. Using your God-given wisdom, you shine in the eyes of upper-level management because your problem-solving and team management skills address organization and personnel needs.

As a team player, you are usually in the leadership role. You can see the big picture and develop a plan of execution as if by second nature. Dividing the project into sections, and delegating to others who report directly to you, makes execution look easy. Your best ally in the business world is Elegant Flamboyant. Her strong planning and people skills will enhance your role.

Since you are usually in a leadership position, others are sometimes threatened by your consummate appearance and high standards. These qualities may make you appear unapproachable. Don't let this shake you. It is important to realize and understand why others may feel this way. When you encounter this situation, ask the Lord for guidance. It is sometimes hard for others to see their gifts, especially when they are concentrating on you and your gifts. Be aware of this and seek the Lord.

He created you and your Harmonic Refined qualities. He wants you to seek Him on how to use them properly. As long as you follow His lead, you will never go wrong. You will always be the perfect role model for all when you are led by the Holy Spirit. In dealing with all your sisters (and brothers), your Harmonic Refined spirit shines through to keep things orderly and organized. The Lord will give you the actions, the words, and the proper time and place to use your gifts to tear down spiritual walls. He wants you to continually acknowledge that His way is perfect and His word is proven. He will always be your shield as you seek to do His will. Guess what? He will do everything decently and in order. Like your biblical sister Priscilla, the Lord will guide you in your leadership role.

> *A*s for God, His way is perfect; the word of the Lord is proven; He is a shield to all who trust in Him.
>
> II Samuel 22:31

Priscilla

Leader and Minister of the Early Church

> After these things Paul departed from Athens and went to Corinth. And he found a certain Jew named Aquila, born in Pontus, who had recently come from Italy with his wife Priscilla. . . .
>
> Acts 18:2

News of the imperial edict spread rapidly: All Jews were to leave the city. As Priscilla and her husband gathered their belongings, they heard people shouting and soldiers marching in the streets below. They were given a one-day notice to vacate the premises. They felt the tension in the air, but never believed that this would actually happen. As she looked around, Priscilla's heart sank. She had to leave many familiar things behind. There was no room for the large vase she used for oil. She had to settle for taking a smaller one on the long trip. Her favorite plate lay at her feet, broken in what seemed like a thousand pieces. Today everything in her life seemed to be in the same condition as her plate: broken and lost to her forever.

Later, when she really thought about it, material possessions seemed unimportant. At least she and her husband were able to safely leave the city. It had not been so easy for many of their neighbors, who were mobbed or thrown out in the streets by Roman citizens laying claim to each home with all its contents. After all, they were only Jews living in Rome, and in Rome, Romans ruled.

Priscilla and her husband were not sure where they would go. Many cities appealed to them, but the name *Corinth* kept coming up in her thoughts. As they talked quietly, they soon decided they would travel to Corinth. Walking out into the Roman streets soon drowned out thoughts of the life they were leaving behind. This was no longer their home. As night closed in on the travelers, they saw the lights of the city transform into tiny, dim candlelights. They now had no choice but to think about a new start in a new city; in a new home. As they headed into the evening mist, Priscilla and her husband knew their lives were about to dramatically change. What they did not know was that Corinth held spiritual treasures set aside just for them. Their lives were about to change for the glory of the Lord Jesus and the uplifting of His church. The Lord had called out of Rome your Harmonic Refined sister Priscilla, the teacher, and her husband, Aquila.

Priscilla was an Italian Jewess who lived at Corinth and later at Ephesus. She and her husband, Aquila, left Rome when the Emperor Claudius expelled all Jews from the city. Priscilla was known as one of the most influential women in the New Testament church. We know this because three out of the five times that her name was mentioned in the Bible, it appeared *before* that of her husband. This is the evidence that shows she must have played a significant role in the early church.

Her home was a rendezvous point for many early Christians, including Paul. Priscilla and her husband were tent makers, the same trade as the Apostle Paul, so they shared not only in the faith but also in a lifestyle. When Paul left Corinth for Ephesus,

Priscilla and Aquila went with him. He committed the work of the church in Ephesus to them. He would entrust something as precious as a new church only to someone he held in high esteem. In his first letter to the Corinthians from Ephesus, he mentioned Aquila and Priscilla, and the church in their home. In II Timothy 4:19, Paul sent greetings to Prisca (again mentioned before her husband) and Aquila.

The fact that he used "Prisca," a more intimate form of her name, showed that they shared not only a love of the Lord, but a godly love for each other. We find another example of their closeness in Romans 16:3–4. Paul sent greetings to Priscilla and Aquila, and stated that they had risked their own necks for his life, showing again the great affection they had for him.

We can imagine that Priscilla was a beautiful woman of stature. Her presence had to be unforgettable, in order for people to listen to and retain her teachings. This was especially true in those times when the role of women was very different from that of today. We can picture Priscilla in a lavender woolen dress with multicolored trim and a matching headdress. A soft white sash gently encircled her waist. She wore a simple pair of golden earrings and a small gold ring. Her sun-kissed skin was flawless. As she taught, Priscilla's countenance was set aglow from her internal torch, the Holy Spirit. His fire burned intensely within her heart as she taught the word of the Lord. She was God's woman, a born leader on a mission to tell others about the Lord and His saving grace!

As the people gathered, they listened with great interest. They stood amazed at her insight regarding the Scriptures. The Lord used her to feed their hungry souls with the bread of life, His Holy Word. With her discerning spirit, she could see areas of teaching that needed clarification and pick out those in the group who needed individual instruction. She made herself available to answer questions and give guidance to church members. She was not intimidated by challenging questions, nor by the age or gender of the members. Her confidence was in the Lord, and He had fully equipped her for the task at hand. She was an exceptional Harmonic Refined woman of quality, armed with the Sword of the Lord.

An example of Priscilla's exceptional quality was shown when she was able not only to instruct but also to expound to Apollos, an Alexandrian Jew and eloquent speaker said to be mighty in the Scriptures. This was no small feat for a woman of her day and time. The Bible tells us, in Acts 18:25–26, that Apollos knew only of the baptism of John, and Priscilla instructed him in the way of God more accurately. Apollos discerned that this woman was spiritually in tune with the will and way of the Lord. For him not to receive her words would have been a great spiritual loss. This also shows us that Apollos was a man seeking the true way of the Lord, since he willingly accepted teaching from the Lord's chosen vessel, your Harmonic Refined sister Priscilla, the teacher.

There is no doubt that Priscilla had great influence on the early church. After the death of Claudius, Priscilla and Aquila returned to Rome. There they continued in their work for the Lord. Evidence of Priscilla's work lingered long after her death. One of the oldest catacombs of Rome, the Coemetarium Priscilla, along with the Titulus St. Prisca—a church on Rome's Aventine—were named for her. Early Bible scholars have even suggested that Priscilla was the author of the book of Hebrews, since there is evidence it was not written by Paul, but by someone under his tutelage.

Her fire for the Lord burned brightly for all to see and still shines in the heart of today's church. Like you, her present-day Harmonic Refined sister, Priscilla ensured that the church received the correct teaching and was in line with God's Word. She required that all things be done decently, in order, and beautifully Harmonic Refined!

> *A*lthough my house is not so with God, yet
> He has made with me an everlasting covenant;
> ordered in all things and secure. For this is all
> my salvation and all my desire; will He not make
> it increase?
>
> II SAMUEL 23:5

Great Career Choices for the Harmonic Refined

Diplomat
Attorney or Judge
Minister or Teacher
Architect
Accountant
Event or Conference Planner

The Outer You

HARMONIC REFINED CLOTHING CHOICES

The two D's, Defined and Disciplined, are quality keys for dressing in Harmonic Refined style. You are an enlightened, conservative dresser who prefers classic, tailored lines. Other image types take cues from you to succeed in the business world. Balanced styling, classic and conservatively tailored suits, and polished accessories are your necessities. The style of your shoes must be in harmony with your suit, your suit must be in harmony with your purse, and so on. Every item must be harmonic or it is eliminated.

Controlled elegance is your style signature. Smooth, clean, crisp, elegant lines define all your clothing choices. Anything bulky or light and airy with lace and ruffles does not fit your wardrobe. If you do wear a lace blouse, the lace on the collar and cuffs is hand-sewn so it lies flat and stays in place. A style or fabric that moves or bounces is not Harmonic Refined. Everything must be in place and anchored down, yet remain elegant. Light and airy styles are for your sister Chantilly Graceful. You gladly step aside and let her wear them. The "frill of it all" is just too much for you.

When describing your wardrobe, the word *quality* comes to mind. Harmonic Refined style is the essence of quality. You prefer natural fabrics such as leather, wool, cotton, and silk. Investing in clothing with timeless styling and natural fibers is the epitome of your image type. Silk linings grace all your suits. Your shoes and purses are leather. Your everyday accessories are of the highest quality available. For a special evening event, your accessories are always elegant. Your favorite evening handbag is black silk with tiny rhinestone accents. Your matching pumps shine as the rhinestones catch the evening lights. You will not have too much glitter, but just enough to add a touch of class. You leave the large rhinestone accents to other image types, who wear them with style. For you, it is all classic or nothing. If you cannot find accessories with just the right size of stones, then you opt for the plain, simple elegance of black silk pumps and matching bag without accents.

At casual events, other image types may feel you are overdressed. This is especially true for sporting events, where you are comfortable in dressed-up casual. You always prefer tailored slacks over jeans, and your favorite pair is silk-lined wool for cool temperatures, or a cool, crisp linen for warmer seasons. If you do own a pair of jeans, they will be of the highest quality available. The length and fit will be perfect, and you wear them with a silk tee top and a classic jacket. Worn with your stylish Italian leather slippers, this casual look is a hit for the Harmonic Refined. Underneath, you are sure to have on hose. If you wear socks, they closely resemble hose and are in a classic pattern that perfectly matches your outfit.

Wearing jeans is an adventurous move for your image type. This move is disarming to others and makes you appear more approachable. Instead of choosing your classic silk blouse, try a soft cotton pullover under your classic tailored jacket. Learn to relax with clothing shapes as well as fabric. The relaxed pullover is just a softer version of style. You can also try an unstructured blouson—for example, a flight jacket in silk, with a matching silk tee. This look is casual yet is still dressy enough to meet your standards.

Sometimes softening your structured stance adds spice to your life. You will also make some wonderful discoveries about yourself and others. It opens doors to witness and share the Gospel. It opens doors to the fountain of life, the Lord Jesus. You bring Him glory as you shine, lifting up the name of the Lord as He uses you to draw others to Him.

> *A*nd I, if I am lifted up from the earth, will draw all peoples to Myself.
>
> JOHN 12:32

Harmonic Refined types frequent certain stores to buy individual items. For example, you buy your favorite shoes at one store, your suits at another, and your blouses and jewelry at still another. You also like using the services of a personal shopper. Your shopper scans stores for your wardrobe favorites and sets up appointments for fittings and home showings. He or she knows exactly what to look for, having learned your style preferences. When selecting your personal shopper, you check references and ensure the prospective shopper has a proven track record. This saves time, because you want to work with a sound businessperson. Having a personal shopper is the Harmonic Refined way to go: It helps you do things decently and in order.

If money is no object, you work with a personal designer. Designer home showings are also definitely in line with Harmonic Refined shopping tastes. Your designer brings the items, lays them out, and shows each piece individually and with its proper accessories. You view each ensemble while sipping tea from a china cup with a matching saucer. The designer then helps you choose the right pieces and combinations that will carry you through the season. As the season progresses, you pick up a few accessories to accent your new pieces, but forgo any additional shopping. You expect a call from your designer if anything new becomes available. You then arrange to have the items delivered to you.

This only happens after you have established a trusting relationship with your designer. If this type of arrangement is not within your budget, you buy quality items one at a time until you have the complete ensemble. You would rather have one good outfit than two or three of lesser quality. Not having the full amount to pay for an item does not bother you since you set goals and have learned to shop at the right time and place for your type of clothing. You are an expert at layaway. You are a smart shopper and you have a schedule as to when and where to buy all your wardrobe favorites. Once you have established your loyalties, your search ends.

Since organization and time are valuable, catalogs are an important part of Harmonic Refined shopping. You enjoy feeling relaxed and pampered, knowing you will not have to fight the crowd. You are loyal to only a few catalogs since each one represents a piece of your image puzzle. You are patient and diligently seek the perfect source for each Harmonic Refined item.

You know your footsteps are ordered by the Lord, and you represent Him in all you do, even your appearance. Like the Lord, who upholds you with His Mighty Hand, you believe all things must be done decently and in order, including your beautiful Harmonic Refined wardrobe.

> The steps of a good man [woman] are ordered by the Lord, and He delights in his way. Though he [she] fall, he [she] shall not be utterly cast down; for the Lord upholds him [her] with His hand.
>
> PSALMS 37:23–24

HARMONIC REFINED FULL-FIGURED CLOTHING CHOICES

Fashion has finally remembered the Harmonic Refined full-figured woman. Most designers have created collections exclusively for you. There are classic, tailored styles in your size that are comparable to those of your smaller sister. Timeless, straight lines with elegant accessories are Harmonic Refined image builders. Since you are full-figured, you can add a bit more drama with your accessories than your smaller sister. Take a cue from the Elegant Flamboyant in the accessory department. Larger, more dramatic, yet still classic styles are wonderfully yours for the asking. Look for something midstream between your basic Harmonic Refined and the Elegant Flamboyant to be on target.

Look for Harmonic Refined basic accessory styling and then go one step beyond to try something a little larger with a touch of drama. That choice should be perfect. You can carry the larger accessories well because of your classic Harmonic Refined presence. Go on and experiment a little! You will see wonderful results. Add a scarf with an oversized but elegant scarf clip. The clip keeps the scarf from shifting, giving you the controlled elegance you need. If you do not feel comfortable with a scarf, try wearing a large brooch on your suit lapel. Add matching earrings and you have the perfect full-figured Harmonic Refined look.

It is important that your clothing fit properly, because ill-fitting clothing ruins a wonderful appearance. If your hips are the fullest part of your body, use the Fingertip Rule for your jackets. This simple technique enables you to wear just about any type of skirt, as long as it fits properly. If you have full hips, it also acts as a great way to camouflage the fullness.

To use the Fingertip Rule, your jacket should fall approximately a hand length below the fullest part of your hips. Stand with your arms relaxed at your sides. Notice where your fingertips fall. This is the perfect length for your jackets. This length will enable you to wear straight skirts and those wonderful designer knits you love. You know, the ones that seem to hug your curves just a little too close for your tastes? You will be able to wear that classic knit dress you bought last season. Remember the one you just could not leave in the store? After getting home, you had second thoughts about wearing it because of your hip size, and it still hangs in your closet. Now you can take it out and wear it with Harmonic Refined style!

Make sure your jackets fit properly. Even the Fingertip Rule cannot make ill-fitting clothing look good. Always buy your jackets larger rather than smaller if your size is unavailable. It is better for a jacket to be a bit loose than to pull when you raise your arms or move. Forget the size printed on the label; buy what fits properly. You will be thankful, because your clothing is comfortable and looks good. Others in your life will be thankful, too, because your total attitude changes when your clothes fit Harmonic Refined perfect.

> *F*or You are my lamp, O Lord; the Lord shall enlighten my darkness.
>
> II Samuel 22:29

KEY WORDS FOR THE HARMONIC REFINED DRESS CODE

Symmetry
Smooth, Clear, Crisp, Clean Lines
Elegance, Tailored
Minimal Detail

HARMONIC REFINED COLOR SCHEMES

Safe, monochromatic color schemes speak the Harmonic Refined color language. You prefer neutrals and blends over contrasts. If you wear a gray suit, you choose a light gray blouse rather than fuchsia because it blends. You leave the gray-and-fuchsia combination for a more dramatic image type or for a time when you want to add a little drama to your life. With your classic purple suit, you wear a soft lavender blouse. The lavender blends with the purple and does not attract attention. You own several white and eggshell blouses. They beautifully display your conservative styling and the orderliness of your image type.

Subdued elegance also sings your color theme song. Black, beige, and brown overwhelm your closet. If you have blue, it is usually navy. This is not to say that you do not wear other colors. To put it simply, you are conservative and prefer a more subdued look. Muted, safe, stable coloring is Harmonic Refined color styling. Everything, including your wardrobe color choices, must be in line with your central image theme of controlled elegance.

Many variables affect your color choices. One is your present career. If you work in banking or another conservative field, there is safety in navy blues and browns, accented with eggshell, gray, burgundy, and subtle hints of white. If you are in a more relaxed profession, such as the fashion industry, you still remain true to your basics but use controlled accents of energy colors like purple or red. On a rare occasion, you might be found in large, bright splashes of color, but most likely those bright splashes are not your style and attract undesired attention. If you decide to wear a bold color, it will usually be one wardrobe item—a red dress, for example, but topped with a black jacket and black shoes. Your sister Elegant Flamboyant would wear a red-and-black jacket with red-and-black pumps. On her head would be a matching hat. Except for special occasions, you leave the high drama for her and opt instead for a conservative stance.

When extra impact is needed, however, you have no problem taking a cue from your Elegant Flamboyant sister by stepping out in brighter colors. The colors may be flamboyant, but your styling and accessories will still be very Harmonic Refined. Reds, purples, and electric blues waltz to the Harmonic Refined symphony. Your red power suit will be the talk of your business meeting. Your regal purple suit easily stops any show when you enter the professional arena. Wear these outfits with one of your beautiful white blouses and your trademark pearls, and the sweet smell of success permeates the room.

Your own personal coloring is also an important factor. If you are fair-skinned, you may feel more comfortable in soft camel brown or beige. If you are medium- or dark-skinned, you may choose to be a bit more adventurous and wear purple, red, or electric blue. It really depends on your individual tastes and coloring. Every color selection helps you maintain color balance and controlled elegance. If you have an eye for color, begin experimenting to discover hues that suit your lifestyle and look best with your natural coloring. If you need assistance, consult a color analyst for expert advice on how to use colors effectively and still maintain image credibility. A consultation saves time and money in the long run. It also gives you Harmonic Refined information on helping achieve your desired outcome in clothing color choices.

Classic and elegant coloring always make up the Harmonic Refined color palette. Blending with just a touch of contrast makes your heart sing. You step out with classic styling like no other in the fullness of Harmonic Refined beauty. Setting the stage for keeping things in line and in order, you are a beautiful creation in lovely Harmonic Refined color schemes. The Lord is well pleased as you glorify Him and unwrap His precious first gift, your beautiful image, for all the world to see.

> *M*any daughters have done well, but you excel them all.
>
> PROVERBS 31:29

HARMONIC REFINED JEWELRY

As the creator of classic, you choose jewelry that fits your image. Using one large piece as a wardrobe theme, you coordinate accent pieces to complete your look. Dangling, moving, or shaking pieces usually do not appeal to you. Most of your jewelry has to stay put so that it does not detract from Harmonic Refined balance. Remember, controlled elegance is the nucleus of Harmonic Refined image stability.

You prefer fine jewelry over costume. Since you like precious stones, diamonds, emeralds, and rubies speak your language. If these stones are not in line with your budget, then you own beautiful imitations. Although you buy imitations of the stones, the settings will be the real thing. Sterling silver and gold hold your precious replicas in Harmonic Refined style. If you wear costume jewelry, it will be high quality; no one will know it's not the real thing. If it's inexpensive, it will be so tasteful that no one can tell the difference.

Your jewelry box is neat and orderly. It is important to keep all your ensemble pieces together. Your collections are packaged in smaller boxes and kept together so you do not have to search when you want to wear them. You have a special drawer set aside in your dresser when your jewelry box becomes overcrowded. Keeping your jewelry scratch-free is important for Harmonic Refined image credibility.

A piece of furniture made just for the Harmonic Refined is the standing jewelry chest or armoire. It stands approximately chest high and serves as a jewelry box and accessory storage all in one. It has several small drawers in the center for your jewelry and a large ring storage area on top. The sides swing outward and reveal hooks to hang necklaces and scarves. The bottom half has larger drawers to store your boxed sets or silk scarves. It is a true treasure chest and an elegant place to store your jewelry. It is also a wonderful-looking piece of furniture and perfect for the orderly Harmonic Refined.

Just as you have favorite places to buy your clothing, the same holds true for your jewelry. You have loyalties to certain lines. Your expertly trained eyes seek out Harmonic Refined jewelry pieces, and know exactly where to find them. You also know exactly what you need and when you need it. Just as you do with your clothing, you enjoy buying entire jewelry collections. If you like the earrings, then you look for the matching necklace, brooch, and bracelet. You are confident with your style and know it is better to get things when you see them, for you will wear them over and over again. In this, as in all areas of your life, you prepare for life's adventures by doing all things decently and in order. You are a vessel of honor prepared to do the work of your Lord in all your Harmonic Refined beauty!

> Therefore if anyone cleans himself from the latter, he [she] will be a vessel for honor, sanctified and useful for the Master, prepared for every good work.
>
> II TIMOTHY 2:21

Harmonic Refined Hair

Your typical hairstyle is neat and elegant. A blunt cut falling just at the shoulders is sure to be a favorite. You also like a perfect short, tapered cut. Both will satisfy your Harmonic Refined taste for elegance. Your well-groomed hair is always in place. Even on a stay-at-home day, you comb and style your hair to prepare for unexpected visitors or events.

Going to the salon on a weekly basis is not a luxury because having your hair done is a necessary part of image maintenance. You are loyal to one hairstylist. Once you find your stylist, you have a standing appointment, unless you are out of town. Because of this loyalty, you usually will not allow anyone else to touch your lovely tresses.

Other image types try home perms, but not you. You believe in letting the professionals do their jobs so there will be no mistakes with your hair. Your stylist uses only one line of hair care products and instructs you in proper care between appointments. Because you believe in doing things decently and in order, you follow those instructions to the letter. You know your hair and crowning glory will be the direct beneficiary of your obedience.

Your hair is always well groomed, but that does not mean it is always in the most becoming style. Be sure to choose a style that enhances your face shape. Sometimes you wear a style because it has looked right for the last few years and always worked for you. Ease up on your conservative stance and experiment a little. Evaluate and, if necessary, update your look at least every two years. It may mean changing that bob cut you have been wearing for the last three years. Go on, live a little. It will give you a fresh new look and make you feel better, too. Make sure the style is complementary to your face shape before taking the plunge. Your stylist should have a face shape guide for you to check out new styles. Face shape is extremely important and could be the difference in your looking older or younger. Your style should also be in line with your lifestyle and image type.

In the hair-coloring department, you lead the way for women of color. You are always careful to make sure your hair blends with your natural coloring. You know that a deep rich auburn, a cocoa, or a chestnut brown looks wonderful against your radiant skin. There are also some wonderful burgundies on the market that give hair a brilliance and luster in any lighting. They look great with golden to brown skin tones as well. You choose your coloring wisely to complement your honey-gold, caramel-brown, walnut, cocoa-brown, or ebony skin tone. You know that the Lord presented you with the natural gift of awesome coloring, and you refuse to destroy it with an uncomplimentary hair shade.

Harmonic Refined women of Latina, Asian, or Native American descent know their magnificent black hair is beautiful the way it is. Nothing man has created can compare with your dark, rich tresses. You already know that ash-blond hair does nothing for your natural coloring, so you do not try to wear it. If you do experiment, you try some of the burgundies described above. You know they classically enhance and do not detract from your God-given beauty. Burgundy also blends with your natural skin coloring to give it that special Harmonic Refined polish.

You stay ready to meet the challenges of hair management with Harmonic Refined style. Staying with a classic strategy in your hair routine, you never go wrong. You radiate happiness with Harmonic Refined styling and show an inner beauty that comes only from the Lord.

> *H*e [She] who heeds the word wisely will find good, and whoever trusts in the Lord, happy is he [she].
>
> PROVERBS 16:20

Harmonic Refined Makeup

Harmonic Refined makeup application is always harmonically perfect. You want others to notice your face and not concentrate on your makeup. Before you choose cosmetics, you first work on your skin. It must be as clear of blemishes as possible. For you, it is important to have a beautiful piece of canvas before you can paint your Harmonic Refined picture. Once you have mastered a skin maintenance routine, you move on to the next logical step, color application.

You research and investigate until you find the cosmetic line that offers skin care as well as beautiful colors for your lips, eyes, and cheeks. If the line offers skin care, you see it as credible. Your image type does not believe in mixing different lines of cosmetics and will use only one line at a time. Once you have found it, you remain faithful as long as the line remains faithful and retains its quality. The line must offer everything from cover-up to a wide range of colors for it to be a true Harmonic Refined image asset.

Using a facial cleanser is just as important as your favorite lip color. You never want to run low. You buy an extra supply of all your cosmetic items and keep them in stock. If you travel frequently, a full set of your personal necessities is set aside just for trips. You also have a full set that stays put on your dressing table. Since organized elegance is a key to Harmonic Refined cosmetic success, you use a checklist to ensure you do not run out.

A skin care consultant who makes house calls fits in well with your lifestyle and beauty needs. If there is a line on the market that offers such a service as well as a quality product, you are one of its best customers. Just as with your clothing selection, you would be comfortable looking over the line in the comfort of your living room while sipping tea. This saves time and allows you to relax while keeping up with your image needs. It also gives you two critical factors that a Harmonic Refined requires: personalized care and the time just for you.

If you are medium- to dark-skinned, your skin is the canvas for your classic picture. Your evenly applied foundation always blends with your natural skin tone, and you use burgundies, plums, and coppers to enhance your radiant dark beauty. Expertly highlighting your ebony, bronze, or olive skin with controlled, elegant coloring is your trademark. You define your lips, cheeks, and eyes with classic brushstrokes. Deep navy, smoked purple, and rich copper sing your Harmonic Refined song.

Subdued, elegant coloring permeates your palette, and the beauty of your countenance—from café au lait to deepest ebony—shines for all the world to see. You are as beautiful as your biblical sister Priscilla when she instructed Apollos in the ways of the Lord. In Harmonic Refined style, whatever your ethnic heritage, you are the Lord's creation and beautiful to behold. You are ready to speak your classic language without saying a word. Your polished appearance says it all for you. Once you have made your final choices and have applied your look, it is easy to see why others take cues from you in the makeup department.

Others can see that the Lord has His hand in your life as you shine in Harmonic Refined style. Whether your ethnic heritage is that of the European queen, the Asian empress, the Latina *condesa*, the Native American or the Nubian princess, you give God glory with a classic, polished appearance. You highlight and color your eyes, cheeks, and lips harmonically together, harmonically in line. Just like your image type, Harmonic Refined!

> The Lord is good to all; and His tender mercies are over all His works.
>
> Psalms 145:9

4. *Elegant Flamboyant*

Vivid, bold, dramatic with flair,
the Elegant Flamboyant, the Lord's jewel rare!

The wicked flee when no one pursues,
but the righteous are bold as a lion.

PROVERBS 28:1

The Beauty of Elegant Flamboyant

Do you use hats, capes, and scarves for drama in your dressing? Do others often compliment your style and fashion savvy? Do you hold your own private dress rehearsals before you wear any new outfit? Do you enjoy making dramatic entrances? Then you are Elegant Flamboyant. Your image type epitomizes style. You like sleek, classic styling with a dash of high drama.

There are times when others think you are showing off with your flamboyance. Let no one be fooled: What they see is the real you. The Lord created you with dramatic flair and boldness. This drama cannot be imitated. It is a gift from the Father that was interwoven into your being during the creation process before your birth. In other words, it is the real thing. Your dramatic beauty makes you stand out in a crowd.

You do not mind being noticed because you were created Elegant Flamboyant. Standing out in a crowd comes with the territory. You could not blend in even if you tried. Your walk, talk, and actions are noticeably dramatic, yet you are also elegant and chic. Your style of dress speaks the fashion language with authority, and your spirit only confirms that authority. Your lifestyle and appearance are fashion-forward with flair!

The Inner You

You do not believe in doing things halfway. It is all or nothing for you. Your need for excitement and drama easily converts the smallest mundane tasks into great adventures. People are motivated by you, and one of your most positive traits is being able to see the gifts of others and giving them the space to use these gifts. You enjoy seeing others flourish and prosper.

Because you are secure in your own right, you encourage others to fully use their God-given talents. You are able to see a bigger picture than most and to see the Lord exalted in all things. You feel that when everyone uses their God-given gifts, then He receives all the honor. You firmly believe that it is the Giver and not the gift that must be glorified. Elegant Flamboyant's second nature is to be encouraging and let others know just how special they are to the Lord.

> *H*aving gifts differing according to the grace that is given to us, let us use them. . . .
>
> ROMANS 12:6

Most people see you as larger than life and very exciting. Your natural gift of motivation places you in great demand in many circles. Watching others prosper is an Elegant Flamboyant energizer. People look to you to bring action to any given situation because your energy and enthusiasm are contagious. You enjoy letting others know that the Source of your energy is the Lord, and He freely gives to those who are open to receive it.

When you meet people who are uncomfortable with your style, try to be sensitive to their feelings. The first thing you should do is go before the Lord. Prayer keeps you focused on the things of God and not on the responses of others. If you decide to focus on the people and the behavior, you will become angry and respond with harshness. When you keep your focus, you realize that the Elegant Flamboyant spirit and appearance can be overwhelming to more reserved image types. This is not to say that you can control others or how they choose to perceive you. You are just sensitive and acutely aware of the impression you make.

Just remember how the Lord Jesus, with His flamboyant style, was so unpopular that they crucified Him. Just thinking of what He went through for you will make you stronger and better equipped to face rejection.

In friendship, you are loyal and have high expectations. Many times, people are hesitant to explain that your expectations seem impossible in their eyes, and they just cannot meet them. Since they love you, they do not want to fail in your eyes, so they exit the kill zone or abandon the relationship. It is during these times that your friends seem to drift away from you. You see this as rejection and disloyalty, when this is usually not the case at all. Sometimes you forget that others may not share your vision of friendship.

Your view is that you do not ask any more than you are willing to give, so in your mind the situation is clear-cut. Stop and pray! When you notice others disengaging, take it to the Lord in prayer. Review your expectations and ask the Lord for guidance. The Holy Spirit will faithfully give you answers. If your expectations are too high, He will gently let you know. He will also help you become more tolerant of others. He will give you the appropriate words when discussing the situation with your friend. Try to remember that yours is not the only viewpoint involved. You may not have communicated your perspective clearly from the beginning. Friendship is a beautiful experience that can last a lifetime. Nurture it with the fruit of the spirit: love, joy, peace, long-suffering, kindness, goodness, faithfulness, gentleness, and self-control. After all, where would you be if He were less tolerant of you with His expectations?

Learn to forgive and accept your friends, faults and all. If you do not, you will experience disappointment and loneliness. The Lord did not create any perfect human beings. We all must strive to be more like Jesus. If we were perfect, what need would we have for the Lord? He created us finite human beings with faults and frailties so we would learn to depend on Him and His mercy and grace. Praise Him, for His mercy never fails.

Oh give thanks to the Lord, for He is good! For His mercy endures forever.

I CHRONICLES 16:34

Being direct and exerting authority are strong traits of your image type. When led by the Lord, you use these traits wisely. You are usually not harsh but clear and direct—what others call assertive. At times, others feel your assertiveness is harsh. It's sometimes difficult for others to absorb your direct nature and dramatic appearance simultaneously. Always try to keep this in mind and take the time to explain your position in a nonthreatening, calm manner.

Do not become impatient when others misinterpret your words and actions. Remember, Ms. Elegant Flamboyant, you are majestic and dramatic, and your appearance may sometimes be a distraction. Others may not hear what you say in the beginning. Patience and kindness will go a long way. Learn also to listen for what others may *not* be saying. Ask the Lord for help in discerning. He will give you godly wisdom and fine-tune your spiritual ear so you can listen to the language of the heart.

During a crisis, people turn to you because of your problem-solving ability. You are able to take control. Your calm appearance is a definite asset during these times. To others, you may appear to be unfeeling, because you remove those who are not productive and put those to work who are ready and willing. Your built-in radar makes a quick analysis of the situation, and a mental printout of the desired results becomes your plan of action. It is during these times that you need to use a little patience. Your usual crisis motto—"Lead, follow, or get out of the way"—may seem harsh. This does not mean you should discard it. There will be times when you must use it to cut through the enemy's devices.

Just remember, you still represent the Lord, and He is always in control. Cover all life's events, before acting, with prayer.

If the situation is one where you have no expertise, you will be in charge of crowd control and keep others back until help arrives. You are the type that responds to a crisis and clears up the problem—then the full impact of the situation hits you and you collapse, but only after everything is under control. It is as if you have a strong Hand holding you, and a fine-tuned Guidance System kicks in during trying times. Your strong Hand and Guidance System are the best available. They are Jehovah Jireh, your Provider, ready and willing to act when you call Him and allow Him to guide you.

> *F*ear not, for I am with you; be not dismayed, for I am your God. I will strengthen you, yes, I will uphold you with My righteous right hand.
>
> ISAIAH 41:10

On the flip side of this, when you're not in tune spiritually, things become unbalanced. You may become forceful or totally withdraw to get your way. This forceful manner can be offensive to others. Again, be aware of how your actions affect others and explain your thoughts and reactions so there will be no misunderstandings. The enemy will use this area if you allow him. Do not give him an opening.

You use a great deal of energy. If not managed, this can lead to stress and a withdrawal from the public. When you withdraw, it creates a vacuum because you are usually in the thick of things. Your silence cuts the air like a knife. You become moody and irritable. Because you are so visible and high-powered, your attitude is very contagious. You can unintentionally cause others to adopt your mood. This is not to say you are responsible for the actions and feeling of others. To put it quite simply, you have a charismatic presence. You have a tremendous influence and impact on people everywhere you go.

This is a great responsibility or honor, depending on how you look at it. The Lord has given you the ability to effect change in the lives of others. You are what others call a "persuader of people." Depending on whom you serve, the Lord or His enemy, you have the ability to influence others to go either way.

God created you for honor and awesome responsibility. You are His elegant warrior, and He would not have you any other way. You may be the only Jesus someone sees, and your actions are a part of you. Yes, being able to influence others is a great responsibility, but you can handle it, if you hold on to His unchanging hand. To whom much is given, much is required—and, my Elegant Flamboyant sister, the Lord has blessed your life abundantly. He expects little compared with the generous gifts He has given you.

It is imperative to keep your prayer life intact by keeping an open channel to the Lord and by reading your Bible. Daily talking with Him makes all the difference and keeps you plugged in to your Power Source. He gave you the elegance and flamboyance to show His glory and majesty! Having balance in all you do ensures that you remain a beautiful, willing vessel for the Lord. No woman in the Bible represents the Elegant Flamboyant better than the Queen of Sheba.

> *F*or everyone to whom much is given, from him [her] much will be required; and to whom much has been committed of him [her] they will ask the more.
>
> LUKE 12:48

The Queen of Sheba

BEAUTY THAT RULED A NATION

Now when the Queen of Sheba heard of the fame of
Solomon, she came to Jerusalem to test Solomon with
hard questions, having a very great retinue, camels that
bore spices, gold in abundance, and precious stones, and
when she came to Solomon, she spoke with him about
all that was in her heart.

II CHRONICLES 9:1

Each day brought more new and exciting news of this king of
Jerusalem. Caravan travelers, merchants, and neighboring heads
of state described his palace halls. They talked of his luxurious
furnishings and the vastness of his wealth. They told stories of
how even his servants lived in luxury, eating from golden plates
and drinking from golden goblets. They described the size of his
household and how all Israel prospered. Under the rule of this
monarch, this wise king of Israel, everyone seemed healthy,
wealthy, and satisfied.

Storytellers told of how the king settled disputes with such
insight that it amazed all who stood in his company. They told of
how he judged the conflict between two women over a child.
Each woman claimed the child as her own. The king told the
women that he would resolve the issue by taking his sword and
cutting the living child in half. He then would give each woman
half a child. The real mother, not wanting her child to die, relinquished her claim and told him to give the child away so that the
child could live. The king, Solomon of Israel, knew immediately
that she was the real mother and restored her child to her. All Israel feared and revered him. They knew that his wisdom was a gift
from his God.

The Queen of Sheba had heard enough. The time had come

for her to go and see this great king for herself. She, too, reigned over a kingdom and was known for her keen intellect. She, too, had great wealth and power. In these times, she held the highest position in her domain. Everyone paid homage to her, for she was queen. She had the final say on all matters in her kingdom.

During this time in history, women of her country held high offices and commanded the same respect, authority, and honor as men in the same position. The queen's Elegant Flamboyant qualities, no doubt, enhanced her ruling ability. She was regal, dramatic, and impressive, even to men. They respected her not only as a monarch but also as a beautiful, powerful woman. This monarch, this beautiful Elegant Flamboyant who was about to make one of the most historic journeys of all times, was your sister, the magnificent Queen of Sheba.

We can imagine that the Queen of Sheba was a majestic, impressive woman who from her youth received life's best training. The magnificence of her appearance and grace was stunning to all who saw her. She dressed in the finest purple silks woven with golden threads. She wore her hair in elaborate braids that her attendants pulled back and then covered with a matching headdress. On her ears, she wore heavy golden earrings, encrusted with jewels. Golden bracelets hung from her wrists, and rings from the royal treasure chests adorned her fingers. Jewels sparkled from each piece. On her head was the ultimate symbol of her power: A golden crown, lavishly decorated with precious jewels, announced to the entire world she was sovereign. She did everything with a dramatic flair. She was Elegant Flamboyant at its royal best.

She ruled the land of Saba, which was located in southwestern Arabia. Ruling a country was no small feat, especially for a woman of her day. Keeping up with royal business and the constant flow of news was exhausting. One piece of news constantly stimulated her curiosity, interrupted her thinking, and stayed on her mind. No one person could possibly be as rich, wise, and as honored as Solomon, king of Israel. The Queen of Sheba decided to go and see for herself if all the stories brought before her were true.

She knew the journey would not be easy. She knew she would be exposed to heat and heavy sandstorms. She knew her huge caravan would attract the attention of all who saw it. She also knew she would not have the comfort of her palace. None of these factors stopped her from making the trip. She lost sleep because these stories so consumed her life, but she had no choice. She had to go and see Jerusalem and this mighty King Solomon for herself.

Great drama surrounded her journey. Over arduous terrain in the heat and sand, the queen and her caravan traveled, until they reached Jerusalem. The Bible tells us in I Kings 10:2 that she came to Jerusalem with a very great retinue (company), with camels that bore spices, much gold, and precious stones. Your Elegant Flamboyant sister came prepared to see the great king and to pay homage with her gifts.

We can imagine that your Elegant Flamboyant sister, after her long journey, had her attendants bathe her in scented waters, massage fine oils into her sand-stroked skin, and then ready her for her entrance. She approached Solomon's palace in her finest royal robes, her most extravagant jewels, and her most magnificent crown. The Bible says she came to Solomon and spoke with him about all that was in her heart. He answered all her questions above and beyond her satisfaction. In II Chronicles 9:4, the Bible says that after she saw his house and the display of his wealth, there was no more spirit in her. In other words, she fainted. You know Solomon and his kingdom must have been totally awesome for that to have happened! She now believed all the reports concerning the king. She blessed the name of the Lord, his God, for making Solomon king over Israel. This is significant, since Sheba was an idolatrous country.

The Queen of Sheba was a woman of determination and power. She was not only satisfied with what she saw, but praised

the name of the God of Israel for the blessings she beheld and received. She knew that only a God could have made such prosperity and wisdom possible. This queen was a determined woman
who liked to discover things for herself. Although she heard the
reports and did not know if they were true, she went prepared
with gifts fit for a great king. Her visit made history, not only because she was a queen, but because of her character. Her visit
marked the beginning of a new era of commercial expansion for
Israel.

Like you, her present-day Elegant Flamboyant sister, the
Queen of Sheba stood out as a righteous woman who sought truth
no matter what the cost. Harsh winds and rough terrain could not
stop her. Heat exhaustion and physical discomfort would not
make her turn back. After her arrival, your Elegant Flamboyant
sister discovered that the real source of life, health, and prosperity
was the Lord God of Israel!

Elegant Flamboyant Strengths in the Body of Christ

Evangelist
Counselor
Church Fund-Raising Chair

Elegant Flamboyant and Family Life

As a mother, you appear to do it all. You have your home, career,
and family activities under control. Even your children admire
your style. They love the way Mom can do almost anything and
still look great doing it. You are patient and encourage them to do
whatever they desire. As a loving mother, you do your best to

guide them down the right path. You see their gifts and help them explore areas where they can fully use those gifts. You are wise enough to know that when people freely use their gifts, they operate at their best.

When they are involved in a difficult task, you encourage and motivate your children. You are always available to help, but you want them to meet challenges head-on. When you allow your children to work through their problems, they sharpen their skills. With patience and timing, while carefully monitoring the situation, you ask the right questions to guide them to the solution. Their radiant smiles tell you they have savored the sweetness of a desire accomplished.

> *A* desire accomplished is sweet to the soul. . . .
> PROVERBS 13:19

You realize your children are individuals and try to treat them accordingly. Sometimes you may be a bit too direct and unknowingly hurt little feelings. Be aware that these little ones look up to you with love and admiration. Your straight-arrow remarks can hurt. Children are individuals who think, feel, and act differently from Mom. If you have a child who has a temperament similar to your own, you may be harder on him. If your child is different from you, you may want her to be more like you. Sound difficult? You bet it is! Being a parent is one of the toughest jobs on earth, but you know it is also one of the most rewarding.

Stop and take a long, hard look at the situation and personalities involved. Then stop and reflect on your own sensitivity. Think about how you would feel if you were in this situation with your own mother. (Now, that should be challenging enough for you!) How would you want her to respond to you and your feelings? What words would you long to hear? How would you want to feel after a disagreement? Ask the Lord to guide you. You can still get your point across without hurting feelings. Remember, your children are clay and you are the earthly sculptor. Impressions in this precious clay last a lifetime.

Your maternal radar works overtime. You see and feel when your little ones are in distress. You know just when to ease up and give some of those famous Elegant Flamboyant positive strokes. They love it because no one strokes them like you. Using love and encouragement, you guide your children to excellence. You are an exhorter and an expert at building self-worth in your children. Elegance and flamboyance become definite assets in this area.

Your little ones love your sense of adventure. Since you like doing things in a big way, even the most boring activities become animated excursions with you in the driver's seat. They hold on and you take them on a whirlwind tour of adventure. Whether it is cleaning their rooms or washing the dinner dishes, you know just how to make it fun and exciting. That is your trademark. Elegantly fun, elegantly exciting, elegantly flamboyant—and they love you for it! They go to school and describe your adventures, and other children envy them. You have to set visiting hours at your home because other children love to come over. Do they come to see your children—or their Elegant Flamboyant mom? Your children know that their home is the hot spot in the neighborhood and they know why. They have a jewel of a mom and they want all the world to know it!

For you, it is critical that your children be educated not only in the natural, but also in the spiritual. You let them know the house rules, and also warn them that you will clean out their rooms regularly. You will not give the enemy a place in your home. Your children know to come to you if there are questions about items they think may be unpleasant to you or the Lord. He established the home as a safe haven, and Mother Elegant Flamboyant stays in a constant battle stance, working with the Holy Spirit to keep it that way.

You teach them to set and attain goals. Learning this early in life leads to later success. Like your sister Harmonic Refined, you believe in planning for success and teaching your little ones the same lesson. You differ from your Harmonic Refined sister because you still like spontaneity in your life. Sometimes you hold impromptu celebrations for your children's accomplishments. You call the school and arrange a surprise lunch date or shopping trip for your little one. These surprises are jewels your children are sure to carry in their lifetime treasure chests. You are sure to fill those chests to the brim with Elegant Flamboyant love.

> *H*er children rise up and call her blessed; Her husband also, and he praises her.
>
> PROVERBS 31:28

Like your biblical sister Phoebe, you find that your family and close friends bask in your generous, godly spirit.

Phoebe

DEACONESS AND EVANGELIST OF THE EARLY CHURCH

I commend to you Phoebe our sister, who is a servant of the church in Cenchrea, that you may receive her in the Lord in a manner worthy of saints, and assist her in whatever business she has need of you; for indeed she has been a helper of many and of myself also.

ROMANS 16:1–2

Excitement filled the air as the news spread through the Christian community like wildfire. An important visitor was coming within the next few days. She always brought love, warmth, and her own special brand of kindness. Her smile lit up their lives like a bright summer's day. On her way, she'd be visiting other churches, so she was sure to bring news. Anticipation floated through the air like a flurry of butterflies and would not settle down until she arrived.

They all knew this godly servant would do all within her power to ensure that their church prospered. She freely gave of all she had. Nothing was too good for the Lord's church. She always invested her time, knowledge, and money in feeding His flock. Being firmly rooted and grounded in God's word, she came prepared to teach and advise. When she arrived, some came because they needed new clothes. Some came just to get a compassionate hug. Some came for prayer. And still others came to feast on new teachings and much-needed words of encouragement. When she was with them, she had something for everyone. This was to be a time of great rejoicing, for the Lord was sending her to minister to His people.

They anxiously awaited her coming like children waiting for ice cream cones on a hot summer day. The women busily prepared meals, and the men set about making any needed repairs. Even the children did their chores without being asked. A quiet place was set aside for her to rest after her long journey. She asked for nothing, but always gave so much. The least they could do was give her a place and time of rest. Everything was ready and in order.

This servant of the church knew just how to dry a tear and help mend a broken friendship. She always listened to the young and held the hands of the elderly. This sister of the church and friend of the friendless never came expecting to receive, but always to give. Her visits excited everyone. This great woman of the church, this jewel of God known for her compassion and re-sourcefulness, was your Elegant Flamboyant sister Phoebe.

Phoebe was a devoted worker in the early church. She lived at Cenchrea, a port city east of Ephesus. She was a deaconess who traveled about freely visiting many of the early churches. This was unusual for a woman of her day. Since she traveled about so freely, it is safe to say that Phoebe was an influential woman with wealth and position. Phoebe "hid in plain sight" on her mission for the Lord. As a woman of means, when she traveled she did not stop to ask questions. She boldly went where and when she wanted to go. She was always led by the Lord's precious Holy Spirit.

We know Paul traveled by boat when he left Cenchrea en route to Ephesus. There is no record of how Phoebe traveled. She may have used an overland route, traveling by caravan. This was the preferred mode of travel for women in her day. Using this route, Phoebe could easily stop at the new and budding churches along the way and bring greetings from Paul and news from other sister churches.

We can imagine that Phoebe was a woman of noble stature—a picture of elegance and feminine strength, with her head held high and her carriage erect. Her scarlet ankle-length dress was beautifully embroidered with multicolored threads woven into a lovely pattern. She pulled her dark brown hair away from her face and knotted it into a long coiled braid, resembling a copper crown set on top of her head. A golden net covered her crownlike hair-style. These nets were common accessories for women of means. Large golden earrings adorned her ears. On each hand, she wore golden rings; on her wrists hung golden bracelets with lapis set-tings. A blue veil that doubled as a shawl draped her lovely head. Around her waist was a blue silk sash, with hints of golden thread. Phoebe was the vision of Elegant Flamboyant at its best.

Phoebe never came to visit empty-handed. On a stop at one new church, she discovered they needed food. She generously gave to feed the hungry. Phoebe instructed the younger women in how to stretch the food so it would last. She took several dresses from her bags and distributed them among the women. She had the men unload bolts of wool and linen to make clothing for less fortunate church members. Yet she brought more than things for physical comfort; she also brought love and an understanding ear for her brothers and sisters in Christ for spiritual comfort. She was God's woman on a mission.

Upon her arrival, another church had a dispute over a misunderstanding of the Scripture. Phoebe patiently listened, explained the Scripture, and ministered to the members involved. She did not want the enemy to have any openings in the Lord's infant church. She felt that a new church was like a new baby. It was susceptible to germs and could become ill because its immune system was not yet strong enough to fight off disease on its own. If so, it needed immediate attention and medication. This attention and medication came only from the Lord and His word.

Phoebe was not only a woman of financial means but also a minister of God's word. Having spent countless hours with Paul, and with the Lord through prayer, she was equipped to discern the truth in any situation. She prayed with the members and reminded them to give no place to the enemy. She reminded them that the Lord Jesus paid a dear price on the cross. As she left, she blessed the churches, encouraging them to run a good race and keep the faith. Because of her helpfulness, Paul called Phoebe a "succourer" or patroness and protector of many. She was always there to aid converts and fight battles for the oppressed. He called her a "succourer of myself" also. It is easy to imagine that because of her resources and position, Phoebe helped Paul escape from many unpleasant situations. Speaking up for him, finding safe passage, and providing food and shelter for God's anointed were within her power. Because of her position, it is safe to say that her home was also a meeting place for church members.

Paul also called Phoebe "our sister" with great affection, and a servant of the church at Cenchrea. The word *deacon* is derived from the Greek word *diaconos*, which means "servant." Phoebe could definitely be called a deaconess. In the early church, it was more of an honor to be called a servant because unlike some of today's churches, little was made of position as opposed to office. Phoebe was indeed a servant of the church, as her actions proved time and time again.

The book of Romans became a record of all Paul and others owed Phoebe for her faithfulness and service. That was evident in Romans 16:2, when Paul introduced her and asked the Romans to "receive her in the Lord in a manner worthy of saints, and assist her in whatever business she has need of you; for indeed she has been a helper of many and of myself also."

While this statement was a wonderful compliment, it was not the highest honor Phoebe received. Her most significant honor came when Paul entrusted her to deliver his precious epistle to the Romans. In those perilous times, when Christians were openly persecuted, Phoebe took the risk and guarded the writings with her life. By doing so, she safeguarded a precious part of God's Holy Word that has been passed on to us today. Such an honor would only be given to someone of high integrity—someone like the deaconess from Cenchrea; someone like Phoebe, your beautiful, bold Elegant Flamboyant sister.

The Elegant Flamboyant Spouse

Drama and the unexpected are the main themes in your marriage. Your very essence is drama, and this special feature carries over to your marriage. You keep your mate on his toes by dropping little notes in his shoes, sending flowers, or whisking him into a warm bubble bath when he gets home from work. You want to make sure he never knows what to expect. When you do something, it will be first-class or not at all. You have no problem showing up at your husband's office with a large bunch of balloons just to show how much you love and appreciate him. He gets a big thrill from your surprise and can hardly wait for the next adventure. His male co-workers envy the attention and want to know his secret. To him, it is no secret. He married a vivid, bold, beautiful Elegant Flamboyant!

Your husband loves your boldness and creativity and gives you free rein to express your true spirit. Although you are assertive by nature, you know how to expertly give your man his place of honor in your life. He is definitely the head of your household as the Lord intended. That was a hard lesson for you to learn, but learn you did. You realized that true freedom is possible when you get out of the Lord's way and allow your husband to take his rightful place in the home and in your life. He grows spiritually, and you are a direct beneficiary of that growth. You breathe a sigh of relief every time he takes the lead. You feel wonderful in the support role. Prayerfully and beautifully supporting the man you love is just what the Doctor, the Lord of Hosts, ordered!

Just as Christ loves the church, the Lord daily teaches your man how to love and appreciate you. You stay in prayer so you will not get in the Lord's way. Your spouse knows he is abundantly blessed and has the best of both worlds. You are a woman who performs like a champion in the work world, yet knows how to let him take the driver's seat at home. You gently show him the cruise-control button as he allows the Lord to guide your marriage to prosperity.

You may become impatient with your spouse when he moves with caution. He may like to take his time in making decisions, especially when the decisions involve others. You, on the other hand, want to fight until you settle things. Learn to be patient with your more cautious mate. The two of you make a good balance for a wonderful marriage, if you each learn to work with and accept the other's style. In the long run, you will see that some-times Elegant Flamboyant does need to stop and take a breath be-fore proceeding. Your man will help you do just that! Believe it or not, he can see things that you sometimes cannot. Things always turn out better when two walk in agreement.

> Can two walk together, unless they are agreed?
>
> AMOS 3:3

Your husband, being the wise man he is (he must be wise—he married you, didn't he?), always consults you before making deci-sions. He loves your independent spirit and feminine strength. He also respects your intellect and sound thinking. He does not feel threatened by your abilities because you use them to glorify the Lord. You ask his opinion on your projects and people you are working with, knowing he can give you a fresh perspective. Your man feels you are all he could ask for in a woman: intelligent, beautiful, and of course, dramatic!

When you and he disagree, you listen to every word and see every action. With your eloquent gift of speaking, you manage to persuade him to see things your way most of the time. When you see you cannot win or you know he is right, you graciously submit and ask for forgiveness. You know that pride comes before a fall, and you do not intend to fall or fail in your marriage. On the flip side, if your spouse is definitely wrong, you allow him to vent and get out his feelings. You want to hear everything he has to say. Many times he will realize, after he gets things out and hears him-self, that he was wrong. Allow the Holy Spirit to do the convict-ing. In other words, stand still and see the salvation of the Lord. If you keep quiet, you will see the salvation of your marriage as well.

This is where it takes a special dose of that Elegant Flamboy-ant patience. You know he was wrong, he knows he was wrong, so allow him to keep his dignity and ask for your forgiveness. When he does (patience, patience, he will get around to it), accept it graciously. You did not get married to fight. You come together, simultaneously asking for forgiveness. The best is yet to come because making up is Elegant Flamboyant fun!

You both are wise enough to realize that there was a little fault on both sides. You speak words of love and forgiveness to your man like no other. Your sweet words land on his heart as you bask in the glow of his love light. Wonder where you learned that lesson? You guessed it! From the Lord, and you are more than happy to share that lesson with your spouse to enhance your marital relationship. You want to get on with the business of marriage. After all, why fight when you can love each other? Life is too short to spend fighting!

> *A* word fitly spoken is like apples of gold in settings of silver.
>
> PROVERBS 25:11

Elegant Flamboyant Working Style

Your manner of dress says you are in charge, and others believe it. You appear to be larger than life and always in control. This sounds good, though it can be a disadvantage at times. Because you are so dramatic, people sometimes expect the impossible from you—but you are able to deliver. You might take on a seemingly impossible task just for the challenge and the thrill of the hunt. Most of the time, you pass with flying colors, but at what cost? You put everything else in your life on hold while meeting this challenge. Your relationships, personal and professional, sometimes suffer during these times. A suggestion would be to share the project with others, making your piece of the pie bite-sized. Learning to delegate is one of your difficulties, but once learned, you are a true master.

For you, hard work is like child's play. When you are involved in an organization, you always rise to a position of leadership. Others respect your dedication and creative thinking. You get the job done, even if you have to do it all yourself. This attitude, however, could lead to quick burnout and a loss of interest on your part. Learn to relax and trust others when you assign or delegate. Allowing others to thrive can be a rewarding experience for you and all involved. It frees up your time to pursue other, larger projects and to network with other professionals. This also helps create a pleasant working environment for all concerned. The reward is being able to sit back and freely observe the gifts in full operation, working harmoniously together for the glory of the Lord.

Under Elegant Flamboyant management, your department gets any new and difficult policies set for implementation. You are known for your savvy, creative ingenuity, and ability to open doors often closed to others. You learned these qualities directly from skilled networking. You make it a point to develop relationships with personnel at all levels. You are a gifted networker, and realize that the "gatekeepers" (secretaries and administrative workers) have access to important information and people. In your eyes, they are really important people.

You believe in treating everyone with dignity, and the gatekeepers love you for it. Many people may not realize it, but you started your career as a gatekeeper. You were promoted through the ranks because of your savvy. With your kind and gracious attitude toward these gatekeepers, you quickly gain access to the decision makers. They let you know the best times and places to catch the power people at work and play. You know that your Father in heaven is pleased that you are respectful of others.

If you work for a corporation, it is important to mirror their image to ensure that your personal image blends. At times, elegant flamboyance may be a bit too dramatic in the eyes of management. Watch for unspoken cues and observe the culture of your organization. You should have little problem in this area, however, since the skillful art of role camouflage is your specialty. Once you get into the executive's seat, you can wear what you please, but you have to get there first! Use some of that Holy Spirit wisdom as a check and balance in making your working-wardrobe decisions.

If it looks as if you have hit the glass ceiling, do not be afraid to cut your losses and move on to greener pastures. Moving on could involve finding another job or even owning your own business. Entrepreneurial ventures suit you because you are a risk taker. Once you have made up your mind, plan your exit, and execute your plan. Make sure to include plenty of prayer and guidance from the Holy Spirit in your plan. If you rely on Him, your chances of success multiply by leaps and bounds. Being an Elegant Flamboyant is a fun-filled adventure. With the Holy Spirit as your Guide, you shine and give God glory! No matter what you do, however, like your biblical sister Lydia, you can be a great influence in others' lives.

> Commit your way to the Lord, trust also in Him and He shall bring it to pass.
>
> PSALMS 37:3

Lydia

THE SELLER OF PURPLE

Now a certain woman named Lydia heard us. She was a seller of purple from the city of Thyatira, who worshipped God. The Lord opened her heart to heed the things spoken by Paul. And when she and her household were baptized, she begged us, saying, "If you have judged me to be faithful to the Lord, come to my house and stay." And she constrained us.

Acts 16:14–15

The streets were filled with the sights, sounds, and smells of the market. Today he was looking for something extra special. As he searched the assortment of wares, he did not know exactly what he was looking for, but he'd know it when he saw it. His wife, to his disappointment, had recently embraced this new religion that was sweeping the land. He had heard her chatter about someone named Jesus, but had tried to ignore her. Because of this Jesus, his marriage and life had dramatically changed. Maybe if he bought her something beautiful, something special, she would again come to her senses and abandon this insanity. Maybe she would again become the woman he had married. Maybe she would again love the things that he loved. He was desperate. He had to find something at this market that would give him back his life.

During his travels, he had heard that the Philippi market had special merchandise. Upon his arrival, he saw gold, silver, jewels, and all sorts of luxury items, but not what he was searching for. He had bought her jewels and now she never wore them. He had bought her gold and silver and she kept them in her chest. She only wore them on special occasions—and even then, only to please him. To his disappointment, since she had embraced this new religion, material things did not mean a great deal to her. Although she had changed, there was one thing he knew would please her. It was her favorite color. It was a color he had yet to see in this crowded marketplace. If he could only find it, he knew she would be pleased. As his eyes conducted a desperate search, he felt this color was his last hope.

As he turned the corner, something dazzling caught his eye. It was beautiful and majestic. It was just what he was hoping to find.

It was fabric in the most lavish of colors—a magnificent purple. He was magnetically drawn to the table where all different types of fabric and shades of purple were displayed. There was linen in the softest purple and wool in a deeper shade. There was even silk in a royal purple. Everything was brilliant and beautiful. How could he decide when all was so lovely?

As he looked through the fabrics, he talked with the merchant behind the table. There was something different about this merchant. She was not brash and pushy like many of the others. She spoke with authority, yet she possessed a softness. She held her head high, yet she was not proud. She was not what many would call beautiful, yet her countenance had an unexplainable glow. As he watched and listened, something about this woman made him want to stay and talk. It was beauty of spirit that he had seen before, but he could not remember where.

As she helped him with the cloth, he asked questions. After making a final selection, he realized that he had not only found the beautiful purple silk for his wife, but also accepted an invitation to an evening meeting. He decided to go, not knowing why. He only knew that he had to go. There was an Unseen Force guiding him that day, and with curiosity he decided to follow Its leading.

That evening, the friendly merchant greeted him at the door. As the meeting began, the people were discussing a subject with which he was all too familiar. They started talking about this Jesus. How on earth had he ended up here? He had planned this business trip just to escape the mention of this dead Performer of Miracles. He had to get out. As he stood and started toward the door, words spoken pierced his heart. Before he knew what was happening, tears wet his cheeks. Was this real? Was he imagining all this? All of a sudden, he felt the emptiness of his heart fill with an unexplainable peace and joy. This was a new experience, one he had never known before.

He felt that same Unseen Force that made him accept this invitation, but this time things were clear. It was as if scales fell from his eyes. He suddenly remembered where he had first encountered the spiritual beauty of the merchant. It was in his own home, with his beautiful wife. He could hardly wait to get home. He could hardly wait to see her and hold her in his arms. He now knew this Performer of Miracles was not dead as others had said. He was very much alive. For this Performer was the Lord Jesus, and He touched and filled the emptiness in his hungry spirit. Jesus was real and He loved him. Yes, the rumors were true. He did find that extra-special something at the Philippi market. He had discovered the real meaning of his life. He found the Jesus Christ, Son of the true and living God.

When the meeting ended, he tearfully thanked the merchant. As they prayed together, he knew he would never forget her. She had taken a great risk in inviting him to this meeting, but by doing so she had saved his life. She had followed the Holy Spirit and extended her hand in Christian love and friendship. This merchant of Philippi, this seller of purple, was your sister, the beautiful, bold Elegant Flamboyant Lydia.

Lydia was a successful businesswoman who lived in Philippi. In her home was the church the Apostle Paul called his joy and crown (Philippians 4:10). It is easy to imagine that because she was in business, Lydia was one of the most successful and influential women in the city. She was a native of Thyatira of western Asia Minor. It is not clear when she came to live in Philippi, but she had been there long enough to establish herself as one of its prominent citizens.

Lydia came from an area where the Lydian market had once been a center for trade and commerce. We can imagine that she still had fond memories of her homeland because she was named for the ancient city of Lydia that was in her native province. Lydia, being a true professional, may have also been a member of the Dyers Guild, a professional organization of that time. Ancient inscriptions bearing its name were found in her home province of Thyatira. Because of this evidence, it is safe to say that Lydia learned her trade in Thyatira and carried it with her to Philippi.

We can imagine that Lydia was a striking woman who wore the wares she sold. She wore dresses of regal purple, yet she had a kind and gentle spirit. Her hair was pulled away from her face and held in place by a golden net she bought from a traveling merchant. Her brown eyes twinkled as she greeted customers and sold her purple. On her head, she wore a multicolored headdress that gently covered her head and shoulders and encircled her waist. On her ears, large golden Elegant Flamboyant earrings sparkled in the sun. She wore gold rings on each hand, and golden bangles accented with precious stones adorned her wrists. She represented the new woman of the era, a smart, savvy, successful entrepreneur.

Lydia was not only successful in business, but also wise. She did little to push a sale. Just the sight of her wearing the deep, rich, vibrant purple made others want to buy. It made them feel richer and more alive simply to be around Lydia and her purple. Was it just the sight of the purple that so stirred the hearts of her customers? Lydia knew that nothing of this earth could really make her business successful. She knew the Holy Spirit pierced the hearts of men as they viewed her purple, and He moved them to buy.

We can imagine many of her customers were Romans who bought the purple finery for temple decorations, and to wear for their many celebrations and ceremonies. Merchants who came through Philippi also knew Lydia and sought her out to buy purple. It is safe to say that Lydia sold to the wicked to finance the work of God's church. Only an Elegant Flamboyant could make the enemy work for the Lord without him knowing it!

Lydia was a woman of determination and generosity, and she was a seeker of truth. She possessed a unique personality to survive as a businesswoman in that day and age. She was gentle enough not to offend the male population, but strong enough that they would not take advantage of her. She was humble enough not to offend the women but firm enough to command their respect. She was a shining example of how to be a woman's woman working for the Son of man, the Lord Jesus. Fortunately for Lydia, your Elegant Flamboyant sister, this was not difficult. She held her household and business together with Elegant Flamboyant style.

The Bible says that Lydia and her household were baptized. She boldly witnessed to her family, convincing them of the virtues of salvation. With this act, she made a bold decision and accepted the Lord Jesus as her personal Lord and Savior and Christianity as a lifestyle in a pagan society. This decision was significant not only because it ensured her eternal life, but also because it made Lydia the first convert in Europe. After her baptism, she begged Paul and Silas to stay at her home. She wanted to know more about the Lord Jesus.

To ensure that she had the facts, Lydia extended hospitality to His disciples. It is a testament to Lydia that she would stop and offer hospitality to strangers, especially a group of Christian missionaries. She hungered for the word of the Lord and knew Paul could tell her what she needed to know. She humbly asked them to stay at her home. In Acts 16:15, she said, "If you have judged me to be faithful to the Lord, come to my house and stay." Lydia listened, the Lord opened her heart, and the Bible says she attended unto the things that were spoken of Paul.

We can imagine that because of her Elegant Flamboyant spirit, once she was converted, Lydia did not care what her customers or the citizens of Philippi thought of her decision. She held church meetings in her home, which also served as a rendezvous point for visiting missionaries. Lydia witnessed to and helped convert many of the city's skeptics. She was as bold as a lion in a day and time when Christians were killed for their faith. The thought of death did not squelch her inner fire. She was a righteous woman who knew that eternal life was not found in what others thought or said about her. Like you, her Elegant Flamboyant sister, she boldly proclaimed the word of the Lord and helped others accept the Light of the world, the beautiful Lord Jesus.

> **O** Lord, our Lord, how excellent is Your name in all the earth!
>
> PSALMS 8:9

Great Career Choices for the Elegant Flamboyant

Fashion Coordinator or Model
Administrator
Entrepreneur
Public Relations Director
Actress or Talk Show Host
Special Event or Conference Planner

The Outer You

ELEGANT FLAMBOYANT CLOTHING CHOICES

Even your most casual attire is flamboyant. The two F's, Fascinating and Fabulous, are Elegant Flamboyant image keys. You are a trendsetter. Others look to you to set the stage for fashion. Many times, others mislabel your flamboyant spirit, not realizing that the Lord created you for boldness. They do not realize that your boldness plays a necessary part in the body of Christ because you prompt others to action. Even if you are generally quiet, your boldness shines through in your dress, because you cannot hide it.

Like the Harmonic Refined, you love classic lines, but you always add special dramatic touches to create an extraordinary look. A large brass, silver, and gold brooch with matching earrings and a cuff bracelet announce Elegant Flamboyant style. Add to that a large shawl or cape draped dramatically around your shoulders and you are at your magnificent best. As you make your entrance, others can see, feel, and experience your drama with just one look.

You are the only image type that can effectively wear clothing that has a masculine flavor. On most of the other image types, masculine styling looks like a costume, but you pull it off like a dramatic, elegant pro. A perfect example of Elegant Flamboyant styling is a pair of man-tailored slacks and matching vest worn with a silk blouse, and accented with a hand-painted silk ascot. A large matching bracelet, necklace, and oversized earrings top off your Elegant Flamboyant style. You have also been known to wear suspenders, neckties, and boleros to accent your look. Although these accessories are associated with men, you know there is definitely nothing masculine about them once you have them on. Others will know it as well. Your strong feminine fragrance easily overpowers any hint of masculinity.

Your pantsuits are composed of separates that you expertly pull together. Since you love men's wear, you have quite a few vests of many fabrics and colors. The T shape, square-shouldered jacket with straight skirts or slim pants, speaks your language. Your jackets almost always have large, square shoulders tailored with sleek lines. Even when fashion says *Shoulder pads are out,* you still wear them. The Joan Crawford shoulder is the only one for you. You wear them to achieve your full, dramatic effect. Your most flamboyant brooches and scarves are supported on those square shoulders. They are one of your main style signatures. Because you like them so much, you are known to shop in the men's department for jackets. The cut fits, and you make them all your own. Once you've adorned them with Elegant Flamboyant accents, no one would ever guess where you bought them.

You are an independent dresser and set the stage for others. You wear what you want, and others usually copy your style. Fashion staging is the trademark of Elegant Flamboyant style. While looking through fashion magazines, you adopt and redevelop ideas and make them yours. Others imitate the way you tie your scarves or wear your jewelry, but they can never really copy your style. When you see your styling on someone else, you smile, knowing in your heart that imitation is the sincerest form of flattery. From a sister Elegant Flamboyant, you get a nod of approval as she uses your new scarf knot—and it, too, becomes one of her trademarks.

No ornate pleats, cinched waists, or lace inserts fit your image type. Your blouses are simple and elegant. Silk tees in brilliant colors fit your wardrobe needs superbly. They become the canvas where you paint your Elegant Flamboyant portrait. There are times when a man's shirt, complete with French cuffs and your most extraordinary pair of cufflinks, will be the perfect topping for a dramatic suit or pair of slacks. You have your jeweler make earrings and a ring to match, and you are ready for any Elegant Flamboyant event.

You also wear hats majestically. During winter, you wear many shapes, sizes, and colors, including headbands. If you cannot find one to match your newest outfit, you have one made. In warmer months, straw brims complemented with colorful scarves and your favorite sunglasses arrive on the scene. As an Elegant Flamboyant, you are always on the cutting edge of style in any season and a fabulous lead for others to follow in the fashion game.

You use dramatic pieces to make your entrance. While others may sometimes feel you are over the top, you and your heavenly Father know better. You are as He created you, a stylish woman who can wear fashions like no other. That beautiful golden thread of drama interwoven into your spirit at birth by your Father allows the fruit of the spirit to spring forth in full bloom!

> *B*ut the fruit of the spirit is love, joy, peace, long-suffering, kindness, goodness, faithfulness, gentleness, self control. Against such there is no law.
>
> GALATIANS 5:22–23

You dazzle in jeweled sweaters. As with your sister Sensual Exotic, large faux jewels and eye-catching details dance in Elegant Flamboyant style. Leather and suede suits also fill your closet. When you wear flared skirts, they are long. Again like your sister Sensual Exotic, you wear car wash skirts with flair. They drape your body dramatically and move with your every footstep. You wear them with one of your many pairs of boots or your favorite pair of pumps. The skirt length depends on your mood and the occasion. A long flared skirt with your favorite boots and a box-shouldered jacket is definitely an Elegant Flamboyant entrance maker.

An ultrasuede jacket, a knee-length straight skirt, suede pumps, and coordinating gloves make the ultimate Elegant Flamboyant fashion statement. Accented with a hand-painted silk scarf, this outfit speaks your language beautifully. You are His vivid, bold jewel set afire by the Holy Spirit. In Elegant Flamboyant style, you are ready to do His will. He has promised to go before you to prepare the way. He acts as your rear guard as long as you give Him the glory. You have His word to remind you.

> *F*or you shall not go out with haste, nor go by flight; For the Lord will go before you, and the God of Israel will be your rear guard.
>
> ISAIAH 52:12

ELEGANT FLAMBOYANT FULL-FIGURED CLOTHING CHOICES

As a full-figured Elegant Flamboyant, you feel right at home in your uniqueness. Follow the same rules as your smaller sister in choosing your wardrobe staples. Large, unusual accessories are your fashion trademarks. Being full-figured, you can wear accessories just a little larger than most. You wear an extra-large brass-and-onyx brooch with matching earrings and belt buckle with elegance and flair. Hammered brass and sterling silver accented with tortoiseshell are majestic on you and in tune with your Elegant Flamboyant presence. Any jewelry that seems extreme on others suits you to perfection. You wear it all with magnificence.

It is important for every piece of your ensemble to match. The theme of your wardrobe pieces must follow the same lines. If you wear animal prints, then your jewelry should also be of an exotic theme. Like your sister Sensual Exotic, you look for shell, wood, or hammered-brass accessories to pull everything together. African prints with matching wood and brass jewelry are just what the Master ordered.

Elegant Flamboyant wears masculine-tailored styling like an expert. You have many vests in brilliant patterns and wondrous fabrics. Worn with your straight skirts or tailored slacks, they are one of your preferred looks. This styling is comfortable and elegant, with just enough drama to make it Elegant Flamboyant. If you wear blouses with front buttons, make sure they are large enough so they do not pull open across your bustline. Take time to try these and all your clothing on before buying.

To ensure you have the correct fit, try using this simple technique. With a blouse on, lift your arms over your head and then bring them back down and hold them in front, level with your bustline. If the buttons do not pull, then you have the correct size. If the buttons pull or the blouse opens while doing this, get the next larger size. If there is not a larger size available, get another blouse style. A great alternative is a pullover blouse with a back keyhole opening. Take note of the sleeves and under the arms. How do they feel? Is there extra stress on the seams? Remember, the extra stress means your blouse will not look good for very long and may soon rip under the arms.

Being full-figured does not change your image type. You wear the same clothing styles as your smaller sister. The only difference is the size. Different clothing lines may mean you will wear one size in one line and a different size in another line. Size is unimportant as long as the garment fits. Your main concern should be how you look and feel in a particular piece of clothing.

If your hips are the fullest part of your body, use the Fingertip Rule to judge the fit of your jackets and cardigans. Using this simple technique when dressing enables you to wear just about any type of skirt, as long as it fits properly. Stand with your arms relaxed at your sides. Notice where your fingertips fall. This should be the perfect length for your jackets. If you have short arms, add two inches. Your jacket should fall approximately a hand length below the fullest part of your hips. Those straight sweater skirts you love will no longer be off-limits because of your hip size. The Fingertip Rule will enable you to wear them all you want!

An electric blue pantsuit with matching duster and a shawl dripping with swirls of blue and gold announces to the world you know that you are a daughter of the King. That announcement is one you do not mind making. You use your shawl to pull together the ensemble and make one of your Elegant Flamboyant entrances. Swirls of blue with your hammered-brass, silver, and onyx jewelry dramatically say *elegance* and majestically say *flamboyance*—two words that are near and dear to your heart as you radiate with praise for the Lord. You look and feel just the way He planned in beautiful, bold, Elegant Flamboyant style!

> *S*trength and honor are her clothing; she shall
> rejoice in time to come.
>
> Proverbs 31:25

Key Words for the Elegant Flamboyant Dress Code

Dramatic
Sophisticated
Elegant
Lavish

Elegant Flamboyant Color Schemes

The Elegant Flamboyant spirit seeks color, and you have an innate sense of it, using it like an expert. Your favorite hues permeate every area of your life, including your office, bedroom, and wardrobe. Everything is color-coordinated, right down to your fingernails. Just the thought of wearing an outfit with matching undergarments of the same color excites you.

If you decide that your bedroom color is purple, then you paint a wonderful monochromatic picture. The walls are soft, blush lavender accented with an elegant border of purple and gold. A luscious purple-and-lavender comforter and dust ruffle adorn your bed. At the windows hang dramatic purple-and-lavender drapes. Even the carpet is in the purple family. You painstakingly search for each piece until you have the right dramatic setting. Your home fluently speaks your dramatic color language.

You use colors so expertly that others notice only the drama. There is no need to tell you to get your colors done. For Elegant Flamboyant, this is common sense. You invite others to have their colors done as well. Once done, the adventure begins. You refer to your palette while shopping and purging your wardrobe. You wear bright colors and boldly use tones not in your seasonal palette. You follow your color palette and add touches of your own, borrowing colors from other seasons. In the Elegant Flamboyant mind, there is no excuse for bad color judgment when there is so much help available.

Using dramatic colors is an important facet of Elegant Flamboyant communication. You speak colors even in your everyday language. Others do not realize just how important color is to you. When asked how your day is going, you respond by saying, "Oh, today is a purple day. It's been a great day." If your day is not going well, others hear, "Today is a gray day. I just do not know why everyone around here is so down in the dumps." You stay in your office and do paperwork on those days. The decorations in your office keep you up and working at full speed. You never forget to add your daily Bible devotions. They keep you at your royal best and Elegant Flamboyant fabulous!

Your conservative styling is a bit different from that of your sister Harmonic Refined. You take everything a step farther and take more risks with styling and color. You expertly incorporate dashes of drama into even the most conservative ensembles. When wearing your favorite red suit, you feel powerful and ready to take on any task. Attending a conservative meeting, you wear a gray or navy-blue suit. Holding true to your Elegant Flamboyant spirit, accents of purple highlight the gray, and fuchsia dances with the navy. Your classic gray ensemble is a straight skirt with a long coat and large silver buttons. Your fuchsia silk blouse announces your entrance in Elegant Flamboyant color style.

You will not rest until "happy" colors surround you. Because you feel so strongly about appropriate color use, you take on the task of educating others. You learn all there is to know about the effect of color on people. Soft pinks and gentle baby blues help calm an angry temper. Yellow encourages others to talk. Brown reminds people of home and stability. Red evokes strong emotions and prompts people to action. Wisely using the Lord's wonderful gift of color is the Elegant Flamboyant way of doing business. You honor Him by helping others see the beauty and majesty of the Lord through His magnificent gift of color.

> *H*e comes from the north as golden splendor;
> With God is awesome majesty.
>
> Job 37:22

Elegant Flamboyant Jewelry

Jewelry is the most important piece of your image puzzle. Large, dramatic pieces with sharp angles are your trademarks. Rounded edges are too soft for your authoritative posture. Large squares of hammered metal speak your language. These sharply angled geometric shapes accented with large stones glimmer as they dance in the light. Bangles, rings, and earrings of mixed metals dominate your treasure chest. Oversized matching necklaces adorn your neckline because you were born to wear what others call extreme styling.

Watches stimulate your taste buds. Timepieces of all types and shapes fill your jewelry box. Since your Elegant Flamboyant persona overwhelms dainty styling, the larger and more unusual an accessory is, the better it suits you. Your oversized silver pocket watch blends perfectly with your masculine-cut pantsuit. A sterling-silver chain, bought at an antiques shop, cleverly holds it in place. Another favorite is your gold lapel watch brooch. Its faux jewel frame sparkles and catches the gleam in your eye as you wear it with Elegant Flamboyant flair. You always look for sophisticated extravagance to sing your image song.

Nothing delicate suits you, so if you want to express your femininity, you wear oversized, exaggerated lace and ruffles. You accent this romantic look with oversized, elaborately framed cameo earrings and a matching brooch. The earrings are as large as the brooch or they are not Elegant Flamboyant. Since it is difficult to find cameo-type earrings in an extra-large size, you find the pieces and create your own. If you do not have the time or cannot find what you want, then you have someone do the work for you.

Good-quality costume jewelry is your signature. You have the unique ability to make inexpensive costume jewelry look expensive. If you decide to use inexpensive pieces, no one knows unless your purpose is to have a scaled-down chic look. You are in complete control of every detail. You know how every piece of jewelry is to look. Each piece has a purpose and announces your image type to all you meet, because jewelry is your ultimate style statement.

Mixing metals is one of your strong points. Many times you buy identical pieces in different metals to mix and match them. It is not unusual for you to wear two large identical necklaces, one gold and the other silver. You then wear a dual-metal watch and matching earrings, showing the creative side of Elegant Flamboyant. Others look on as you transform traditional fashion pieces into your style statements.

In warm weather, you look fabulous in large jewelry in wooden, geometric shapes. Hand-carved wooden beads reminiscent of the jungle and angular shapes of unusual materials are found in your jewelry box. A large ceramic bangle and matching necklace, or a sterling-silver-and-brass brooch are also great choices. You go to great lengths to add that Elegant Flamboyant dash of high drama. You wear dramatic jewelry like no other.

You artistically mix ceramic, wood, and metal. This unusual combination is sure to be a hit. The more unusual the combination, the better it suits you. No one except a sister Elegant Flamboyant, Creative Poetic, or Sensual Exotic would think of wearing things your way. A ceramic bangle is easily transformed into an elegant belt buckle. Taking one of your favorite scarves and exquisitely securing it with the bangle makes a conversation piece at your next outing. You are a red-hot magnet that attracts the unusual. Whatever you choose, it will always be fashion-forward with flair. You are vivid, bold, and beautiful to behold. Exhorting and encouraging others to be who they are in Christ Jesus, you magnify the name of the Lord in Elegant Flamboyant style!

> Oh, magnify the Lord with me, and let us exalt His name together.
>
> PSALMS 34:3

ELEGANT FLAMBOYANT HAIR

Your hairstyles always accentuate your face. Wearing your hair pulled back in a bun or French twist makes room for Elegant Flamboyant image creativity. Your version of a bun or French twist is never simple. You strategically place golden beads in your hair to catch the sun's rays and enhance your style. If you are not in the mood for beading, you use a large, exotic hair comb accented with faux jewels to secure your twist. Others may think this styling is conservative, but you know just how to wear this pulled-away style with dramatic impact. "The sleeker, the better" is the Elegant Flamboyant hairstyling motto. When your hair is in place, it does not take away from the overall effect of your drama. You use styling mousse or gel to get the desired effect. No hair will be out of place, for you have rehearsed every head turn for full dramatic impact.

You love to wear elaborate braiding. You do not mind sitting for long periods of time as long as you leave the stylist's chair looking the way you want. This is an investment in your image, and it pays off. You use your braids for added drama—they mirror your personality and style. Even in your most conservative attire, your braids blend beautifully. When you are in a creative mood, you have your stylist strategically place designer beads of gold and silver that catch the gleam of your jewelry. You are the only image type that thinks of matching your jewelry to the beading in your braids.

If you wear short hair, it is expertly styled to complement your face. It is imperative for you to keep it cut and trimmed to maintain that look of elegance. Your hairline is an important image factor. If your hairline is not neat and clean, you feel totally unkempt. It does not matter if your outfit and makeup are otherwise perfect. An uneven hairline leaves you less than perfectly groomed.

In the hair-coloring arena, you are a style setter for women of color. Like your sister Creative Poetic and Sensual Exotic, you can get away with more than most in this department. You are one of the few who take risks with your hair coloring. If you decide to wear blond streaks, then blond streaks you have. Bearing this in mind, make sure your dominant color blends with your skin tone. A deep rich auburn, cocoa, or chestnut brown looks fabulous against your radiant skin. You are the expert on the wonderful burgundy hair coloring. It gives hair brilliance and luster in any lighting. Burgundies also look great with golden, brown, mahogany, and ebony skin tones. Choose your hair coloring wisely to complement your café au lait, honey-gold, caramel-brown, walnut, or cocoa-brown skin coloring. Adding touches of drama, you can expertly complement your awesome skin tone with wisely selected hair coloring and highlights.

This word goes out also for women of Latina, Asian, and Native American descent. You know that your magnificent hair is beautiful the way it is. Nothing man has created can compare with your deep, rich tresses. If you feel the need to experiment, try some of the burgundies described above. They will add dramatic highlights without detracting from your God-given beauty. Burgundy will also blend with your natural skin coloring to give your appearance an Elegant Flamboyant glow.

You most likely have a favorite stylist who takes care of your hair and keeps your cut neat and clean. If your stylist is not available, you have no problem learning to do your own hair. You watch and learn each time you go the salon. Learning by doing is an Elegant Flamboyant trait. It would not be a surprising for you to attend cosmetology school, just to gain knowledge for your personal use. You would buy your own permanent and hair clippers and do it yourself. Image maintenance is time consuming, but you are willing to work hard because you represent the Lord. You are His chosen vessel for vivid beauty and bold loveliness. You are His Elegant Flamboyant daughter whom He called out of darkness into His marvelous light!

> *B*ut you are a chosen generation, a royal priesthood, a holy nation, His own people, that you may proclaim the praises of Him who called you out of darkness into His marvelous light.
>
> I PETER 2:9

ELEGANT FLAMBOYANT MAKEUP

Your makeup is lavish and dramatic even for daytime wear. High gloss and sheen are your trademarks. Vivid, bold lips and strong cheeks and eyes announce your presence. You brilliantly use vibrant colors to complement your wardrobe choices. You prefer deep fuchsia, luscious red, and any other highly dramatic and exciting color. If you are not dramatically made up, it is simply because you've decided to have a subtle day. Still, you do at least wear vibrantly colored lipstick. You are one of the few people who do not need to consult a makeup artist for help—you *are* the ultimate makeup artist. You take care to match your eye shadow with your lips, and they both blend perfectly with your skin tone and chosen outfit. If you cannot find just the right eye color, you forgo eye shadow and line your eyes with a deep, rich eye-defining pencil. Whatever look you choose, it will be sharp and completely together.

Unlike the Harmonic Refined, your cheek color need not always match your lips. You experiment with hues from radiant reds to deepest plums. These colors are attention getters and first on your preference list. Your fair complexion wears the Coco Chanel look with style. You expertly use foundation to lighten your skin tone and give it a milky texture. Add your red lips and cheeks, and you express glamour at its finest. You dramatically line your eyes in the darkest navy or charcoal gray. With your eyelids dusted in charcoal gray, all see an Elegant Flamboyant masterpiece in a matter of minutes.

If you are medium- to dark-complexioned, your skin is the canvas for a dramatic picture. Using reds, plums, and fuchsias, you enhance your radiant dark beauty. Expertly highlighting your ebony, bronze, and olive skin with rich, spirited coloring is one of your dramatic trademarks. You vibrantly color your lips, cheeks, and eyes with your appealing flair. Deep navy, paradise purple, and electric blue sing your sweetest Elegant Flamboyant song. Vibrant teal dashes through your color scheme. The beauty of your countenance from café au lait to deepest ebony shines for all the world to see. You are as radiant as the Queen of Sheba during a royal ceremony in all your Elegant Flamboyant beauty.

Whether your ethnic heritage is that of the European queen, the Asian empress, the Latina *condesa,* the Native American or Nubian princess, you are the Lord's creation and an example of His love for His Elegant Flamboyant daughters. You are ready to speak the Elegant Flamboyant language without saying a word. Your dramatic appearance says it all for you.

*B*lessed is the man [woman] who walks not in the counsel of the ungodly, nor stands in the path of sinners, nor sits in the seat of the scornful, but his [her] delight is in the Lord and in His law he [she] meditates day and night.

PSALMS 1:1–2

5. *Creative Poetic*

An original, a beauty,
She'll capture your heart.
The Creative Poetic, our Lord's work of art.

I will praise You, for I am fearfully and wonderfully
made; Marvelous are your works, and that my soul
knows very well.

PSALMS 139:14

The Beauty of Creative Poetic

Are you often described as creative and spontaneous? At work, do you take the lead on creative assignments? Do you travel in several social circles? Do you form your own independent opinions and way of doing things? Do you dress according to your moods and refuse to be governed by the fashion standards of others? Then you are the Creative Poetic image type.

You are your own person. Your independent spirit is sometimes hard to spot because you appear to be easygoing. While this may be true, your independence surfaces when people try to change you or your lifestyle. If they attempt to impose changes, they hit a brick wall as your Creative Poetic spirit appears—and then everyone had better look out! You will not tolerate others imposing their values upon your life, and you don't mind telling them so. You are governed by the Holy Spirit. If these people come in the name of the Lord and offer suggestions that confirm His will for your life, then and only then will you respond in a positive manner.

The Inner You

You have a warm smile and the ability to make others feel comfortable and accepted. Because of these qualities, others sometimes make the mistake of thinking your life is an open book. There is only a small circle of people who really know you, and only a select few of that group are allowed inside your inner circle. You are quick to let others know that you choose the time, place, and people to share your Creative Poetic delights. You value privacy and independence above all else, and guard your personal life closely.

You are not the type to ask personal questions unless you have permission. Even then, you often shy away from asking because self-disclosure does not interest you. You appear to be a happy, cheerful person to those who do not know you, but that happiness can be a facade and a means of keeping others from probing too deeply into your life. Unfortunately, when you desperately need the prayer, love, and acceptance of others, you are not able to let them know for fear of "being discovered."

The Lord is faithful and knows your heart. Seek Him and He will send true friends to minister to you. If you really want healing, love, and acceptance, you must first be open when help does come into your life. Pray and ask the Lord for your needs. Sometimes we have to stop hiding from ourselves in order to be healed. It is now time to stop hiding and receive your healing. All you have to do is believe and trust the Lord to bring it forth. You have His promise that He will be your rear guard. What more could you ask for? The next move is up to you.

> *T*hen your light shall break forth like the morning, your healing shall spring forth speedily, and your righteousness shall go before you; the glory of the Lord shall be your rear guard.
>
> ISAIAH 58:8

Because you march to the beat of your own drummer, you sometimes have a difficult time conforming. A note of caution here. There are times when, because of your independent spirit, it appears that you do not respect authority. For example, when involved in a group effort, you might agree to complete a task by a certain time. In the midst of the project, you decide to change the deadline because your new time line better suits your purposes and those of the people working under you. While this sounds good, it is wise to inform those overseeing the project, to head off any problems. It is wonderful that you are an independent thinker, but when working with a group, live up to your commitments as agreed. The Lord has not raised us to be rebellious but to render to Caesar what is Caesar's, and to God what is God's. In other words, submit to authority. If you cannot live up to your original commitment, then say so in the beginning. Evaluate your decision regarding the group. If you find you cannot live up to your original commitment, then it is time to move on.

If people want your participation on a committee or project, they should prepare to answer a barrage of questions. You want to know the whos, whens, wheres, and hows before making a commitment. If they can give straight answers, then you commit. If there are no straight answers, or you do not agree with the cause, then you know the project is not for you. For you, honesty is always the best policy. You will not commit to any project or program that goes against your belief system. If there is any area that creates inner conflict, then the activity is not for you. Compromise, especially in your spiritual life, is out of the question. Jesus is Lord and for you, that is enough. He gave His all for you. Since you represent Him in all you do, you give all or nothing.

Because you like simplicity, activities requiring a great deal of structure do not appeal to you. Your new computer comes with a three-hundred-page manual that you never read. Learning to program your new VCR does not interest you. As long as it records and plays movies when you need it, then it's just fine. You would rather spend your time involved in interesting conversation or painting a new mural for your living room. Things that would upset or irritate a more structured image type are, to you, like water rolling off a duck's back. They are just not important. Give you simplicity and the company of a few friends and life is full and rich.

You have little patience for stressful, competitive activities unless they are all in fun and there is something in it for everyone involved. Your image type must have coined the phrase *win–win* because you operate using that principle most of the time. You are noncompetitive and believe there is enough of God's goodness for everyone to enjoy. You do everything within your power to make sure others know it in Creative Poetic style!

> Oh, how great is Your goodness, which You have laid up for those who fear You, which You have prepared for those who trust You in the presence of the sons [daughters] of men [women]!
>
> PSALMS 31:19

You have little tolerance for people who are rigid in their viewpoints. You believe legalism does not leave room for love and acceptance. You feel uncomfortable around rigid attitudes. You have the same feelings regarding overly competitive individuals. When you encounter someone you feel is overly competitive, you usually "disappear" from the scene, leaving others to deal with the behavior. When the dust settles and others look around, you have moved on to something else. Your intention is not to abandon the project or the people, just the behavior.

As much as the behavior bothers you, you still have compassion. You pray that the Lord will help you be more accepting of others in this area. You do not like to see others hurting and believe these behaviors are the outward manifestations of inner pain. In your mind, these individuals do not have the right focus. You believe that when Jesus becomes Lord of your life, He curbs those excessive behaviors, putting them in check and keeping things in balance.

You have your own time schedule. You are often late but manage to eventually get wherever it is you happen to be going. This attitude and behavior can be irritating to more urgent image types. If you work for a more time-oriented individual, things can become tense, especially after you arrive late for an important meeting. To some people, *lateness* is another word for "apathy." As far as you are concerned, nothing could be farther from the truth, but remember that others usually have a different perception of your actions.

When you are scheduled to meet a friend, try to arrive at the time agreed upon. If you are more than fifteen minutes late, do not be upset if they don't wait. They were on time; you were not. Be aware of how your behavior affects others. Others may think you do not care about their feelings and begin to question your level of commitment to the relationship. Through the power of prayer, the Lord will help you keep things in balance. With the Holy Spirit as a guide, you will not only be on time, but keep your commitments as well. Hand in hand with the Lord, you certainly can do all things through Christ who strengthens you.

> *I* can do all things through Christ who strengthens me.
>
> PHILIPPIANS 4:13

Most of the time, having closure is not important to you. You leave many loose ends and unfinished projects in your life. Unfinished painting, music, and craft projects fill your home. This characteristic also carries over into your relationships. You sometimes make commitments and do not keep them. When scheduled to meet a friend, you run into a colleague who is in the middle of a crisis. Guess where you wind up? With the colleague and the crisis, doing all you can to help. This is your way of setting priorities. Whatever happens to be the most important at the time is what gets your attention. To your Creative Poetic heart, what could be more important than a friend in need? Like your biblical sister Dorcas, you are a compassionate friend to those in need. (But if you don't call the friend you were supposed to meet to explain, assuming that she will understand the situation, you jeopardize your relationship.)

While your concern for a colleague in need is wonderful, you also owe an explanation and apology to your friend. She was looking forward to spending the evening with an important person in her life, and that someone is you.

A phone call is sometimes all it takes to prevent the breakup of a precious relationship. Do not give the enemy an opening, for he will be sure to take it and cause confusion and pain. Use your gifts of communication and making others feel special. Ask your friend for forgiveness and for the chance to begin again. When you honor friendship, it will honor you. By honoring your friends, your relationships enhance your life over and over again. The Lord will also smile on the Creative Poetic picture you painted just for Him.

> *A*s iron sharpens iron, so a man [woman] sharpens the countenance of his [her] friend.
>
> PROVERBS 27:17

In your professional and personal relationships, you may sometimes have to change your drumbeat to accommodate others. Work on communicating your thoughts and views, so others will better understand your different way of thinking. Your Creative Poetic spirit allows you to bear no malice toward people who differ from you. Accepting others and their differences is one of your most beautiful traits. You pray they will learn to accept you and yours.

Your need for variety demands interaction with different

types of people on different levels. Because of this trait, you have several circles of friends. It is not unusual for you to share your life's story with a single parent on a fixed income or with a head of state. You are equally comfortable with both. Making people feel special is one of your first and best gifts. You love people and see through positions to their hearts. This quality endears you to many and keeps you in great demand for social functions because you know just how to float around and use this special gift. Your Creative Poetic spirit sends forth God's love light everywhere you go.

> The spirit of a man [woman] is the lamp of the Lord, searching all the inner depths of his [her] heart.
>
> PROVERBS 20:27

You never meet a stranger. At a party, you seek out the person sitting alone in the corner. After finding out he really did not want to attend, you work hard to make sure he has a good time. If he's new to the area, you arrange a lunch date and introduce him to others. If he really just wants to be left alone, you leave, but go back periodically to check on him, bringing a refreshing cup of punch or a plate filled with wonderful party treats. If he's open to it, you shower him with attention and encourage him to look for new opportunities during the evening. You graciously assist your host or hostess with the guests. Even if you are not hosting the event, you want everyone to have a good time. Loaded with refreshing drinks, you roam through the crowd with tray in hand, and help the evening shine. After all is over, you even stay and help with cleanup. You are the example of a perfect party guest. You realize it is hard work entertaining and want to show your appreciation for an evening well spent.

Dorcas

COMPASSIONATE FRIEND OF THE POOR

> At Joppa, there was a certain disciple named Tabitha,
> which is translated Dorcas. This woman was full of good
> works and charitable deeds which she did.
>
> ACTS 9:36

Wandering through the streets, she looked for the large stone house near the sea. She believed if she found this place, she would find what she needed. When her husband died, she became penniless and homeless. Her children were now also gone and she was left all alone. Where could she go? What could she do? No one seemed to have room for her. Things were not supposed to turn out this way. If she did not soon find shelter, she knew that she would die.

Her old, tired body ached as the night closed in around her. She felt her feet becoming numb. With each step, pain echoed its haunting laughter through her limbs. As she turned the corner, she pulled her ragged cloak tightly about her as the night wind blew through her clothing. She desperately needed warm clothes to protect her body from the elements. The weather during the summer months was mild, but now it was winter, and the wind coming off the sea sent icy needles of cold air through her, cutting into her skin like sharp, silent daggers.

As she knocked on the door, she hoped the rumors were true. She hoped this woman of influence could help. She was rapidly losing her strength. A warm dress and woolen overcoat would be like a dream come true. Color was no object. She needed something to warm her aging body.

As the door opened, a woman with a gentle face invited her inside. Entering the large room, she immediately felt the warmth of the fire. The aroma of fresh bread baking filled the air. This could not be real. This friendly woman did not know her, yet she was so kind. She did not remember what happened next, because the pleasantness of the moment overwhelmed her. As she collapsed into a crumpled heap before the roaring fire, everything around her, including her coldness and pain, became a blur.

When she awoke, the kindly woman was sitting at her bedside, gently stroking her brow. As she got up from the bed, the woman served her a bowl of soup and some warm bread. After finishing her meal, she was escorted into a room filled with colorful dresses and overcoats. The kindly woman then helped her select two outfits, both fit for a queen. As she tried them on, a river of tears wet the front of one of her new dresses. This was like a dream, yet she knew it was real when she felt warm arms encircle her old, tired body.

After the fitting session, she and the woman prayed together, then she was escorted back to the bedroom. As sleep's fingers slowly closed her eyes, she could barely contain all the day's events without her mind whizzing out of control. She had started out today in the cold, without even a decent dress to wear or a place to sleep. Now she was lying in a warm bed with a full stomach and two warm new outfits. Drifting off to sleep, she silently praised the Lord for this kind woman. She turned on her side and sobbed as tears of joy streamed down her wrinkled cheeks. This woman, without knowing her, had welcomed her into her home. This woman, who'd fed and clothed her and given her a warm bed to rest her weary bones, was indeed sent from the Lord. Yes, all she'd heard was true. This gracious woman, who became her patroness, was your sister, the beautiful, Creative Poetic Dorcas.

Dorcas lived in Joppa, an important city for the early church. It was a port city, and many traveled through its gates. Dorcas had great compassion for the widows and orphans of the city. The people of Joppa loved her because she freely gave of all she had for the less fortunate. She was always available to help anyone with almost any cause without complaint. For those who did not need her help financially, she always had a kind word, a blessing, or a prayer. She was a true ambassador for the Lord in her ministry to the hungry and homeless.

It is safe to say that Dorcas or Tabitha, as she was also called, was a woman of affluence. We can imagine she dressed creatively in multicolored linen and wool. Because of her creative spirit, Dorcas expertly combined colors and fabrics. She did not worry about matching colors. She skillfully blended gray, scarlet, and blues together, guided by Her Guardian, Guide, and Stay, the Holy Spirit, to create a beautiful Creative Poetic picture. Although she could very easily have afforded silk, she spent her money on the less fortunate rather than on herself.

She pulled her dark auburn hair away from her face. Her one item of adornment, a hand-carved ivory comb, held it in place. Over her head, she wore a soft headdress that protected her head from the sun as she walked along the city streets, gathering in the poor and homeless.

With her built-in radar, the Holy Spirit, she saw the needs and invited others into her home for fittings of new clothing and hot meals. These people were accustomed to wearing clothing made from rags that washed up on the shore, and eating whatever they could find, wherever they could find it. They would leave her home not only feeling renewed from the new outfits and full stomachs, but also with a fresh knowledge that He who sees all heard their prayers.

Once in her sewing room, Dorcas worked furiously, weaving together all types of clothing for the perpetual needs of the city's poor. Hard work left its mark on her hands. We can imagine that although Dorcas was an affluent woman, her hands more closely resembled those of a fisherman's wife, rough and covered with calluses. For every callus, there was a story. For every needle prick, there was an outfit on the back of a widow or an orphan in the city streets. Her work was never done. Her appearance was secondary to her ministry of helping those less fortunate than herself. She was Creative Poetic at its spiritual best.

It can be said that Dorcas probably spent her personal wealth on the wards of her city. The many people who knocked on her door, and those she discovered on her daily walk through the city streets, consumed her time, energy, and effort. When she helped, she never expected anything in return. The Holy Spirit guided her every act. Everything she said and did came from the kindness of her heart. It seemed as if the more she gave, the more the Lord blessed her to give even more. Dorcas gave so much of herself that even when she became ill, she did not stop working.

She ignored the signs of illness that overtook her usual endless pool of energy. Then the full impact of the sickness hit, swift and deadly. This unexplained illness, with its foul stench, came in like a ravenous wolf. Before anyone was able to do anything to help, the beautiful Dorcas lay dead in the upper room of her home.

What would they do now that their patroness was gone? The widows whom she had helped stood weeping and mourning her death. Never had there been one so kind and caring as this Dorcas. She had blessed so many lives and now she was suddenly taken from them.

During this sad time, the apostle Peter was preaching in Lydda, which was about ten miles from Joppa. It is safe to say that news of Dorcas's work spread throughout the early church. The disciples sent word for Peter to come quickly to Joppa. It was a fervent, desperate prayer of a city that needed Dorcas. There was no one who could take her place. It was a time and place ripe for a miracle. It was a time and place ripe for the Lord to make Himself known to the city of Joppa.

Peter arrived and discovered Dorcas in the upper room surrounded by weeping widows—perhaps the very widows she'd dressed and helped, and in the very room where she'd worked.

They had already dressed her for burial. He dismissed the weeping mourners from the room and knelt and prayed over Dorcas. He knew that His Lord was able to do exceedingly and abundantly above all he could ask or think. He knew that God was able to raise Dorcas from her slumber. Peter laid his hands on her and, using the Aramaic form of her name, he spoke a simple command to her in a strong voice: "Tabitha arise" (Acts 9:40).

With the utterance of these words, the Bible says that she opened her eyes; and when she saw Peter, she sat up. Can you imagine the initial surprise and the following celebration after the people saw their Dorcas alive? We can be sure there were shouts of praise to the Lord on that day. The Bible further tells us, in Acts 9:42, that because of her resurrection, many more believed in the Lord. This was one of her greatest triumphs. Through her death and resurrection, people believed in and accepted the Lord Jesus as their Savior. Hallelujah!

After her miraculous resurrection, Dorcas continued her work with a newfound energy. She was a living miracle. God had given her a precious gift—the gift of a second chance. Knowing this, Dorcas decided to make the most of it. True to her new strength, she left her mark even on today's world. Her work began the Dorcas Sewing Societies that are now known worldwide two thousand years later.

Just like your Creative Poetic sister Dorcas, you serve as an inspiration to others with your Creative Poetic spirit. Your love for others is seen in all you do. You know there is enough of God's goodness to go around. Your mission is to spread His word, letting others know that they need no longer strive for the things of this world, which will never satisfy. You let them know, through your words and actions, that only Jesus can bring true joy, peace, and satisfaction. Like your sister Dorcas, you are true to your name: an original, a beauty that captures hearts. You are a beautiful Creative Poetic, and the Lord's work of art!

Creative Poetic Strengths in the Body of Christ

Psalmist—Writer or Singer
Hospital Outreach Chair
Church Historian

Creative Poetic and Family Life

You have your own unique decorating style. Soup and peanut butter jar labels replace traditional wallpaper in your kitchen. Unmatched individual place settings make up your favorite china. Dried flowers hang in bunches from the window and door frames. Wind chimes made from antique earrings gently catch the breeze in your living room. Everything in your home is what others call "decorator interesting."

Very little in your home is new. You collect antique or senti-mental pieces and use them as the center of your decor. Behind every item is a story that reflects your creative spirit. You found a china service for eight at a garage sale, but talked the owner into selling only one or two place settings. Another plate was discov-ered at the local discount store while the coordinating (notice I did not say *matching*) cups and saucers were bought at a high-end specialty shop. This is not to say that you do not like matching china. If you do find a pattern that meets your standards for Cre-ative Poetic style, then concern for expense goes out the window. If you don't have the cash on hand, you save for it or put it on your credit card. The bottom line is, if you like it, you will not rest until you have it.

Your home is also unique and what others call "engaging." Folks never know what to expect because your environment changes with your mood. You are an expert at pulling together different furniture styles for an eclectic look. You enjoy variety and stay away from mainstream decorating trends. Your couch might be Queen Anne and your coffee table contemporary. Your favorite chairs are just plain old comfortable. Today you drape beautiful silk scarves over all your lamps for a romantic effect. To-morrow you replace them with traditional shades. Your mood is the thermometer that shapes your entire choice process.

Since variety is the spice of your life, you do not feel you must give up something to have a good time. You make all your choices according to your mood. You put life on cruise control and enjoy the scenery. For example, if you and your conservative husband go out for ice cream, he orders his standard chocolate and vanilla sundae, prepared in the traditional way. You, on the other hand, order pistachio, peach, and mocha almond ice cream with butter-scotch sauce topped off with bananas and cherries.

While others might frown on your choices, you do not let their disapproval bother you. You are secure enough to accept their traditional approach to life. Constant prayer and reading your Bible help keep your self-image at a healthy level. You are a joint heir with Christ, and He died to give you the power of choice. You, for one, will not let that precious sacrifice be in vain. You take full advantage of all life's choices as you glorify your Lord in Creative Poetic style!

> The Spirit Himself bears witness with our own spirit that we are children of God, and if children, then heirs—heirs of God and joint heirs with Christ, if indeed we suffer with Him, that we may also be glorified together.
>
> ROMANS 8:16–17

Your children love your creative spirit. You enjoy having fun with them. Whatever the activity, they enjoy full creative freedom while you act as observer and safety manager. In the kitchen, you instruct them in the proper use of the microwave and other appliances. After proper training and passing all tests, they prepare their own meals when Mom is busy with one of her many projects. This helps promote a sense of self-worth that is sure to last a lifetime.

Holiday times are great fun for your children. They bake their favorite treats and decorate them to their hearts' content. You allow them to pull out all the stops and be fully creative. By the time things are finished, the kitchen is filled with wonderful smells and beautiful, disfigured holiday treats. You watch proudly and munch loudly on the one-legged gingerbread man with green squiggly hair and cinnamon drop eyes. For you, this is one of those precious, irreplaceable moments of childhood, and the creation of this mutant ginger treat is a labor of true love.

You are the mom who organizes a painting party. You cover everything in the bedroom and leave one wall bare. Small buckets of paint in an array of colors await the attack of child-sized brushes. You give out instructions, and the painting begins. As you allow them to decorate their wall with colors and designs of their choosing, you stand back and watch with wonder. They can hardly sleep recovering from the day's excitement.

That night, as you peek into their bedroom, you catch the glint of a hidden flashlight that is quickly extinguished as you enter the room. You smile as you close the door, knowing they were viewing the day's handiwork. This was a day their young hearts will not soon forget. The wall is full of beautiful designs born from youthful enthusiasm, all compliments of the Lord and their mother, His beautiful Creative Poetic daughter.

All entertainment activities are carefully screened. Any movie or book that you feel may defile their precious spirits does not stay in your home. If one of your little ones does happen to bring something suspicious in, you openly discuss your feelings and decisions and state your position. It is critical that your children be educated not only in the natural, but in the spiritual things as well. You let them know the house rules and help them clean out their rooms regularly. Your children know to come to you if there are questions about items that might be unpleasant to you or your heavenly Father. The Lord established the home as a safe haven, and you always strive to work with Him to keep it that way.

You take time out to spend individual time with each of your children. Getting to know them first as little people and understanding and accepting their differences is a priority for you. Learning about them as individuals helps you plan outings more suitable for the entire family. It also helps in planning Mom-and-children activities and cuts down on conflict that stems from miscommunication.

Since each child receives "Mom" time, your little people share secret thoughts and desires, and you focus on every word. These are treasured times because you know they will not stay young forever. You also know that if they do not share with you during early childhood, adolescence will be a rocky road. Your battle plan is to prepare for war during peace. You know the enemy stays prepared and waits for any opening. Your maternal armory is stocked with the things of God: His Holy Word and prayer.

During adolescence, children become especially vulnerable to outside influences. Teaching them early in life that they can come to you with anything is the best battle plan for family protection. By taking time out for each child, you teach them about His precious first gift, being made in His image. They also learn firsthand how to accept others, for others, too, are beautifully made in the image of the Father. You let them know that your source of knowledge is the Lord, who teaches you so you can teach them. Like your biblical sister Hannah, you believe in the power of prayer to guide you as a mother.

> *A*ll your children shall be taught by the Lord and great shall be the place of your children.
>
> ISAIAH 54:13

Hannah

THE FAITHFUL MOTHER

> Moreover his mother used to make him a little robe, and bring it to him year by year when she came with her husband to offer the yearly sacrifice. . . .
>
> I SAMUEL 2:19

Every year it was the same. Hannah and her family went up to Shiloh and offered sacrifices to the Lord. Every year she endured taunts for being a childless woman. She could stand the heart-ache no longer. The Lord just had to hear her prayer and grant her petition. Did He really hear her prayers? Was He really listening? Did He even care? She was young, healthy, and desperate for children. She was married to a wealthy man who lived to please her, but that was not enough. She knew her husband loved her better than his other wife, but this knowledge did not fill her empty womb. Only a child, a male child, would make the deep pain in her heart disappear. As they continued the journey, she knew she had reached a crossroad in her life. This journey had to be different. She had made her decision. She would meet Him face to face, if need be. When they arrived in Shiloh, she would go to the temple and talk with the Lord.

The next day, she arose early. She dressed and attended to her duties as mistress. Thoughts of what she would say flooded her mind. What words would she use? How would she say it? What would make this time different? The Lord had to grant her request. Her body longed to be filled with motherhood's blessing. It was for this purpose she was created. No one could tell her any different. No one except the Lord God Himself.

As she left the safety of her camp, she knew this was a journey of purpose. This was to be a day she would remember for the rest of her life. She walked through the streets, hearing the laughter of children and the shouts of mothers calling to them. Oh, how she wished to be one of them. Tears blinded her as she searched for the street leading to the temple, leaving the peals of laughter behind her. Her veil was soaked with tears of sorrow. She felt as if her heart were broken into a thousand pieces. Her body shook with the heaviness of grief. She grieved for her unborn children. She grieved for her many unanswered prayers. She felt they never reached heaven, but instead hung like dangling ribbons from the clouds of her life's gray sky. Hers was a grief so real that she openly sobbed as she caught sight of the temple.

Her pace quickened as her feet suddenly felt light as feathers blowing in the wind. She dried her moist eyes and stepped inside. The quietness of the temple was almost frightening, but today she decided to be brave. Nothing else mattered. Today He had to give her an answer. As she approached the sanctuary, her body felt so heavy that as she entered the holy place, she literally fell on her face and began to weep. She had finally arrived in His holy place, where He would surely speak to her. Hannah, your Creative Poetic sister, had come to the temple of the Lord to ask for a child.

Elkanah was a wealthy man with two wives, Peninnah and Hannah. Peninnah had several children but his favorite wife, Hannah, was childless. This was a sore spot between the two women. The Bible tell us, in I Samuel 1:6, that Peninnah always "provoked Hannah severely," making Hannah miserable because she had no children. Every year when the family went to Shiloh to offer sacrifices to the Lord, Peninnah harassed Hannah and caused her to cry and not eat.

One year, while on their trip, Elkanah spoke to Hannah and asked her why she was so miserable. He just could not understand why she allowed Peninnah to bother her. He treated Hannah better than his other wife and better than ten sons. In her culture, to be treated as good as one son was an honor, but better than ten sons—especially for a woman—was unthinkable. It is easy to imagine that this special treatment angered Peninnah. She had given Elkanah many children and Hannah had not even been able to give him one son.

Under any other circumstances, Elkanah's special treatment would have been enough, but in the area of motherhood, it was not. Elkanah's heart ached for Hannah because he loved her so very much, and while his love and concern were precious to Hannah, they just weren't enough.

We can imagine that Hannah was a beautiful young woman who dressed in shades of scarlet, blue, and purple silk and wool. On her hair, she wore a golden net; her skin was radiant and gently kissed by the sun. On her ears were golden earrings. She wore a golden ring, one of the many gifts from Elkanah, and on her wrists hung golden bracelets. This gold looked wonderful on her but did not fill the emptiness of her heart. Hannah would have traded all her silks and gold for a child. She would have traded it all for the touch and feel of a precious baby. She would have traded it all for a son.

As she prostrated herself before the Lord, she was so overcome with grief that she did not have the strength to speak. Only her lips moved as she prayed. She knew the Lord would search her heart and hear her prayer. While she prayed, the priest Eli watched, and because he could hear no words coming from her mouth, he thought she was drunk. He could only see her lips move as she prayed silently.

As he began to rebuke her, Hannah explained her situation, telling him that she was not drunk but instead was a woman with a sorrowful spirit. His anger cooled against her, and in verse 17 Eli told her to "go in peace and may the God of Israel grant your petition which you have asked of Him." After this blessing, she went away, ate, and was no longer sad. At that moment, Hannah believed the Lord had heard her prayer. This was the first time in a very long time she'd been able to relax. Not even Peninnah's taunts could destroy her faith. She would wait on the Jehovah Jireh, her Provider.

Hannah was a woman who did not take prayer lightly. We do not know just how much longer Hannah waited, but soon after that encounter, Hannah's prayer was answered. She became pregnant and bore a son. She named him Samuel, which means "asked of God."

After Samuel was born, Hannah took care of his every need. She did not leave his care to anyone else. He was to be brought up with a special purpose: serving the Lord God of Israel. Hannah had vowed that since the Lord granted her petition, she would return His gift to Him. Samuel would spend his life in the temple of the Lord and be trained for the priesthood. He would be exposed only to the word of the Lord and things of holiness. Hannah was so serious about Samuel's upbringing that on one occasion, she would not accompany Elkanah to the yearly sacrifice because Samuel was not yet weaned. Once he was weaned, she took him to the temple and presented him to Eli. Samuel was then dedicated to temple service. After the sacrifices were offered, Hannah said good-bye to her son. This was her gift of honor to her Lord, Who had heard her prayer.

Each year when she returned to Shiloh, Hannah brought Samuel a new linen ephod made by her own hands. Knowing Hannah, the robes were made of the finest linen available. Hannah created these beautiful works with her hands to honor God. While she sewed the deep blue linen, interwoven with golden threads, her Creative Poetic spirit permeated each piece. Garments of this pattern were worn only by members of the priesthood, and Hannah was proud to have a son in the Lord's service. We can imagine that Samuel owned several ephods because Hannah made sure he had only the best. He wore them honorably because they were made by his mother's loving hands. He wore them honorably because his life had been dedicated to serving the Lord.

Hannah trained him well, and the Lord was well pleased. Samuel's beautiful, faithful, Creative Poetic mother placed her son on the path of righteousness, and he became a great judge over Israel. In typical Creative Poetic style, she cared not for gold, silver, or jewels. In typical Creative Poetic Style, she cared not for robes and dresses of fine silk and wool that were hers for the asking. She even held her peace when taunted by Peninnah. With her gentle spirit, she humbled herself before her God. Jehovah Jireh heard her prayer and gave her the desire of her heart. He gave her not only her beautiful, righteous son Samuel, but also three more sons and two daughters. These children were a tribute to undying faith; the undying faith of Hannah, your beautiful, Creative Poetic sister.

The Creative Poetic Spouse

Your husband loves your freedom of expression. You often catch him off-guard. On any given day, he might come home and discover you have re-created your bedroom into a tropical paradise. As he enters his new, erotic surroundings of tropical flowers and animal prints, you transport him from his hectic day into the world of Creative Poetic joy. Creating different moods at unusual times and places keeps the fire in your marriage burning brightly for years to come. Knowing this, the Creative Poetic is just the woman to keep things interesting.

Experience has taught your husband to stay on his toes and constantly watch for the unexpected. You keep his life interesting and exciting by coming up with daily surprises. You act as a rejuvenating force after he has had a long, tiring day. You have that special knack for making him feel special, and he adores you for it. Sometimes your Creative Poetic energy can be exhausting for him. Be aware of this and learn to watch his reactions and moods. He may need just a few minutes to unwind before he can enjoy one of your surprises!

When you call his office and hear frustration in his voice, there is a warm bubble bath waiting when he comes in the door. After he gets out of his bath, his robe and a cool drink are ready. You allow him to relax and give him some quiet time alone. When he is calm and relaxed, you serve his favorite dinner. The children are put to bed and you surprise him with a massage. He then tells you about his day as the two of you relax in each other's arms.

Because of your creative, independent spirit, there are times when you will become immersed in one of your many projects. Make sure you come up for air and give your husband his much-needed attention. He may feel neglected and not tell you because he loves to see you happy and does not want to stop your creative flow. Take a break and give him an affectionate hug. Ask him about his day and allow him to talk freely without interruption. This not only relaxes him physically but also helps him smoothly transition from work to home. If he had a hard day, make a special effort to take care of his needs before going back to your project. After unwinding, he will be more open to hearing about your day as well. You think of creative ways to help him relax and poetically use your wifely wisdom to help him experience unforgettable evenings. He could write a book about your Creative Poetic beauty.

Your project will still be there waiting patiently for your return. You honor your husband by putting him first. He may not say anything at that moment, but he will remember. When you honor him, you are planting seeds of love, and the harvest will be plentiful. You are a wise woman who knows the value of making your mate feel important. Doing your best to satisfy him gives you plenty of room to use your Creative Poetic gifts. By doing so, you gain his undying support and affection. The Lord has given you gifts of boundless energy and creativity to use for His glory. You crown your husband with excellence as you make his life rich and free!

> *A*n excellent wife is the crown of her husband. . . .
>
> PROVERBS 12:4

Creative Poetic Working Style

You look for the flip side of every issue. You are curious but never what others consider nosy. For you, there is always more to a situation than meets the eye, and you generally find it. Your curious nature makes you suited for career fields that involve investigative work. You find clues and search them out for authenticity. You discover the facts and are especially good at keying in on the feelings of people involved.

Your love of people helps you find the perfect combination of feelings and getting to the bottom of the news. Because you have mastered this trait, you get the necessary information without hurting the people involved. If your job is reporting the news, you gently let them know that you must report the facts, but will guard their privacy as much as possible. You are the one who always gets the story because of your reputation. People always know you care about the human factor, so they tend to give you hidden information. They know you will report it fairly while keeping the feelings of others in mind.

Working under pressure suits you only when you have a definite deadline yet still enjoy room for creativity. If you are a columnist, for example, you know you must write a number of words on a certain subject by an appointed time. You are responsible for this output on a recurring basis and work tirelessly to come up with the details and make the articles interesting. Last-minute breakthroughs are commonplace. You handle everything with joy because these things come with the job. Your love for the unexpected makes this type of job ideal for you. You thrive when outcomes of daily situations are uncertain and you have the power to make changes as you go along.

There are times when you allow job pressure to affect your judgment and cause stress. There may be an unpleasant story you have to cover. Just seeing the condition of the world is enough to make you want to retreat and hide from it all. During these times, go to the Lord and hold on to His unchanging hand. He created you just the way you are, and He knows how things affect His Creative Poetic daughter. He wants you to come boldly to His throne with your every concern.

> *L*et us therefore come boldly to the throne of grace, that we may obtain mercy and find grace to help in time of need.
>
> HEBREWS 4:16

As a team player, you are in your element. Still, if you are to be a productive part of the team, you must first trust your team leader and be sold on the team's purpose. If others could be hurt because of team actions, then you have a difficult time cooperating. You confront the issues with ease and expect assurances that all will be well. If you decide to continue with the team, you work hard to ensure that it keeps its integrity. For you, integrity in personal and professional relationships is a must. Many a Creative Poetic has been known to quit a lucrative position because a company falls short in the integrity department. You allow the Holy Spirit to lead you in all your actions because He is integrity at its finest.

You do not like being tied to a desk. Your love of freedom demands that you not be in bondage. You thrive in jobs where you can spread your creative wings and fly. If you do happen to take, for example, a secretarial position, you quickly evolve into an administrative assistant who regularly coordinates and interacts with other departments. The people aspect of the job makes it tolerable until something more suitable comes along. If you do not especially want to interact with others, you do well as a graphic artist or art assistant. In such a position, you use your creative talents in a more quiet working environment. As long as your creativity flows freely, you let your work do the talking.

Your image type goes far in creative circles, but your mode of dress may hamper your promotion chances in more conservative career fields. You may be misjudged as unpredictable by more conservative types. Do not be discouraged. Remember, you were interviewed for the job you now hold, be it wife, executive, or even friend. The one important thing you should remember is that you were selected! Do not forget that. There was obviously something about you and your style that opened the door to your present position. Remember, you now hold the position, so apparently the person who interviewed you liked your style and believed you could do the job.

You are a thoughtful and considerate leader. Your team members know that you care not only about them, but about their families as well. You allow them to take personal time off, as long as it does not interfere with the mission at work. Flextime is one of your favorite work options because it allows you and team members to take care of personal business yet still do the work necessary to keep things rolling. People like having you in charge because you believe that the "people factor" is critical to organizational effectiveness. Like your biblical sister Miriam, you are a born leader who feels the hearts of others.

Pray without ceasing, for the Lord will do battle for you. Whatever your position, your heavenly Father is always ready and waiting and will never let you down. You have His promise as long as you trust Him. Remember, you are fearfully and wonderfully made in His image. Isn't that just like Him to create someone wonderful like you, just like Him?

> *B*ut he [she] who puts his [her] trust in Me shall possess the land, and shall inherit My holy mountain.
>
> ISAIAH 57:13

Miriam

FIRST PATRIOTIC SINGER OF SONGS

> Then Miriam the prophetess, the sister of Aaron, took the timbrel in her hand, and all the women went out after her with timbrels and with dances.
>
> EXODUS 15:20

Holding back the long reeds with her small hands, Miriam could barely see the basket as it floated away. The water level already reached her waist, and she stood on tiptoes to keep it in sight. As she watched, the large basket became caught in the river's current and began to travel at an accelerated speed. Trying to keep up with it, she almost lost her balance as her tiny feet became tangled in underwater weeds. Yet she did not fall, because she was on a mission. She was determined to keep watch over her family's precious cargo.

Fear suddenly gripped her heart as she noticed a group of Egyptian women bathing in the basket's path. As she worked her way through the river's green jungle to get a better look, Miriam noticed that one of the women wore the Egyptian royal family's emblem around her neck. As she drew even closer, she heard their conversation. Could her eyes and ears be deceiving her? Was this the daughter of a murderer? Was this the daughter of the pharaoh who had just decreed that all infant males of Israel be put to death? As the basket came within inches of the bathers, Miriam moved slowly through the water and held her breath. She prayed for a miracle. As she prayed, she moved to get a closer look. Suddenly, she froze in her watery footsteps. As she grasped the long reeds of the river in her tiny hands, she saw that the basket had floated among the bathers. The basket had floated into the arms of the princess of Egypt.

Panic gripped her heart, and fear began to gnaw at her spirit. What would she tell her mother? How could she have prevented this from happening? There was nothing she could do but wait. As the Egyptian princess opened the basket, Miriam beheld the unexpected—the inquisitive glance melted into a beautiful smile. After sending away her fellow bathers, the princess brought the basket out of the water and gently lifted the precious contents into her arms. When the tiny babe began to cry, the princess pulled him to her chest. Tears welled up in her eyes, and she began to rock him in her arms as if he were her very own son. The princess then wrapped the baby in a cloth bearing the Egyptian royal symbol.

Standing quietly in the murky waters of the Nile River, Miriam drank in the sight of the woman and child. She breathed a sigh of relief, knowing the child was out of danger. While she watched the bonding begin, Miriam knew what to tell her mother: She had just witnessed a miracle. The basket holding her infant brother had just floated into the future. For he was now

under the protection of the very family that had previously con-
demned him to death. As she loosened her grip on the wet clump
of reeds, Miriam realized she had witnessed the mighty hand of
God move the waters of the river to save her brother. Your Creative Poetic sister Miriam had witnessed the Lord save Moses, the
future leader of Israel.

Miriam was the older sister of Moses. Even as a child, she displayed an inner strength and wisdom that were unique for one so
young. Her ability to think and act quickly and intelligently was
shown as she spoke to the daughter of a murderous pharaoh, who
had just decreed all Israel's male babies be put to death. Upon her
discovery of the baby Moses, the pharaoh's daughter was over-
joyed. Miriam, seeing her reaction, immediately spoke up and offered to find a Hebrew woman to nurse the baby. The pharaoh's
daughter accepted her offer, not knowing that Miriam was the sister of her newly found bundle. Neither did the pharaoh's daughter know that her act brought joy to the family of Israel's future
leader. This little girl, by her act of courage and quick thinking,
saved her brother and reunited her family.

We can envision Miriam as a tall, strong woman who stood
out among her peers. It is easy to imagine that she had the spirit
of a leader. Even the dark pits of slavery could not extinguish the
fire that burned within her heart. It shone brightly in her eyes.
She knew that the day of delivery was not far away. Her dark
brown hair with its golden highlights was worn in a braid that
hung down her back under her headdress of light-colored wool.
Her long, sand-colored, woolen dress and overcoat draped loosely
around her form and were cinched at her waist by a light-colored
sash. On her feet, she wore sandals. Since she was a slave, she did
not wear golden jewelry, but her beauty did not need the adornment of gold. Because she worked in the sun, her skin was a deep,
golden brown that resembled copper. Her hands were callused
and dry, but in her heart burned the Spirit of the living God.

Her life in the black pits of slavery was not easy. She and the women cooked, cleaned, and worked in the fields to gather straw for the bricks for the great Egyptian cities. We can imagine that when the plagues of Egypt came upon the land, Miriam instructed her people by helping to prepare them for the coming catastrophes. Once her brother Moses returned, we believe she served as a spokesperson for him.

She gathered the women together and told them to fill their water vessels before the upcoming water shortage. Miriam's word spread throughout the nation from house to house. All the women knew that if this word came from Miriam, it was indeed true, and they immediately filled their vessels. They waited, like little children, with great anticipation for the unknown calamity that was sure to come. Miriam also supervised the baking of the unleavened bread in preparation for the great Passover. She knew the Lord God was moving and using her family for His great purpose.

Her days were filled with joy, and she hummed songs of praise from her heart. Little did she know at the time that she would become a symbol of patriotism for all generations. All she knew was that every day the Lord was working miracles on Israel's behalf. At the Red Sea, Miriam led the women through the waters. With walls of water on both sides, her spirit of courage was needed to save her people. The Lord knew that He could depend on Miriam and that she would come through for Him on that day. Singing and praising the Lord with her songs, she saw the pharaoh's chariots being barred by the pillar of fire. She raised her voice even louder as a path was opened in the midst of the sea before the children of Israel.

As they marched down the path, praises, songs, and great joy filled every heart. They knew that only the hand of God was holding back the great walls of the sea. Miriam was there to see it all. She saw the drowning of the pharaoh's soldiers as they had the nerve to march through the midst of the sea after them. She watched as the Lord God removed His mighty hand and the sea swallowed them, chariots and all. Never again would Israel see the Egyptian army advance against them. They could go on to the Promised Land without fear.

Miriam was the first woman on record to openly display patriotism with the gift of song. She led the women of Israel in the oldest of national anthems. Her people had just been delivered from four centuries of hard bondage in the land of Egypt. This event ushered in a new era in Israel's spiritual evolution. It was Miriam who led the way with her glorious song to the Deliverer of her people, the Lord God Jehovah. In Exodus 15:20–21, Creative Poetic Miriam took a timbrel in her hand and led all the women with timbrels and dances before the Lord in a song of praise.

Miriam was called a prophetess by her people. In Hebrew, the word *prophetess* refers to a woman inspired to teach the will of God or the wife of a prophet or a singer of songs. There is no record of Miriam ever being married, so it is safe to say that she gained this title by teaching the will of God and singing hymns of praise.

Miriam was not always in a place of honor with Israel. She was caught in a conspiracy against her brother Moses with her brother Aaron. They both murmured against him. Miriam was not pleased with her brother's choice of wife. In Numbers 12:1, the Bible tell us that Moses had married an Ethiopian woman. It has been said that Miriam was angry because at the time, the Ethiopian people were known idol worshipers and of another race. Whatever her reason, the Lord did not agree with her attitude and actions. It is obvious that the Lord saw nothing wrong with this biracial marriage. In fact, He was so displeased with this sin that He passed immediate judgment on Miriam.

In verse 2, she and Aaron agreed that the Lord not only had spoken through Moses but had used them also. The Lord heard them and became angry. In the next few verses, we read how the Lord rebuked Miriam and Aaron, but only Miriam was struck with leprosy as a punishment for murmuring against Moses. It is clear from this passage that she was the leader in this incident and had probably given Moses the hardest time. It is also clear that Miriam was indeed influential, and her attitude was a critical factor in leading the people.

Because of his love for his sister and his humbleness of spirit (Numbers 12:3), Moses pleaded with the Lord for her healing. The Lord so loved Moses that He healed Miriam. Since leprosy was considered to be unclean, Miriam was kept out of camp for seven days before she rejoined her people. Her importance was shown in Numbers 12:15, where the Bible tells us that the people did not journey on until Miriam was brought in again.

Even when she was not at her best, Miriam can still be remembered as a woman of honor. Her people needed her Creative Poetic spirit to help lead them to the Promised Land. It is easy to imagine that her character was changed after her encounter with leprosy. She repented before the Lord and asked her brother for forgiveness. She now knew that her brother would never do anything against the Lord of heaven, so who was she to judge him? She grew to fully trust him and his choices, even his choice of wife. She went on to continue singing her Creative Poetic songs of praise for the Lord God, who deserved all the honor and praise. She continued to share her beautiful Creative Poetic spirit to glorify God and encourage her people. Like you, her Creative Poetic sister, she influenced those around her to worship the Lord God with songs of praise!

Great Career Choices for the Creative Poetic

Photojournalist
Interior Decorator
Hairdresser
Fashion Designer
Artist
Writer

The Outer You

CREATIVE POETIC CLOTHING CHOICES

Your working wardrobe is full of variety. Like the Jaunty Esprit, you like comfort, but you remain loyal to the two U's, Unique and Unusual. As long as something is unusual, it is uniquely yours. Boots in all lengths, from ankle to over the knee, in an array of colors, are your wardrobe staples. They match your favorite outfits and different fashion moods. Dressing in layers is also typical for you. The more layers you wear, the better you feel. An oversized sweater with a vest and long skirt and your favorite ankle boots, complete with leggings, speak your language. Dressing is a Creative Poetic art form, and a way to express your personality and individuality.

Your outfit of the day depends on your mood. People watch with interest to see what you wear because you look different every day. Today you may wear a straight skirt with a silk blouse and vest. Tomorrow a suede skirt and boots with a matching duster, a cowl-neck sweater, and a long flowing shawl will be more your mood. Still another day you wear an ankle-length skirt and boots with an oversized jacket and a bulky tunic with your Spanish mantilla.

Each time you dress, it is a creative adventure. If you want to express a European mood, you wear an oversized man's shirt and vest with leggings. You top it off with an authentic Parisian beret. When in an ultrafeminine mood, you wear an antique panne velvet dress with a high lace neckline and matching lace cuffs. Starting with an empty canvas, you create a Creative Poetic original every time you adorn your body.

Unusual leg wear is also one of your passions. Hosiery in many styles and colors is a Creative Poetic wardrobe necessity. Your style preferences are always on sale because only you and your sister Sensual Exotic would buy them. Electric orange and outrageous purple are yours for the taking. Shocking pink and sunshine gold await your coming. Your first, second, and last choices are unique, and only a select few would dare wear them because they are simply Creative Poetic!

The same holds true for your shoes. They range from those over-the-knee boots to electric-colored sandals. Your style signature shouts with every pair. You are the first to try a new fad. Stack-heeled styling with multiple straps is sure to be in your closet. Although you like style, you also want comfort. If you like a style and find it comfortable, even if it is out of style for the rest of the world, you wear it because it meets your needs and boldly displays the Creative Poetic image.

Your wardrobe includes vests in many different fabrics and colors. You wear a vest over your favorite sweater dress or evening outfit. One Creative Poetic friend is so uniquely individual, she wears her vest on the "wrong side" with the labels showing simply because she likes the color and texture of the lining. When people tell her she is wearing the vest inside out, she simply lets them know she fully intended to wear it as it is. She lovingly lets everyone know she is an individual and enjoys charting the unknown, even in the realm of fashion. With her Creative Poetic spirit, she teaches people to be more accepting of others and their differences. What other image type would take something as simple as a vest and use it to minister? Only you or your sister Creative Poetic could be so creative.

> The wise in heart will be called prudent, and sweetness of the lips increases learning.
>
> PROVERBS 16:21

Unlike your Harmonic Refined sister, you do not have fashion and shopping loyalties to certain stores and catalogs. Your shopping standards are what could be called diverse. You are not into designer names and convention. Status means little to you. You frequent boutiques, department stores, flea markets, and craft shows to find your Creative Poetic treasures. If you see something you like, you buy it. It doesn't matter where you find it; if it speaks to you, it's yours. It can be a jeweled vest from a Parisian boutique or a poet's shirt from the local thrift shop. If it has Creative Poetic style, you find it and buy it. While you may look through fashion magazines, you are not influenced by the look of the season. You are an individual and enjoy creating your own style. Your style of dressing is always interesting, creative, and individually unique.

You establish a rapport with store owners and designers. They learn to recognize your tastes and hold unusual pieces for your return to their shops. They know that if they please you and your unique tastes, the rest will be easy. You set the stage for challenge and help them stay on track with the newest fashions. They soon learn your fashion secret. Many of the world's top designers are the Creative Poetic image type—and rightly so. You and your sister Creative Poetics allow your creative juices to flow freely. You make the world around you its creative best.

Your creative style makes you seem very different from the mainstream population. Your style of dressing says you are definitely an individual who does not conform to the standards of this world. For this reason, it is so important that you constantly pray to ensure that the world you do belong to is the one of the King of kings and Lord of lords. It is also important for you to remain true to your image type. With prayer, daily Bible reading, and devotion, you stay in tune with the Father and maintain the balance and freedom that are so typically you. His Holy Spirit gladly shows you how to do all things in full Creative Poetic style!

*B*ehold what manner of love the Father has bestowed on us, that we should be called children of God! Therefore the world does not know us, because it did not know Him.

I JOHN 3:1

CREATIVE POETIC FULL-FIGURED CLOTHING CHOICES

Unstructured, loose-fitting layers work best for you. Your clothing choices mirror those of your smaller sister. An unstructured chemise, coupled with your favorite boots and topped with a duster, spells comfort and Creative Poetic style. A vest worn over an extra-long, loose-fitting blouse and leggings with your new ankle boots makes a great casual look. Wearing it in Creative Poetic style, you are comfortable and ready to tackle any project. Full-cut, unstructured fashions with artsy accents shout to the world the beauty of your image type.

You wear different styles to match your moods and your job. If you are a busy executive, you look for classic lines with relaxed detail. Unstructured jackets with tea-length skirts give you elegant, creative styling. The look gives freedom of movement and still maintains Creative Poetic image credibility. Creatively draped scarves and shawls give that extra dash of artistic presence. Underneath, you wear a simple blouse and vest to keep in step with the layers you love so well.

Cotton knits allow your skin to breathe and take you from summer to winter with few wardrobe changes. These knits dance with your movements, and cotton breathes naturally with every step. Long, unstructured skirts and oversized cardigans with side-seam slits are fashionable yet creatively unique. You use these pieces as your base and add Creative Poetic touches for pizzazz.

Separates in lively colors and prints dance from boardroom to evening with Creative Poetic style. Top these with multicolored, oversized vests in rich fabrics and you are ready for any adventure.

If you have full hips and choose to wear a straight skirt, use the Fingertip Rule. Using this simple technique will enable you to wear just about any type of skirt, as long as it fits properly. To use the Fingertip Rule, your jacket should fall approximately a hand length below the fullest part of your hips. Stand with your arms relaxed at your sides. Notice where your fingertips fall. This should be the perfect length for your jackets. If your arms are short, add two inches. This enables you to wear straight skirts if you choose.

You have quite a bit of flexibility as long as you make wise clothing choices. You glorify the Lord with your creativity and freedom. You always keep in mind that where His Spirit dwells, there is liberty. Walking with Him, you glorify your God in Creative Poetic style!

> *N*ow the Lord is the Spirit; and where the Spirit of the Lord is, there is liberty.
>
> II Corinthians 3:17

Being full-figured does not change your image type. You wear the same clothing styles as your smaller sister. The only difference is the size. If you wear clothing from different clothing lines, your size may change according to how the line is sized. Remember, size is unimportant as long as the garment fits. Your main concern should always be how you look and feel. If you are comfortable, then your creative Inner Compass will guide you in all you do. You are an original, a beauty, and you capture hearts. You are a beautiful Creative Poetic and His adorable work of art!

Key Words for the Creative Poetic Dress Code

Artsy
Creative
Unique
Original

Creative Poetic Color Schemes

Your colors let everyone know your identity. You mix and match colors and patterns that to anyone else would seem foreign. You expertly use deep, rich colors with iridescent accents, developing your own color themes. It is not unusual for you to wear color combinations such as pistachio green and salmon pink with purple accents. Combining these with your taste for antique textures and patterns in fabrics is a winning Creative Poetic style statement.

The Creative Poetic color combination code is: "The more unusual, the better." Your colors flow with your mood and blend with your spirit. You can be totally unconventional in the morning, wearing mauve and gold with hot orange accents. That evening you choose deep navy and burgundy with silver-gray accents. This is a classic color combination your Harmonic Refined sister would be proud to wear. Your choices just truly depend on how you are feeling and where you happen to be going. For you, color is a matter of timing and mood.

Others often ask for assistance because for you, color mixing is a creative exercise. You develop color schemes no one else could or would think of using. A collage of purples and greens highlights a yellow bedroom. In your kitchen, black, white, and orange shout your theme. If you cannot find the orange accents, you hand-paint the fabric and then make them yourself. Your dining room is decorated in an art nouveau theme. Your table is an old door painted dark brown and accented with the matching design from your drapes. Everything is a Creative Poetic original work of art.

You always try to top your last color-blending experiment with every dressing event. Teal and orange send tremors through the senses when merged with eggshell as you enter a room. Your artistic nature is free and clear to navigate as color becomes an adventure in Creative Poetic fun. One of your favorite outfits is your purple tea-length skirt, topped with your teal jacket and accented with your oversized fuchsia-and-green fringed shawl and large dangling gold earrings. Your lemon-yellow silk blouse is hand-embroidered with just enough purple to catch the eye and easily blend with the skirt as it peeps from under your jacket.

You are a colorful display of God's glory in your Creative Poetic palette. You create the perfect theme for the perfect adventure to keep you thoroughly free, thoroughly Creative Poetic. You let others know that you are an original and walk in the light of the Lord's countenance.

> *B*lessed are the people who know the joyful sound! They walk, O Lord, in the light of Your countenance. In Your name they rejoice all day long, and in Your righteousness they are exalted.
>
> PSALMS 89:15–16

CREATIVE POETIC JEWELRY

Traditional jewelry becomes unique on the Creative Poetic form. You can take an ordinary conservative pair of earrings and make them speak your language by clipping one on your ear and the other on your lapel for a sensational conversation piece. On the other ear is a different favorite earring, perhaps a star or moon shape in sterling silver or polished gold.

When you find earrings you like, it is not unusual for you to buy two pairs, in two sizes. If you happen upon two pairs of different-sized hearts that are identical except for the size, you have found a coordinated treasure. You choose one earring from each pair and wear them together. One small heart is worn on one ear, the larger one on the other. The look says *Creative Poetic* over and over again. Others always notice your unique jewelry styling, and your earrings become conversation pieces every time.

You also like dangling earrings accented with multiple shapes and colors. Depending on your mood, you wear one or both. You do not need matched sets. If you lose one of your favorites, you are sad but not defeated. You still wear the one earring with pride and adorn the other ear with another unmatched favorite. It takes more than losing an earring to quench your creative fire.

Flea markets hold trunks of Creative Poetic jewelry treasures. Antique beaded clusters and intricately framed, odd-shaped unnamed stones call to you from hidden places. They do not stay hidden for long because you hear them calling and they go home with you. One-of-a-kind bangles made of brass, pewter, and silver are Creative Poetic treasured finds. Antique napkin rings make a dazzling pair of Creative Poetic earrings that are sure to be showstoppers.

Rings excite you. Depending on your mood, you wear several or a singular favorite. Mixing rings of gold, silver, and copper, your hands tell the world you are the true creative, artistic type. One of your favorites has sentimental value, and you seldom take it off. Most of your rings are of precious metals and were found at one your favorite places, the flea market. You always discover your best treasures at these wonderful markets. You love filling your jewelry chest to the brim with wondrous Creative Poetic collectibles.

The Lord gave you a keen eye for everything that suits your image type. The world opens up to you when you step out in Creative Poetic form. You lead the way and help others see they are free as He intended. With every fiber of your Creative Poetic being, you sing praises to the Lord, your God.

> *I* will sing to the Lord as long as I live; I will sing praises to my God while I have my being.
>
> PSALMS 104:33

CREATIVE POETIC HAIR

As with other areas of your life, you style your hair according to your mood. Today you wear curls, crimps, or braids. Tomorrow you change and wear it short and straight. Your short cut is shockingly short on one side, with the other much longer. Highlighted with dazzling color, this dramatic haircut awakens all who see you. When this look grows boring, you wear a wig or have a mane of hair woven in for added effect. You do exactly what you want, when you want. Everything, including your hair, moves in step with your Creative Poetic mood.

Your need for variety may lead you to experiment with odd hair color. It would not be unusual for you to dye your hair to match your gown for an evening event. Enter Ms. Creative Poetic with your regal purple gown and bold, purple streaks highlighting your tresses. You do not stop there. Using color shades expertly, you find another striking color that shouts your message of creativity for daytime. Whatever color you choose, it is sure to be eye-catching and interesting. Your use of colors may shock and amaze others, and they are sometimes a bit envious of your boldness. They cannot even imagine themselves having the nerve to be so daring with color.

You wear beads in your braided hair that dazzle in the sunlight as you walk. For you, it doesn't matter if the beads are multicolored or mixed metals. All that matters is that you like them.

Whether short or long, the braiding will be unusual. You design your very own style and communicate it to your stylist. Your preferred stylist is also a Creative Poetic, and together you create a masterpiece. You leave the chair creatively beautiful for all the world to see. You do not concern yourself with someone not liking your hairstyle, because you don't style your hair for others. As long as the Holy Spirit and you are pleased, then all things are settled. You walk in His glory with your beautiful, creative appearance.

To announce your Creative Poetic individuality, you braid your wet hair and allow it to dry to give it extra crimps and fluff. After it dries, you either let it hang freely or pull it back with a beautiful comb. You own several antique decorative combs that hold your tresses in place and enhance your originality. You pull ringlets around your ears and down your back, and off you go, ready for the next adventure.

You also use your decorative combs in your short hair for an artsy, creative statement. A feminine crew or box cut or an agreeably curious hair design, sculpted by a new hairstylist, speak the Creative Poetic lingo. A short, curly style or short, straight styling with coloring only on the ends also makes for a Creative Poetic entrance maker. You expertly wear your hair in bold, beautiful, independent styles that other image types only dream of wearing.

Creative Poetic women of color love to experiment with hair coloring. A word of caution here. Please make sure your hair color blends with your skin tone. This does not mean that you must limit your creativity. Just stop and think about the end result before using permanent coloring. If you feel you must color your hair in a permanent bright orange or purple, make sure you have a wig available for more conservative outings.

Since you are one of most creative image types and love to experiment with color, you take bigger risks than any of your sisters. Depending on your chosen profession, you should choose coloring that is acceptable and appropriate for that career field. If you are in the entertainment or art field, you have a broader range of hair-coloring options. Bright orange just might be acceptable in this case. If not, a deep rich auburn, a cocoa, or a chestnut brown is a great choice. To whet your creative taste buds, try highlighting your hair with streaks of blond or any light coloring. There are also some wonderful burgundies on the market that you may find acceptable and in line with your creative tastes. They look great with any skin tone. Choose your coloring wisely to complement your café au lait, honey-gold, caramel-brown, walnut, or cocoa-brown skin coloring.

This word also goes out for women of Latina, Asian, and Native American descent. Please try to leave your magnificent hair the way it is. Nothing man has created can compare with your deep, rich tresses. If you must experiment, try some of the burgundies described above. They will add creative highlights without detracting from your God-given beauty. Burgundy will also blend with your natural skin coloring. Remember, the Lord presented you with the natural gift of awesome skin coloring; remember that when coloring your hair.

You are so adventurous and independent with your hair that many see it as your signature piece. If the hairstylist makes a mistake, you do damage control by wearing headbands or hair combs. By strategically placing a piece of jewelry in your hair, you create a one-of-a-kind look and capitalize on the mistake. The mistake then becomes your style statement. No one would believe it was a mistake because you have made it your own. Like the Lord, you take lemons and make glasses of sweet lemonade. You use your hair to bring glory to the Lord. Even in this area, you are humble and seek only to glorify Him.

> *I* will praise You, O Lord my God, with all my heart, and I will glorify Your name forevermore.
>
> PSALMS 86:12

CREATIVE POETIC MAKEUP

You apply makeup heavily or you wear none at all. It really depends on your mood and where you happen to be going. Sometimes the desire for glamour wins over the natural. When that happens, you take a cue from your Sensual Exotic sister. Using your selected colors, you create an electrifying, glamorous portrait. Other image types may describe your look as overdone or garish, but if it is your chosen look of the day, then what they say or think does not matter. You march to the beat of your own drummer and love to look different. For you, this just goes with the territory of being a wonderful, unique Creative Poetic. Your spirit shines through with every stroke of your makeup brush.

Your lipstick colors are always on sale because no other image type, except the Sensual Exotic, would wear them. Shocking pink, brilliant orange, and electric red make up your color palette. You find unusual hues and either tone them down or brighten them with other colors. The artsy side of your spirit enjoys the challenge of blending just the right amount of each color to create something new and original.

Your creative side takes these colors and matches them with just the right outfit. You experiment with your newly chosen colors for different looks. If you want to look Asian, then your makeup reflects a taste of the Orient. You outline your eyes in black, giving them an almond shape by extending the outline almost to your hairline. Your lips and cheeks shine in a luscious red. You speak the language of the region without saying a word.

You are the first to try the new colors for each season. All your eyeliners and shadows come in a multitude of colors, and you wear them all. You mix colors until you get exactly what you want. You also go to great lengths to get your foundation just right. You custom-blend your own if you cannot find the perfect tone. There are times when you consider it fun to wear a foundation shade that does not exactly match your skin tone. It helps keep things free and fun.

If you are medium- to dark-skinned, your skin is the canvas for your creative picture. You use unique colors to enhance your radiant, dark beauty. Expertly painting your ebony, bronze, or olive skin with spirited coloring is your creative trademark. Uniquely painting your lips, cheeks, and eyes with golden brown, paradise purple, or electric yellow, you sing your Creative Poetic song.

Vibrant rose pink dances through your palette, and the beauty of your countenance from café au lait to deepest ebony shines for all the world to see. You are as beautiful as the prophetess Miriam as she sang and danced for the Lord while crossing the Red Sea. Whatever your ethnic heritage, you speak the Creative Poetic language without saying a word. Your artsy appearance says it all for you. You use coloring to create different moods. For an evening of dramatics, gold dusting powder announces your coming. You use it for an allover glow, dusting your face and body. Worn with your new array of colors, it is sure to be a hit.

Whether your ethnic heritage is that of the European queen, the Asian empress, the Latina *condesa,* the Native American or Nubian princess, you are a beautiful creation of the Most High God and His Creative Poetic work of art.

> That our daughters may be pillars, sculptured in palace style. . . .
>
> PSALMS 144:12

6. *Chantilly Graceful*

Refinement, romance, ruffles, and lace,
Chantilly Graceful, God's vision of grace.

For the Lord God is a sun and shield; The Lord will give grace and glory. No good thing will He withhold from those who walk uprightly.

PSALMS 84:11

The Beauty of Chantilly Graceful

Do you love being surrounded by ruffles and lace? Do you prefer to adorn your waist with soft sashes instead of rigid leather belts? Do you long to wear full skirts with petticoats and full-sleeved, ruffled blouses? Do you prefer dressing in Victorian-era clothing? Then you are the Chantilly Graceful image type.

You are the essence of femininity and grace. Your walk is so graceful you appear to float. It looks as if you can walk on eggshells without breaking them. Your gait is soft and flowing, even in heels. No one will ever hear your feet "clunking" on the floor. Your Chantilly Graceful spirit guides each step. Whether you are a size 6 or 26, your gliding footsteps are the same. Size is unimportant. It is your spirit and not your size that make you Chantilly Graceful.

When you make your entrance, it's much like a movie scene where the leading lady is walking through a garden in full bloom. Rose petals layer the carpet of grass beneath your feet as you glide into any room. Others admire, and sometimes envy, your graceful, feminine style. It is your heart's desire that they realize everything about you comes from the Lord and the glory belongs to Him. Chantilly Graceful beauty is a gift from your heavenly Father, and your loveliness comes from a humbleness of spirit, one of God's most beautiful creations.

For the Lord takes pleasure in His people; He will beautify the humble with salvation.

PSALMS 149:4

You are soft-spoken, and there are times when others ask you to repeat your statements. It is rare to hear you speak a harsh word or raise your voice. The only time you truly feel comfortable raising your voice is when you are praising the Lord. Even when you are in a disagreement with someone or your feelings are hurt, you try to safeguard the feelings of the other person. Because of your gentle spirit, you always seem to place the needs of others before your own. This may sound good, but it can sometimes create internal conflict.

When this internal conflict surfaces, you tend to discuss your true feelings with someone other than the person with whom you are having conflict. This causes discord. If you choose to confide in anyone other than the Lord, what you say will get back to the person you were talking about. When it does, it will not be exactly what you said in the first place. The situation will get as sticky as taffy on a summer day if you are not careful and prayerful. It is hard for you to confront and deal with your problems directly, but to prevent more trouble, you must learn. Confrontation, when combined with love and prayer, is one of your strongest allies. Go to the Lord and ask Him for courage.

He will give you the words and the time to speak them. If allowed, the enemy will use the situation to keep you from growing spiritually. He tries to trick us into thinking that confronting our problems causes greater pain and does not give solutions. When we buy into his lies, we stay in the midst of conflict. The chains of conflict are bondage, pure and simple. When guided by the Holy Spirit, we see that our problems are not what we were led to believe. As a daughter of the King, it is your responsibility to go to the other person and resolve the problem.

Many times we find we, too, are at fault and may have unintentionally said or done something that was perceived as offensive. The Lord will use your soft-spoken manner and gentle spirit to heal many wounds, if you surrender to Him. The only thing that stands in your way is the spirit of fear. Fear is blinding and causes you to miss out on blessings. It strangles any and every good thing in its path, including you, my Chantilly Graceful sister.

> Therefore, if you bring your gift to the altar, and there remember that your brother [or sister] has something against you, leave your gift there before the altar and go your way. First be reconciled to your brother [or sister], and then come to offer your gift.
>
> MATTHEW 5:23–24

Be strong and do not be afraid. He will never leave or forsake you. Put your fear and pride aside and take action. The Lord will do the rest, if you take the first step. Do not worry about what others say or do. You answer only to the Lord. Even if the others involved do not respond positively, you do what you have to do. Take a deep breath and move with the Holy Spirit. Above all, pray, take your time, and do not rush. Ask Him for patience and guidance.

He promised to answer if you call on Him. You certainly cannot get any better than that. Trust Him and believe He has already prepared the way. Your Chantilly Graceful spirit combined with the Holy Spirit is a vision of true feminine strength. You are the picture of feminine softness, armed with the strength of the Lord. What a beautiful union: the Lord God of Hosts and your Chantilly Graceful spirit, walking hand in hand. It is a combination that will never fail.

Sarah

> Then God said to Abraham, "As for Sarai your wife, you
> shall not call her name Sarai, but Sarah [Princess] shall
> be her name. And I will bless her and also give you a son
> by her, then I will bless her, and she shall be a mother of
> nations; kings of peoples shall be from her."
>
> GENESIS 17:15–16

Monarchs were known to use any means necessary to acquire women of great beauty for their harems. This time was no exception. Although Sarai was mature in her years, she still glowed with a radiant beauty that drew stares and comments from men many years her junior. Kings wanted her. Men, rich and poor, desired her, but she belonged to Abram. This great beauty's heart belonged only to her husband. She only longed to be the center of his desire. What she did not realize was that the very fiber of her faith would soon be tested because of her beauty.

As they approached the border of Egypt, Abram knew his life might be in danger. He had already decided to tell a half-truth to protect himself from death. Since Sarai was also his half sister, that title was the only one she would use while traveling through this foreign land. She was to act as a sister and not his wife as long as they remained in unfamiliar lands. When they entered the Egyptian empire, they kept guard on their lives by living a half-truth designed to shield Abram from danger.

Things happened just as Abram predicted. When the pharaoh saw her, he wanted her for his harem. Being an obedient wife and fearing for her husband's life, she left and joined the pharaoh's household without incident. She did not want her beauty or actions to be responsible for any injury to her husband or household. Her husband, her earthly protector, had just given her up and hidden behind a lie to protect himself. He had given her up to be possessed by another man.

As the caravan faded into the distance, her heartbeat seemed to fade with it. This beauty seemed a curse. Other women, desiring this supposed gift, did not know or understand the burdens that came with it. Quiet tears softly dampened her veil as the sun set on what seemed like the most hopeless day of her life. She was now being escorted down the great halls of the royal palace. Her dark eyes surveyed the luxurious surroundings with great sorrow, for no jewels, gold, or silver could fill the emptiness of her heart. She was now not just a wife, but a beautiful possession of a king.

The pharaoh was pleased with his new wife and proudly displayed her at court. She had been bathed in scented waters, dressed in the finest silks, and adorned with the most brilliant jewels the pharaoh of Egypt had to offer. None of these things impressed this godly woman. Her heart longed to be with her husband. She prayed that the Lord God would hear her prayers and make a way for her safe return to her home and family.

The household of the pharaoh was soon filled with all manner of afflictions. Everything around him seemed to be troubled. He sat down and began to think about the recent changes in his kingdom. He sent for the royal advisers and priests of the temples. They consoled him with pagan rituals without results. They even sacrificed to their gods, to no avail. What was the problem? What had he done to bring this calamity to his household?

The most recent and major change was the acquisition of his beautiful new wife. He summoned her to his throne room and questioned her. She could sense immediately that the Lord had intervened on her behalf, so she spoke with great boldness to the pharaoh. She admitted that she was not only the sister of Abram but also his wife. This courageous woman of faith was your sister, the beautiful, Chantilly Graceful Sarai.

We can imagine that Sarai was a stately woman whose dark eyes, flawless skin, and graceful beauty mesmerized all who saw her. Her dark eyes burned with the intensity of onyx set in shining, sterling-silver settings. Her dresses of rich, deep teal and scarlet enhanced her radiant complexion. She wore soft shawls that also encircled her delicate waist. Her very presence reminded people of royalty. Her long, dark, braided hair was coiled in a crownlike style on top of her head. On her ears were heavy gold and silver earrings.

Her wrists were adorned with bracelets that were gifts from her loving husband. On each hand, she wore rings accented with small jewels. These jewels lost their brilliance next to her natural beauty. When she walked, she appeared to be floating. Her Chantilly Graceful spirit was apparent to all who saw her. Even in the intense heat, Sarai appeared to handle every situation with a gentle coolness. She handled everything and everyone with the delicacy of a gentle Chantilly Graceful. She was so beautiful that at the time she was taken to the courts of Egypt, she was almost seventy years old. Even in her advanced years, her Chantilly Graceful beauty still mesmerized kings.

The pharaoh immediately sent for Abram. He gave Sarai back to him and sent him on his way, along with all his possessions, and commanded that no man in his kingdom should stop them from leaving. She was now back where she belonged. The Lord had delivered her from an impossible situation. This would not be the last time Sarai's faith would be tested. The Lord had just begun His work in her life; He would reveal Himself again many times in her future.

Although he had selfishly given Sarai up to another man, Abram still had the favor of God. The Lord made a promise that he would father children. Abram was a man of faith who praised God for this promise and decided to wait on Him. Sarai, also now an old woman, desperately wanted to give her husband a son. Although she was now barren and past her childbearing years, she still wanted Abram to be a father. She sent her maid, Hagar, an Egyptian, in to her husband so that he could father a child.

This situation and subsequent birth caused great discord in their household.

When Hagar conceived, the Bible tells us (Genesis 16:4), her mistress became despised in her eyes. It would be safe to say that Hagar exalted herself and flaunted her pregnancy. In those days, a woman's value was often attached to her ability to produce male children. This was a sensitive area for Sarai, but she would not tolerate such treatment, and discussed the matter with Abram. He so loved his wife that he told her to do with Hagar as she pleased. In Genesis 16:6, the Bible says that Sarai dealt harshly with Hagar, who fled into the wilderness. While Hagar was in the wilderness, the Angel of the Lord appeared to her and told her to return and submit herself to her mistress. When she returned, she bore a son. Abram named him Ishmael.

Abram was a man of prayer and in constant communication with the Lord. Because of his faithfulness, the Lord made a promise to him that even today is difficult for people of faith to believe. The Lord told Abram that he would be the father of many nations. At the time of this spiritual encounter, Abram was ninety-nine years old. The Lord then told Abram his name would be changed to Abraham, which means "father of many nations." The Lord then spoke of Sarai. He said that her name from that day forward would be Sarah, which means "princess."

The Lord told Abraham that he would also bless Sarah and make her the mother of many nations. Abraham fell on his face and laughed, thinking in his heart that what he heard was a joke. He was ninety-nine and Sarah was ninety. There was no way they were going to have a child together. Abraham then thanked him for blessing his son Ishmael. The Lord corrected Abraham and told him that the son He would bless would come from the womb of Sarah, his wife. The son would be called Isaac, and the Lord would establish a covenant with him.

Can you imagine the astonishment of the elderly Abraham? The thought of he and the elderly Sarah having a child was mind-boggling. By the next year, the Lord promised, Isaac would be born. Abraham decided to keep this news to himself. He was not even going to tell Sarah. She would definitely think he had lost his mind. He never doubted that the Lord could make it come to pass. He just could not bring himself to tell his wife about the promise. If the Lord said it was going to happen, then He would choose the time and place to inform Sarah when this miracle child would be born.

Sometime after his meeting with the Lord, three Strangers visited Abraham. When he saw the three heavenly Visitors, he invited them to stay and eat at his table. He instructed Sarah to make fresh bread, and he had a young calf prepared. Sarah, being a good and faithful wife, quickly made things ready for the meal. With this act, she became the first woman in the Bible to extend hospitality to guests.

As they were eating, the Visitors asked about the whereabouts of Sarah. Abraham explained that she was in the tent, unaware she was listening to the conversation. At that point, the Lord spoke (Genesis 18:10): "I will certainly return to you according to the time of life, and behold, Sarah your wife shall have a son." When Sarah heard this, she silently laughed, for she knew she was long past her childbearing years. It is easy to imagine that she did not realize that the Visitors were sent from the Lord. As soon as she had the thought, she heard the Lord ask Abraham why she laughed. He repeated her thoughts exactly aloud to her husband. Sarah, being frightened, denied that she had laughed. We can be sure she began to take this prophecy more seriously after this incident.

Sarah conceived and bore a son at the exact time appointed by the Lord. Abraham named him Isaac, which means "laughter." Isaac's birth was a joyous occasion. In Genesis 21:6, Sarah expressed her joy by saying, "God has made me laugh, so that all who hear will laugh with me." Just the thought that she, at the age of ninety-one, could have a child was a great miracle. The

Lord had been faithful and kept His word. He had given Sarah the desire of her heart because of her faithfulness to His servant Abraham.

Sarah's faith was tested many times during her lifetime. The greatest test was believing that she would have a precious son in her old age. Through this miracle, she learned that with God, all things are possible to those who believe. He gives grace to those He loves. Just as for Sarah, your Chantilly Graceful sister, He is your sun and shield. He has given you grace and beauty. As a Chantilly Graceful, you have an unexplainable beauty of spirit that touches and changes lives.

Chantilly Graceful Strengths in the Body of Christ

Hospitality Chair
Church Publicity Committee
Social Chair

Chantilly Graceful and Family Life

Your home is totally feminine and beautiful with Victorian lace and a Tiffany lamp in every room. Victorian styling, floral patterns, and soft textures delight the eye. Pastels with wisps of lace and full ruffles overflow from your spirit into your surroundings.

Your bedroom shows your true spirit of femininity. Lace, ruffles, and other signs of femininity cover everything from floor to ceiling. A matching comforter and dust ruffle adorn your bed. On the dressing table, dainty perfume bottles are displayed. A full, ruffled skirt surrounds the dressing table and matches the comforter. The room is like a soft summer breeze that runs its fingers through the branches of a tree covered in cherry blossoms. The loveliness of your spirit is seen in every facet of the decor.

Your decorating style always has a romantic theme. Full lace sheers and balloon shades in soft pastels and floral patterns decorate your windows. Beautifully framed watercolors hang on each wall. Lamps with ruffled shades or Tiffany styling top your tables. Your furniture style of choice is the romantic Victorian or Queen Anne. The sleekness of modern styling is too harsh for your tastes. Rounded, ornate edgings with curved legs speak the Chantilly Graceful decorating language. *Wispy, soft,* and *flowing* accurately describe your surroundings.

Entertaining is one of your greatest joys. You like a clean and orderly home, but still want it to feel lived in and be comfortable for your family and guests. You are not preoccupied with things being orderly as long as everyone is comfortable. You are the consummate hostess. Other image types learn lessons from you in this area. When entertaining, attending to your guests' creature comforts is your top priority. You keep the room temperature at a comfortable level, and you minister to their every need.

The pillows on the couch are fluffed, and each guest has a thirst-quenching drink in hand. The perfect Chantilly Graceful evening setting has a fire roaring in the fireplace. A beautiful buffet with your finest china, crystal, and silver is pleasing to the eye. Soft music is playing, and your friends are talking and enjoying each other. You have orchestrated an unforgettable evening for all. They knew before they arrived that tonight, they would be pampered by a beautiful Chantilly Graceful hostess.

You personally greet your guests and escort them into your home. With your graciousness, you escort yourself into their hearts. Nothing is too good for them. The atmosphere is elegant and romantic. They leave all problems and conflicts at the door. As they enter your world of comfort, beauty, and romance, they inhale Chantilly Graceful perfume. Your warm smile puts them at ease. They see the ruffle of the drapes, the silver candlesticks, the linen and lace napkins and tablecloth. The crystal and silver punchbowl and cups, the floral-print furniture and the fresh flower centerpieces make them feel as if they had just entered a romantic paradise. This romantic ambience leaves no room for conflict or discord. They breathe sighs of relief as they enter your world of beauty and grace.

The couple who quarreled on the way to your home leave their problems at the door. After their arrival, they realize that the reason for their misunderstanding was not as important as they thought. As you welcome them into your home, you whisper a prayer that the Lord will bless and heal the unions of all who enter and bring Christian mates to the singles who wish to be married. The Lord, hearing the prayer of His maidservant, uses you to work miracles of healing through your gift of hospitality. You watch as the Lord works, and the same couple who entered in conflict now hold hands throughout the evening. They leave early so they can renew their vows in private. You steal into the kitchen and ask the Lord to never let His grace and mercy leave your home. You want your home to continually be a dwelling place for His Holy Spirit. By doing so, you give out treasures of love to your brothers and sisters and glorify your Lord.

> *In* the house of the righteous there is much treasure. . . .
>
> PROVERBS 15:6

As a Chantilly Graceful mother, you love order but still allow your children to be children. If their rooms are a little messy, it's fine, as long as they are working on a project that requires room for creativity. Your first priority is their comfort and happiness. You give them room to explore their areas of interest and encourage them to freely discuss these areas with you. Your young ones feel free to use the family encyclopedias and computer for research. With the keen eye of motherhood, you watch with interest as they thumb through books and punch key after key on the computer, searching for the hidden treasures of knowledge.

Many of these research projects are school assignments, and you continuously stress the importance of a good education. Your little ones know that if they need additional help, Mom will be there. If they need special help, you call a conference with teachers and get the proper tutoring. You let them know that pride has no place in your home, and it comes before a fall. If help is needed and available, then they must accept it without shame. Shame only comes when someone needs help and refuses to ask.

You screen all their recreational activities. Any movie or book that you feel may defile their precious spirits does not stay in your home. You discuss your decisions with them and let them know your position. It is critical that they be educated not only in the natural, but also in the spiritual things. You clean out their rooms regularly so the enemy will not find openings into your home. You never throw out anything without explaining the reasons. The Lord established the home as a safe haven, and Mother Chantilly Graceful seeks His guidance in keeping it that way.

Because you believe in making everyone feel needed, if one of your little ones appears to have nothing to do while the others are working, you create a project where you "need help" and allow your child to do research. You are exceptionally gifted at finding legitimate tasks. Feeling needed, appreciated, and accepted is basic human need, and you make sure this need is met in your children's lives. As a mother, you feel it is your responsibility to guide your children down the path to spiritual and emotional health. If their basic needs are met, then they will be open to receive parental guidance. You rely on the Lord to meet those needs in your life, and you pass His love on to your children in Chantilly Graceful style.

You are a mother who truly believes in her children. You allow them freedom to develop their own sense of direction. Giving guidance when necessary and monitoring progress daily, you sense when they are going the wrong way and give warnings and directions. If the instructions are not followed, then sweet, gentle Chantilly Graceful mom turns into a lioness who sternly disciplines her cubs. Your children may think your chastisement is harsh, because your stance is so firm. You let them know this is the result of not following instructions, and this will happen each time your guidance is not followed. They learn quickly not to take advantage of your gentleness and to listen and follow your instructions to the letter. They also know that each chastisement is given with motherly love.

They also learn that following your guidelines makes life easier. You teach them to plant seeds for the future. They will soon reap the benefits of those properly planted seeds. Your Chantilly Graceful spirit is greatly appreciated when they begin to see the fruits of their labor spring forth on the vines of their young lives. They now know that hard work and listening to Mom are the keys to success. All of a sudden, your stern lioness chastisements seem like pennies from heaven. Your little ones also discover they want bucketsful of those pennies.

In your family plan, spiritual health ranks as one of your top priorities. Before your children learn to talk, you show them how to get down on their knees and pray. During the first lesson, gibberish comes out that is hard to understand, but you know your heavenly Father is smiling and can follow every word. You also know that habits started during childhood are hard to break. Talking with the Lord is one of best habits a human being can have at any age. You honor the Lord by following His word in raising your children. Starting with a solid foundation, they are trained in the way that they should go, so they will not depart from it.

*T*rain up a child in the way he should go, and
when he is old he will not depart from it.
                                    PROVERBS 22:6

The Chantilly Graceful Spouse

Your mate is a romantic gentleman. He had to be in order to capture your heart. He had to court you, bring you flowers and candy,
and above all promise to take care of you. Taking care of you simply means he wants to make sure all your needs are met, and he
wants you to be comfortable. He knows your comfort level is very
important, and he longs to pamper his lovely Chantilly Graceful
companion. Sometimes his traditional way of thinking makes
him appear rigid, but you know he has a heart of gold and will do
anything for you.

When an exhausting project at work consumes him, you send
him flowers. You spoil him with daily phone calls just to say you
love and miss him. He can hardly wait to get home to talk with
his best friend. Ready and waiting when he gets home is his favorite dinner. He loves the sound of your voice as you gently ask
him about his day. You know just how to relax him physically and
emotionally. You are the expert in both departments. You allow
him to vent any anger or frustration from his day. You want him
emptied out for your time alone. You graciously allow him to unwind, knowing that after he has discussed the day's events, he is
then free to hear about your day. Your soft hands relax him as he
talks and you gently massage his shoulders. He is glad to come
home to his Chantilly Graceful treasure, and you are happy he
comes home to you.

You are such a smart woman that you defer to him in most situations. On a daily basis, you use the art of biblical submission.

Many people are a bit confused when it comes to submission, but not you. The Lord gave you the Book on submission, and you follow His directions. For you, submission simply means loving him unconditionally, faults and all. That, of course, is not as easy as it sounds. You sometimes have to bite your tongue, stand still, and allow him to make mistakes. You know the Lord made your husband the way He intended, and you do not stand in His way.

You want your husband to be refined by the Master's hand. When the Lord refines and finishes your man, he will come forth as pure gold! As the Lord refines him, you, too, are being polished, because you are one flesh. The process is not always pleasant. The Lord has a way of revealing unpleasant things. These areas are sometimes buried so deep that only He can reach and clean them out. The process is long and hard and sometimes painful. Remember, His word is like a healing balm. When He decides to clean, He will scrape and simultaneously heal. He knows your husband's limits and will do all things according to his ability to handle them. The Lord is merciful, full of goodness and love. As He refines your husband, He also changes your heart and strengthens your marriage. Once He begins the process, the Lord is faithful and will complete the work He has started. Like your biblical sister Ruth, you know to stay the course until His plan is ultimately revealed to you.

> *B*eing confident of this very thing, that He who has begun a good work in you will complete it until the day of Jesus Christ.
>
> PHILIPPIANS 1:6

Your heavenly Father is so faithful and good. He knows just how to keep you so busy that you cannot try to help or get in His way when it comes to your husband—so why fight a losing battle?

You know that when it comes to fighting Him, you just cannot win. Experience has taught you that the best thing to do is pray for your spouse. Pray that the Lord will place His hedge of protection around him. Pray that he will find favor in the eyes of his superiors on his job. Pray that he will come home to you safe and happy. Those are the kind of prayers your Father loves to hear. As a Chantilly Graceful, you already know because you do it every day!

Ruth

THE LOVING, OBEDIENT DAUGHTER

> Then they lifted up their voices and wept again; and
> Orpah kissed her mother-in-law, but Ruth clung to her.
>
> RUTH 1:14

She had lost all she had. With both sons and her husband dead, her only thought was to return to her homeland. There had been a famine there at home, but now, many years later, word had come that this had ended. As she prepared to go, she looked around at the green hills and the abundant land that now seemed so empty. There was nothing more this land could offer her. In fact, if she ever thought of it again, her memories would only be of her dead husband and two dear sons. It was time to go home. It was time to go back to Bethlehem.

Naomi, with her husband, Elimelech, and their two sons, Mahlon and Chilion, had left their precious homeland to journey to the fertile land of Moab. They started a new life and became part of the surrounding community. Both sons married Moabite women. As time went on, her husband and sons died. Naomi, now an old woman, was left alone with her daughters-in-law. She was an old woman with the desire to live once again in the land of her youth.

As she began her journey, she bid farewell to her daughters-in-law and asked them to return to the home of their mothers. She blessed them for their kindness and prayed they would each find a new home and husband. The three women wept bitterly. They had become family and did not want to leave one another. After much hugging, crying, and kissing, one daughter-in-law decided to stay in the land of her people, but the other made a totally unexpected decision. She decided to go to Bethlehem with Naomi. Naomi pleaded in vain with her to stay in Moab. As Naomi walked away, the young Moabitess followed her every footstep. In the blazing sunlight and heat, she became Naomi's clinging shadow.

As they walked, Naomi remembered the familiar streets and busy marketplace where she once met friends and neighbors, and the city well where she went to draw the day's water supply. She drank in memories of the smells, sights, and sounds of a place she'd left long ago—of this place called home. Her thoughts of sweet Bethlehem were suddenly interrupted by the footsteps on the rocky ground behind her. Her young daughter-in-law still followed with a determination that amazed the aged Naomi. As the day melted into evening, she decided to embrace her future and welcome this determined young woman named Ruth back into her life.

The Bible says, in Ruth 1:14, that Ruth clung to her mother-in-law and refused to stay in Moab. In Ruth 1:16–17, Ruth speaks words of honor and love to the aging Naomi. In one of the most beautiful passages in the Bible, she says, "For wherever you go, I will go; and wherever you lodge, I will lodge; for your people shall be my people and your God, my God." In verse 17, she continues and tells Naomi that the only thing that will part them is death.

It is easy to imagine that the trip was long and hard, so Naomi's silence did not last. They made most of the journey on foot and partially on the backs of donkeys. These were not times when women traveled alone without a guardian or protector. The

Lord surely guided their path and kept His hedge of protection around them, because nothing dramatic happened. As they made their way into Bethlehem, some of the elders recognized Naomi but could not imagine why a Moabitess would come to live among them. There was something special about this beautiful stranger. Her manner was gentle and her countenance radiant. Yes, they could learn to accept this gentle soul.

We can imagine that Ruth was a beautiful young woman of medium stature. She wore her dark hair pulled back into a braid that she wrapped around her head. It was held in place by a simple comb. She wore a dress and overcoat of light-colored wool. On her head, she wore a light-colored headdress that also encircled her slender waist. On her feet were leather sandals. She wore no jewelry. The little jewelry she owned, she sold to a local merchant to buy food. She was a natural beauty with a humble spirit. Little did she know that the Lord was guiding her path and preparing a prosperous future for her and Naomi.

She had taken on the lowly task of following the reapers in the fields and gathering grain that fell on the ground behind them as they worked. Ruth would go home to Naomi, happily display her finds for the day, and prepare the night's meal. One day Ruth was gathering grain at the field of Boaz, a wealthy landowner and a distant relative of Naomi's late husband. Ruth could easily have made herself known to Boaz to gain favor as a family member, but instead was just happy to gather grain. She felt blessed simply to have the strength to care for her mother-in-law and herself. Although they lived far from luxury, the Lord met their needs.

When Boaz saw Ruth, he asked his people about her identity. They told him of her good work and that she was the daughter-in-law of Naomi, who had come from Moab. Seeing that Ruth was a beautiful young woman and could have been easy prey while working in the fields, Boaz immediately asked her to work among the young women and to gather only in his fields. Offering her his protection, he ordered his men not to touch her and to look out for her well-being.

During their encounter, in Ruth 2:10, Ruth fell on her face before Boaz and asked him why he found favor with her, a foreigner. Boaz gave her the full report on her actions of selflessness. He was touched by her giving up all to care for Naomi. He did not take credit for his actions. He gave all the credit to the Lord by blessing Ruth (verse 12) and told her that she was under the Lord's wings; she had found refuge. With her Chantilly Graceful spirit, Ruth had found favor in the eyes of this rich and powerful man. The story of Ruth and Boaz is one of the Bible's most beautiful love stories.

There is no doubt that Boaz was a man of high moral character. He found Ruth attractive not only physically, but spiritually as well. This beautiful Chantilly Graceful, with her gentleness, had touched his heart. At mealtimes, he invited Ruth to eat with him and his servants. She was allowed to eat the grain and to dip it in the master's vinegar. Ruth ate until she was full and kept some back to take home. When she went back to the fields, Boaz ordered his reapers to drop extra grain for her as she worked.

One evening upon Ruth's return home, Naomi noticed that the load of grain was much larger than usual. After Ruth related the day's events, Naomi told her to continue working with the people of Boaz throughout the harvesttime. As the end of the harvest drew near, Naomi told Ruth that it was now time for her to find security for her future; she would instruct Ruth.

Ruth knew Naomi would only tell her what was good and proper. Naomi instructed Ruth to wash herself, put on her best garment, and wait and go to the threshing floor of Boaz during the late evening. Upon her arrival there, she was to hide until Boaz was asleep. Then she was to come out from hiding, and uncover his feet, and lie down. Ruth listened and in loving obedience, without questioning, she told Naomi in Ruth 3:5, "All that you say to me, I will do."

That night, Ruth went to the threshing floor. After he had eaten and his heart was merry with wine (verse 7), Boaz fell asleep. Ruth lay down at his feet. Around midnight, Boaz awoke from his sleep and was surprised to find a young woman lying at his feet. Ruth then asked him to take her under his wing because he was a near kinsman. Boaz was honored by Ruth's actions. He fully understood that she could have chosen any younger man she desired, but instead chose him. He told her not to fear, because he would protect her honor. He told her to stay until morning and he would perform the duty of a near kinsman.

The next morning, when he and Ruth arose, he took her shawl and filled it with grain for her to take home. When Naomi saw Ruth, she was thankful for the gift of grain but was more concerned about what had happened the night before. After Ruth described the evening's events, Naomi told her to stay home and sit still because she knew the honorable Boaz would resolve all matters on that day.

That morning Boaz went to the city gate and gathered with the elders. There was another kinsman who, by right, could have laid claim to Ruth. Boaz wanted to do all things decently and in order. After talking, the kinsman relinquished claim in the presence of the elders. Boaz was now free to take Ruth as his wife. The elders blessed the union in the presence of all.

Ruth's Chantilly Graceful spirit was a catalyst for her future success. It won her the favor of Naomi, Boaz, and the Lord. She became the wife of Boaz and was able to care for Naomi in her old age. Ruth bore a son whom she called Obed, who was the grandfather of King David. The Lord God honored her by placing her in the lineage of Jesus Christ, His only Son. Like you, her Chantilly Graceful sister, Ruth's gentle spirit helped her find favor in all areas of her life. She was a true example of a woman whose actions were filled with the fruit the Lord God loves, the fruit of the spirit. This fruit only manifests in a life seeking after His grace and mercy. Like Ruth, your Chantilly Graceful sister, you are full of His glory and His true vision of grace.

Chantilly Graceful Working Style

Working with people is one of your strong points. You love to make others smile and experience beauty. Your ultimate thrill is when you can help people begin to make positive changes in their lives. You start this process by witnessing and ministering about the love of the Lord Jesus. Although bold evangelism is not your style, if given the proper opening, you will speak without hesitation. You prefer to minister subtly, letting others see the Lord in your actions and in the way you live. In delicate, direct Chantilly Graceful style, your point is well taken by all who see you.

You do not mind making policies that affect people and their well-being. When making personnel policies, you work hard to ensure that all will benefit from your decisions. It is important for you to know the impact new policies will have on workers of all levels. You want to ensure that decisions are fair, and every aspect of them is carefully examined. You consider not only how decisions will affect the worker, but also how they will impact the family.

You are an expert social chair and people manager. You surround yourself with others who have skills and talents you lack. You want your office to run like a well-oiled machine, so your Harmonic Refined colleague is the office administrator. Your office always gets calls for seemingly impossible projects that need to be finished in brief amounts of time. You choose an Elegant Flamboyant to be your special project manager. You need to develop a new creative angle for the office, so you get a Creative Poetic creative director. Everything is under control because the

Lord has gifted you with the people factor. You use it for His glory by placing others in positions where they can best use their gifts.

If you are in a management position, you look for a fellow Chantilly Graceful to handle the prestigious position of social chair for your department. You are wise enough to know that if you take care of your people, they will take care of you and the needs of the office. You work with this person to ensure that she remembers all birthdays, anniversaries, and other special, personal events. She is responsible for every detail, down to the napkins, paper plates, and cups. She establishes an office social fund and coordinates all recognition for special events.

Baby showers, birthdays, and Christmas parties are important to Chantilly Graceful management style, and are all handled with care. It is important that you address the people element in your department, so the productivity level continues to stay at its present level. After all, no work gets done without the people!

You impress upper-level management with the loyalty you receive from your subordinates. It is hard for them to understand how such a soft-spoken, Chantilly Graceful woman gets such productivity out of her people. They do not know your secret is an open Book—the word of the Most High God—and that they, too, can have it just for the asking.

You do not like to make waves and will sometimes stay in unpleasant working conditions for longer than necessary. Many times the Lord has provided a way out; you just don't see it. If others are hurting, your concern for them may overshadow your own well-being, and you will not see the way of escape. Many times He has also given a way out for the other people involved, and they choose not to take it. Learn to stand still, watch, and pray in the face of adversity. Your Father is faithful and is your rear guard in times of trouble. Do not stay if He is telling you to move, even if others refuse to leave. He would rather have your obedience. You are choosing the least profitable way when the Lord is not in charge.

*B*ehold, to obey is better than sacrifice, and to heed than the fat of rams.

I SAMUEL 15:22

As a Chantilly Graceful, you have an ear for others and their problems. Your empathetic, supportive spirit often makes you the unofficial office adviser. While this is a wonderful compliment, it can be draining. It is difficult listening to everyone and remaining objective. If you are not careful, you can become entangled in the very office disagreements on which you are advising. Before you know what hit you, you can become the target of the enemy's darts.

Sometimes people allow themselves to become vulnerable and then regret their vulnerability. The person with whom they share their intimate side becomes a target. To protect themselves, they begin to attack what they feel has become the source of their problem, you. This may sound a little far-fetched, but can and does happen, especially when you are dealing with the secular world. You may have been genuinely trying to help people, and then they turn on you. Remember, you are in a spiritual battle, and the enemy does not fight fairly—and he never will. The Lord has already given you the battle plan. Seek Him, keep up the fight by praying and following His lead, and victory is sure.

*F*or we do not wrestle against flesh and blood, but against principalities, against powers, against the rulers of the darkness of this age, against spiritual hosts of wickedness in the heavenly places.

EPHESIANS 6:12

The Lord wants you to minister to the lost, and the enemy does not like it. He would love for everyone to be unhappy, self-destructive, and unsaved. You do not make his job easier by ministering to others. Please keep your prayer and Bible reading intact. You must keep an open line to the Lord so you can remain objective and minister effectively. Do not allow the enemy to get you caught up in turmoil on your job. Watch and pray; the Lord will show you the way. His Holy Spirit is on the job and will never fail you, especially when you are doing His will.

Great Career Choices for the Chantilly Graceful

Interior Decorator
Personnel Manager
Educator
Floral or Art Designer
Guidance Counselor
Museum Curator

The Outer You

CHANTILLY GRACEFUL CLOTHING CHOICES

Your style of dressing is the epitome of feminine beauty and grace. The two L's, Loveliness and Lace, are the core of your image type. If you dressed the way you really wanted, you would be dripping with lace, ruffles, and petticoats every day. Everything you wear, even your underclothing, is either satin, silk, or beautiful lace that stands alone to proclaim your femininity. Your hose are stretch lace and your shoes are in soft pastels, adorned with gentle hints of graceful styling. Light, airy, and lacy frills let the world know your image type.

You always choose softness over structure. Lace-trimmed collars and cuffs and pearl button blouses are some of your favorites. Full-sleeved blouses with ruffled cuffs and full skirts flow with each Chantilly Graceful step. Soft sashes instead of rigid leather belts adorn your waist, and bows instead of buckles accent your shoes. You use satin bows and ribbons as central themes in your dressing, even when you are wearing jeans.

You own several blouses with either the high Victorian neckline or a lace-and-ruffle collar. Off-the-shoulder, intricately detailed lace blouses and dresses are yours for the asking. Only the Chantilly Graceful woman can wear the elegant poet's shirt the way it was designed to be worn. A poet's shirt with your soft curls or gentle French braid tied with a bow is a look other image types imitate. Since you are the original feminine romantic, the Lord created you as the model of feminine beauty. You are a unique creation, and if you imitate anyone, that someone would be your heavenly Father.

> *B*eloved, do not imitate what is evil, but what is good. He who does good is of God but he who does evil has not seen God.
>
> III JOHN 1:11

Straight, pleated styles are too severe for your spirit. Your idea of a straight skirt is gathered at your waist in a soft bell shape with a tapered hemline. All lines in your wardrobe are soft with rounded or curved edges. Clothing with sharp and tailored lines does not suit you. If you are in an executive position, you may wear some straight styles in order to fit in with the corporate culture. Sometimes ultrafeminine clothing can work against you in the workplace, especially if you want to go into management. Depending on the culture of your company, management may feel you will not be able to make tough decisions because you appear to be so feminine.

Nothing could be farther from the truth, but you also know that this sort of thing happens. Praise the Lord! Attitudes in the workplace are steadily changing. Wise managers look at performance and encourage people to be individuals instead of corporate clones. They are also finally accepting women as women and are not looking for women dressed in men's clothing. While this is slow in happening, you can take a cue from your Harmonic Refined sister and try wearing a tailored suit while adding some Chantilly Graceful feminine touches.

Try a softly draped, lace-trimmed blouse under your tailored suit, for instance. To further soften your look, wear a cameo brooch on your lapel. Add your pumps with bows to maintain image credibility. Make sure you choose shoes with closed-in toes. If you prefer an open shoe, sling-backed pumps are acceptable. The look is still corporate but helps you remain true to your image type. It is still Chantilly Graceful, the true image of feminine strength and individually you.

This role camouflage is not deceptive. It is using wisdom. The Lord told us that we will live in this world, but we are not to be spiritually of this world. Since we live in the world, we must be able to move about and get things done using godly wisdom. Remember, the first thing people see, Christian and non-Christian, is your appearance. They may not consciously judge you, but, my sister, judgment does occur. The truth is, it does happen, so be prepared to overcome as many barriers as possible.

A typical Chantilly Graceful image can sometimes be described as a little-girl look. Many people are shocked when you tell them your age because you look so youthful. While this sounds wonderful, it can be negative, especially when you are in a position of authority. If you are working as a committee chairperson, community leaders may not take you seriously when you show up for a meeting wearing your favorite outfit in pastel pink. In your full skirt, with a soft sash around your waist, a lace blouse, and your angora-and-pearl cardigan, you look beautiful. Although you are a vision of femininity, remember how this image is viewed by others, including other women.

> *A*nd do not be conformed to this world, but be transformed by the renewing of your mind, that you may prove what is that good and acceptable and perfect will of God.
>
> ROMANS 12:2

Before going to your meeting, pray and analyze your audience. Ask the Lord for wisdom. If you are going to present to a group of Harmonic Refined and Elegant Flamboyant women, remember that they like to see control and strength, so you need to project a strong image. Wear the suit we discussed earlier and add just a little something extra, such as a softly colored hankie in your suit pocket. You will speak to the Elegant Flamboyant with your flair. Your suit will speak the language of the Harmonic Refined. It whispers *soft authority* and says that you are in charge.

If the panel is made up of other Chantilly Graceful women, then you have it made. You still need to wear your suit, but add your usual feminine touches and they will listen, because you will be speaking their language. The men on the panel usually give you what you want because you will use your soft, yet determined feminine grace to convince them to support your cause. Your look is still business, but you have softened the severe edges with the femininity of Chantilly Graceful. Your femininity and strength, when combined with prayer and the Holy Spirit, win every time, especially if your cause is chosen by the Lord. He will go before you and prepare the hearts and minds of those making decisions.

> *B*e strong and of good courage; do not be afraid, nor be dismayed, for the Lord your God is with you wherever you go.
>
> JOSHUA 1:9

CHANTILLY GRACEFUL FULL-FIGURED CLOTHING CHOICES

Being full-figured does not change your image type. You wear the same clothing styles as your smaller sister. The only difference is the size. Do not be concerned about the size as long as the piece of clothing fits well. Different clothing lines may mean you wear one size in one line and a different size in another. Your main concern should be how you look and feel in a particular piece of clothing. As long as it is Chantilly Graceful, then it will be truly you.

Your clothing choices are the same as those mentioned earlier. You like soft separates with curved and rounded edges. Scalloped hemlines suit you well and draw the eye downward. The emphasis is on your legs, where you want it, rather than on your figure. Lace and ruffles delight the eye as you waltz into the room. Floral-patterned jackets and long, flowing skirts are some of your favorites.

If your hips are full, then the classic Chantilly Graceful full or gathered skirt is a wardrobe staple. It hides a full stomach, thighs, and hips, and allows you to feel free and feminine. While this type of skirt feels comfortable, it adds unwanted inches if worn with too much fullness. Instead, try a gentle A-line or fewer gathers for a slimming effect. If you like those beautiful sweater skirts, try using the Fingertip Rule to camouflage areas you consider to be figure flaws.

To use the Fingertip Rule, your jacket should fall approximately a hand length below the fullest part of your hips. Stand with your arms relaxed at your sides. Notice where your fingertips fall. This should be the perfect length for your jackets. If your arms are short, add two inches. This will enable you to wear those straight sweater skirts you love, by camouflaging a full stomach, hips, and thighs.

You look best in soft, unstructured, extra-long cardigans accented with pearls and other feminine touches such as ribbons and small details at the shoulders. A Peter Pan collar trimmed in lace, with pearl buttons larger than you would normally wear, will draw the eye upward from your hips and add a wonderful feminine touch. Try also using button covers for extra mileage with your blouses. There are some really beautiful ones on the market. Pearls trimmed with intricate gold that resembles lace and cameos should speak your Chantilly Graceful language.

> $\mathcal{N}$ow thanks be to God who always leads us in triumph in Christ, and through us diffuses the fragrance of His knowledge in every place. For we are to God the fragrance of Christ among those who are being saved and among those who are perishing.
>
> II Corinthians 2:14–15

If you decide to wear pants, make sure they fit properly and that you have adequate room to move about. A pantsuit in a soft pastel with a beautiful watercolor scarf is the perfect Chantilly Graceful look. If you prefer to wear jeans, then choose a denim jacket with lace and pearl details. Denim with your special touches is noticeably nice and feminine. Add your favorite pearl accessories and your Chantilly Graceful song is played over and over again. You were created in the fullness of creation by the Lord God of hosts, and you gently emit your God-given Chantilly Graceful fragrance to all the world.

Key Words for the Chantilly Graceful Dress Code

Delicate
Lacy
Soft
Flowing

Chantilly Graceful Color Schemes

What colors color you Chantilly Graceful? You already know the answer. Soft, gentle pastels and floral prints are Chantilly Graceful color keys. The softer, the better, because you feel your feminine best in gentle swirls of pastel coloring. Soft, picturesque floral prints are also found in your palette. These beautiful patterns remind you of a springtime garden.

You also like watercolors. These colors are a bit more intense than pastels, so you choose them when you want to wear something more daring than usual. Fluid pinks, blues, and lavenders create wonderful rainbows of color for your palette. Soft yellows, greens, and turquoises signal the beginning of spring and announce your arrival in Chantilly Graceful style.

> The flowers appear on the earth; the time of singing has come, and the voice of the turtledove is heard in our land.
>
> Song of Solomon 2:12

A dress in winter white with a pink rosebud pattern worn with your grandmother's strings of antique pearls speaks the romantic language of Chantilly Graceful. A gathered lavender silk skirt worn with a matching cardigan, trimmed with bows and beading, anxiously waits to be worn by you. You wear any color that softly whispers your name. Soft swirls of fluid, pastel colors were made for you and you alone. The colors blend with your softness and gentle beauty. The rainbow is at your command as you waltz with its flowing components.

Hand-painted silks are also an important part of your wardrobe. They emit the Chantilly Graceful fragrance as the colors blend and flow together in soft swirls. A silk artist can design items just for you. These treasures can also be found in just about any department store. Or you can find material painted in your wondrous color schemes and have scarves made by your favorite seamstress. Like a Victorian painting in a soft, delicate color scheme, you are a truly beautiful sight to behold. All your colors dance and move in rhythm with your soft footsteps.

Try using these hand-painted magical strokes as accents if you need a stronger image for a special meeting or for an evening out. Instead of pastel pink, try a deep, rich pink. Accent with a hand-painted silk scarf that uses the vibrant pink as its base color. It should be highlighted with a bouquet of other, softer Chantilly Graceful colors. This will bring about a new color adventure you will try over and over again. You were made to wear them, and they are stimulated by your Chantilly Graceful spirit. Soft, beautiful, whispers of color announce to the world your arrival. You are the picture of feminine grace in Chantilly Graceful coloring. When our God created the rainbow, it was also a promise of things to come. Just like the rainbow, your Chantilly Graceful beauty is a promise fulfilled for all the earth to enjoy!

Chantilly Graceful Jewelry

Cameos framed in intricate, golden webbing were created with feminine, romantic ambience just for you. Although the golden frames are intricate by design, the small details are what makes them Chantilly Graceful. The delicate loops of gold intertwined with small beading resemble dainty rosebuds. When worn by a true Chantilly Graceful, these delicate traces of femininity become touches of gentle beauty.

Nothing chunky blends with your delicate spirit. Your jewelry pieces must not compete with one another and must pass your image credibility test. You are a stickler for romance but also like order. If you decide to wear pearl earrings, then you will wear your antique pearl brooch and ring. If you own diamonds, emeralds, or sapphires, you wear the entire ensemble. The necklace, ring, earrings, and ring adorn your gentle frame. Each piece is encircled by a romantic setting that whispers Chantilly Graceful style and grace.

Your standards are tough, and you prefer real jewelry. Costume jewelry is worn only if it meets your standards. It must closely resemble the real thing. When choosing costume pearls, you closely check the coloring and ensure there are no scratches or spots of chipped paint. The same holds true for each piece of costume jewelry that makes it into your jewelry chest. You know which brands to buy, but shop around for different lines if they carry romantic accessories.

Your chains for your pendants are always thin and delicate. Your pendants are small- to medium-sized. You wear an extra-large piece of jewelry if it has sentimental value. Grandmother's elegant brooch and the pendant she wore on her wedding day, or your mother's large diamond-and-pearl earrings, are kept for special occasions. The earrings are worn with a pearl choker with Victorian styling. When you decide to wear the brooch, you take time to strategically place it in just the right spot. Wearing little other jewelry, the piece stands out as the central theme of your grace and style.

When you feel adventurous, you wear dangling earrings with delicate detail and small chains. Swirls, curves, and clusters with small, ornate details whisper *Chantilly Graceful* over and over again. Any piece that says *romance* and *femininity* was created just for you. Your jewelry collections come alive and are notes on the Chantilly Graceful scale, bringing harmony to your gentle image song.

> *I* adorned you with ornaments, put bracelets on your wrists and a chain on your neck.
>
> EZEKIEL 16:11

CHANTILLY GRACEFUL HAIR

You are drawn to romantic themes even in the way you wear your hair. If you wear it long, curls softly frame your face. You use feminine bows and ornate hair clips to hold it in place. It is not unusual for you to wear wispy curls reminiscent of the Shirley Temple era. To others, the look is old-fashioned, but to you it is magical. Secretly, others wish they could look as romantic and feminine as you do, because your hair reminds them of another age and time.

If you wear your hair short, your curls and swirls will have just enough length for them to gently bounce with your body movements. A permanent adds soft body and just enough curl to gently frame your lovely face. An extra-short cut always has the wisps of curls you love. You may still use the occasional bow or hair clip for your famous Chantilly Graceful feminine touch.

Antique pearl hair combs hold French rolls in place. Loose curls cascading past your ears and gently brushing your neckline sing the Chantilly Graceful song. A French braid caresses your shoulders. Accented with your favorite bow, it tells the world you are the essence of feminine romance. This is one of your best looks because from the front, you camouflage your Chantilly Graceful image with your hair pulled away from your face. Your look is that of a woman with authority. As you walk by, though, others see your braid, and your bow whispers *Chantilly Graceful* to all who see it.

If your hair is fine, hair spray is one of your basic survival items. You use it to achieve that Chantilly Graceful soft fullness. Remember the beehive hairstyle from the 1960s? It was most likely designed by a Chantilly Graceful. There are quite a few of your sisters who still wear that style. Take a look around at those old enough to remember that era and you will see true-blue Chantilly Graceful women who still cling to those feminine styles of yesterday.

Chantilly Graceful women of color love soft hair coloring. If you color your hair, make sure the color blends with your skin's natural coloring. Since you love softness, you already know that soft blending wins over sharp contrast. Deep rich auburn, cocoa, and chestnut brown are softly feminine. If you decide to highlight your hair, use soft streaks of coloring that are sure to complement your coloring. Nothing shocking or harsh will do for your image type. Leave that to the image types that can get away with it. Chantilly Graceful must stay with soft blends and gentle highlights in hair coloring.

There are some wonderful burgundies on the market that give your hair a soft brilliance and luster in any type of lighting. These colors also look great with any skin tone. Choose your coloring wisely to complement your café au lait, honey-gold, caramel-brown, walnut, cocoa-brown, or ebony skin coloring. Remember, the Lord gave you awesome coloring, so if you decide to color your hair, use it to highlight your natural tone.

This word goes out also for women of Latina, Asian, and Native American descent. Try to leave your magnificent hair the way it is. Nothing man-made can compare with your rich tresses. If you feel the need to experiment, try some of the burgundies described above. They will add gentle highlights without detracting from your God-given beauty. Burgundy will also blend with your natural skin coloring and give you a lovely glow.

Soft fluffs, cascading curls, and braids with bows are Chantilly Graceful trademarks and stand out as romantic favorites. Everything about you is soft, flowing, and feminine. He created you in beauty for His glory. You are His masterpiece of loveliness. Your heavenly Father gave you an extra portion of feminine splendor, and you shine like no other image type in the fullness of Chantilly Graceful beauty.

> **Y**our fame went out among the nations because of your beauty, for it was perfect through My splendor which I bestowed upon you, says the Lord God.
>
> Ezekiel 16:14

CHANTILLY GRACEFUL MAKEUP

Your ideal makeover is soft and translucent. You're at your best in a fresh, natural look. To achieve this, use soft, blending watercolors. You will very seldom need or want a made-up look. Every color must blend perfectly with the next and look natural. Colors with names that make your mouth water are part of your makeup palette. Gentle fuchsia, soft hunter green, tender apple green, lemonade yellow, and luscious juicy watermelon or strawberry are perfect examples of Chantilly Graceful colors.

If you use red, you want your lips to look as if you have just eaten a strawberry—not a deep, vibrant red, but a soft, gentle hue reminiscent of springtime. Your cheeks look as if they have been kissed by soft rose petals, and your eyes have feather strokes of soft watercolors. If you choose to wear earth tones, gentle browns, coppers, and peachy peaches accented with soft corals and turquoise blues are the perfect Chantilly Graceful colors.

If you have been color-analyzed, then please use your palette. If you are a Winter, apply beautiful red and gorgeous fuchsia, using gentle strokes. If you are an Autumn, Spring, or Summer, follow the same instructions using your selected colors from your seasonal palette. Makeup applied heavily will only take away from your gentle presence. Your spirit is one of gentleness and softness, and your makeup should be a reflection of your spirit. Listen to your heart when using colors and you will not go wrong. Again, ask your own personal Color Consultant, the Holy Spirit, for guidance.

Your foundation should gently blend with your natural coloring. Nothing artificial will do. If you need a more dramatic look for evening, use your daytime coloring, applied a little deeper and more richly. It should never be vibrant and dramatic; leave that look for other image types. You would rather blend in with your surroundings than dramatically stand out. If you were to stand out, you want it to be because you look lovely and feminine, not brassy and dramatic. Everything you wear, even your makeup, gently whispers *Chantilly Graceful.*

If you are medium- or dark-complexioned, your skin is the canvas for your feminine portrait. Sweet apple reds, juicy plums, and soft pinks and corals enhance your dark beauty. Color softly kisses your lips, cheeks, and eyes. You expertly highlight your ebony, bronze, or olive skin and create your delicate trademark. Your colorful, subdued femininity sings your sweetest Chantilly Graceful song for all the world to hear.

Gentle teal daintily waltzes through your palette, while the beauty of your countenance—from café au lait to deepest ebony—shines for all the world to see. You are as beautiful as

Ruth when she became the wife of Boaz. Whatever your ethnic heritage, you are the Lord's creation and beautiful to behold. You are ready to speak your graceful language without saying a word. Your appearance says it all for you. If you need assistance finding your best colors, do not hesitate to consult a professional image consultant or makeup artist. A trained professional can help you determine the best colors and makeup for you skin tone and type, as well as instructing you in how to apply that fresh, natural look you love.

With sun-kissed softness for a more romantic evening, you glorify the Lord with your Chantilly Graceful beauty. Whether your ethnic heritage is that of the European queen, the Asian empress, the Latina *condesa,* the Native American or Nubian princess, your feminine glow glorifies the Lord. With your Chantilly Graceful countenance, you are refinement, romance, ruffles, and lace; the Lord's true vision of loveliness and grace!

> *L*et me see your countenance, let me hear your voice for your voice is sweet and your countenance is lovely.
>
> SONG OF SOLOMON 2:14

7. *Sensual Exotic*

The Sensual Exotic,
To our senses, she appeals.
Beautiful, God's handiwork,
True loveliness revealed.

Who is she who looks forth as the morning,
Fair as the moon, clear as the sun;
Awesome as an army with banners?

SONG OF SOLOMON 6:10

The Beauty of Sensual Exotic

Are you attracted to soft knits in vibrant colors that show the natural curve of your figure? Do you love the feel of silky fabrics against your skin? Do sequins, glitter, and glamour make you feel alive? Then you are the Sensual Exotic image type. Others view you with interest and would never call you or your appearance boring. You are all woman and not afraid to express your femininity, even in your dress. Because of this attitude, you are sometimes unaware of how your obvious appeal affects others.

Sensual comes from the Latin root word sensus, which means "pleasing to the senses" or "having a strong sensory appeal." Exotic comes from the Greek word exoticus, which means "strikingly or excitingly different or unusual." What a perfect combination of words to describe you and your image type! You are vibrant, exciting, strikingly different, totally Sensual, and totally Exotic. Like your biblical sister Abishag, your beauty is renowned.

Abishag the Shunammite

WINNER OF THE FIRST BEAUTY CONTEST
_____

> So they sought for a lovely young woman throughout all the territory of Israel, and found Abishag, the Shunammite and brought her to the king. And the young woman was very lovely and she cared for the king, and served him; but the king did not know her.
>
> I KINGS 1:3–4

227

The word spread throughout the kingdom. The nation needed a beautiful, virtuous woman to serve the king. This was to be a place of honor, since the king was King David, the great warrior of Israel. Although he was now an old man, it did not matter to the many young women who wanted the chance to serve him. Only one was to be chosen. Only one could enter into the company of the king and become part of the royal household. Only one would come to know the true reason for this intensive quest. This excitement set the palace in a constant state of frenzy as the search seemed to take on a life of its own.

Since the king was now an old man, they sought a beautiful young woman to serve as his nurse and concubine. His physicians prescribed this as a remedy to increase his waning vitality. Not only was this young woman to be beautiful, but she also had to possess a special quality. It was a quality that was hard to put into words; an unspoken quality that rang as clear as a bell to the senses. This special quality belonged only to a Sensual Exotic woman.

Surely there had to be a young woman so ravishingly beautiful that she could revive the king and reignite the once famous fire. Finally, after months and months of viewing countless maidens, they found her in the town of Shunem. Her physical beauty stood out far above all the others. Her spirit was one of humility, and she willingly came forward to serve her nation and king. Her patience with the selection process displayed an inner peace that could only be found in a woman of gentle loveliness and spiritual beauty.

As she walked before the judges, they knew in an instant that their search was at an end. Her dark eyes mesmerized all around her. As she moved through the room, her presence was so sensuous, she appeared to leave traces of her essence wherever she stepped. She held every man in the room captive by her beauty. Every woman who viewed the event from the hidden corners of the palace burned with envy. All except her Sensual Exotic sister

Bathsheba, the queen, who understood the spirit of this woman. Bathsheba appreciated the young woman's appeal. For although she was now mature in her years, she still influenced the royal household. She would gladly welcome her sister. Yes, the search was at an end. This young woman, chosen by the Lord and destined to take her place in history, was your beautiful Sensual Exotic sister Abishag the Shunammite.

We can imagine that Abishag was a statuesque beauty with long black hair and flawless, deep golden skin. Her dark eyes, with painted lids, resembled large pieces of onyx in fine gold settings. Her figure was the image of perfection. Her shoulders were like chiseled marble. The Master Craftsman sculpted her waist to perfection. She dressed in the finest of purple silk. Around her waist was a multicolored sash with golden threads. On her ears were large golden earrings that matched the sparkle in her eyes. Golden rings adorned her long, delicate fingers. Beautiful golden bracelets set with lapis and precious stones were on each wrist. Necklaces of gold and silver hung around her exquisite neck.

We can imagine that all this adornment and luxury were initially shocking to Abishag. She was from a quiet village with green hills where flocks grazed peacefully. There were no musicians entertaining. There were no huge banquets being prepared. There were no servants attending to her every need. Here in the palace, at the snap of a finger, she bathed in perfumed waters. When she rang a bell, servants brought platters of her favorite fruit to her. Tailored to fit her perfectly, each piece of her royal wardrobe spoke her language. With a nod of her head, somebody somewhere would do whatever she desired. It was almost too exhausting for Abishag to even think about.

She was with King David almost constantly. Many times when she attended him, dignitaries visited. She learned that during these times, she was to listen and not speak. Although her duties were to act as his nurse and concubine, and not an adviser, it is easy to imagine that she had some influence over the king. The duty of concubine, however, was not performed, since King David was now old. During one of these many visits, Abishag was to be an important witness to one of the most significant events in biblical history.

Bathsheba, the queen, came in to see King David. The creases in her brow let Abishag know she was concerned about something of great importance. Abishag helped David get comfortable so he could listen. As she looked around, she noticed that someone had dismissed all the other servants from the room.

As Bathsheba began to speak, Abishag noticed Nathan, the prophet, standing in the back of the room. She listened as Bathsheba told the king that his son Adonijah had proclaimed himself king over Israel while he, the present king, was still alive. She heard and watched as Nathan came before the king. She listened as he told of the celebration and sacrifices of Adonijah. She watched and listened as Nathan told of how he, the royal adviser and prophet of the Lord, was not invited to the celebrations and sacrifices.

Abishag heard Bathsheba, her sister Sensual Exotic, plead with David to keep his promise and crown her son Solomon to reign after him. After her plea, she and Bathsheba exchanged knowing glances, for they both knew that this scene shaped history. Abishag watched as she saw a fire rage in the eyes of the elderly king. She heard his words and saw his emotions rise as he gave instructions for the anointing and crowning of Solomon. She heard every word, every syllable, every tear, and every royal instruction. Abishag, the little village girl, was now an important part of biblical history.

She was important not just for winning the first beauty contest, but for serving as an important witness to the future of her country. She was at David's side as he made one of the most significant decisions of his reign. She witnessed the beginning of an era that would become famous all over the known world. She witnessed David name Solomon as Israel's next king. There would be no ruler or kingdom as famous, anywhere or at any time in history, as Solomon. She witnessed the beginning of wisdom.

Abishag the lovely Shunammite was a powerful example of a Sensual Exotic woman. She was beautiful, God's handiwork, true loveliness revealed. Like you, her Sensual Exotic sister, she was awesome as an army with banners!

The Inner You

Because you are so different, no matter what you choose to wear, your sensory appeal is very noticeable. It doesn't matter if you are wearing a large bulky sweater or sweatshirt that covers you from your neck to your knees; your sensuous beauty cannot be concealed. This beauty permeates your smile, your hand gestures—every part of your being. It is what makes you so unique. Your obvious appeal is a gift from your heavenly Father. It is as natural to you as the canvas is to the artist and as flight is to an eagle. It is what makes you uniquely you.

Your presence makes men stand straighter and women take detailed notice of their appearance. Men feel more masculine in your presence. They pull up their drooping trousers, suck in their stomachs, and straighten their posture. Doors are opened and chairs are pulled out for you. There is nothing about you that resembles masculinity. Sweats, jeans, and even traditional masculine uniforms are still electrifying on your Sensual Exotic frame. The reason is clear. Your very essence is strong sensory appeal. Whether you resemble a Nordic queen, an Asian empress, a Latina *condesa*, or a Nubian or Native American princess, you have the same effect on others. Ethnic heritage makes no difference. As a Sensual Exotic woman, your appeal is more than skin deep and shines through the physical.

Other women wonder about your appeal. When you enter a room, there is a silent run to the ladies' room for appearance checks. They may not ask you, but they want to know the source of the special charisma that gets doors opened and chairs pulled out for you. Your Sensual Exotic sisters know the answer. It is a powerful, unspoken beauty. It is a wonderful gift from the Lord. It is your Sensual Exotic spirit, something that cannot be imitated. It is a thread of golden splendor interwoven into your very being during creation by your heavenly Father.

Your sensuous spirit is evident in all you say and do. It is so appealing to the senses that people sometimes misjudge you and your intentions. Many times, your style of dressing, your walk, or even your gestures are misjudged and labeled as "provocative." This is not to say you are responsible for the thoughts and actions of others, but it is important to know how others perceive you. Remembering this, always go to the Lord and ask for wisdom in dealing with others, especially when you sense there is a problem. Do not ignore your intuition. Misunderstanding can often be prevented if we deal with feelings before they become problems. Remember, in a spiritual battle, you cannot give the enemy an opening.

> *F*or we do not wrestle against flesh and blood, but . . . against the rulers of the darkness of this age, against spiritual hosts of wickedness in the heavenly places.
>
> EPHESIANS 6:12

It can be unfortunate, but we humans are visual and prejudge others by what we see. Go to the Lord in prayer and seek His guidance in this area. He created your loveliness and your sensuous appeal. He will use it for His glory if you depend on Him. But our enemy has a way of distorting our gifts in the eyes of others. If allowed, he will twist that very gift to alienate you from others and cause confusion. Just remember, you are covered by the blood of Jesus, and there is no better protection available. You belong to Him and were created in His image.

You may not be responsible for the conduct of others, but you are responsible for how you choose to respond. Choose not to give in to the natural urge to strike out and mirror the very behavior that hurts you. Stand still and wait on the Lord, for He will fight the battle. He knows your heart and the hearts of those who try to hurt you. Leave it at the foot of His throne. As long as you give Him glory, no weapon formed against you shall prosper. He knew when He created you and added that Sensual Exotic portion to your being that things would not be easy for you. He also knew how others would respond to that beautiful portion. Remember, the Lord never changes. You have His promise that He will take care of the situation.

> *N*o weapon formed against you shall prosper, and every tongue which rises against you in judgment You shall condemn. This is the heritage of the servants of the Lord. And their righteousness is from Me says the Lord.
>
> Isaiah 54:17

Physical comfort is one of your top priorities. Your furniture must be made of material that is pleasing to your sense of touch. It must be warm in winter and cool in summer. It must also be comfortable to sit on and made for relaxing. If you live in a cold climate, your ideal home has a fireplace. In a warm climate, air-conditioning is not a luxury, it is a Sensual Exotic necessity. If people want to see you get unbalanced, let them change your physical comfort level. Bingo! They hit the jackpot! Physical discomfort drains you. Take away your cool air in summer and heat in winter, and your entire attitude changes. Instead of your normal sunny disposition, you become whiny, irritable, and have a hard time concentrating on anything but your physical needs. Remembering this, make sure you adequately prepare for the change of seasons.

Atmosphere is very important to you. When eating out, cafeteria dining is not your style. You do not enjoy standing in a long line and waiting to sit on a hard bench or an uncomfortable chair. You would rather go to a place known for its atmosphere than its cuisine. A restaurant with hard wooden benches, paper plates and napkins, and mason jars for drinking is totally out of the Sensual Exotic realm. You only frequent this type of place if your loved ones absolutely insist. If you had your choice, you would dine with candlelight, fine china, crystal, and someone attending to your every need. It doesn't matter if the food isn't great, as long as the atmosphere and service are exceptional. These are the things that make the Sensual Exotic spirit sing.

People are more important to you than things. You feel material things are a temporary part of life. You focus on the things our Lord calls eternal. Your family is important and you place them, their comfort, and their feelings above any of your material possessions. Times such as Christmas and birthdays are special moments; there is not enough gold or silver in the world to replace them or the people involved. You spend extra time preparing meals and making sure things are in order. There is more than enough food and drink, and the temperature is set for perfection.

You are not into keeping an immaculately clean house, but instead have a home that is comfortable and stylish. The physical and spiritual needs of your family come first. You work on meeting those needs. This is not to say you do not like a nicely decorated home. You love your home, but feel the physical comfort of loved ones is priority one. If there is a little dust, it does not bother you. If you do not get the wash done, it only bothers you when it becomes an inconvenience to your family. You do the basic housekeeping duties and enlist the help of your family members. You feel that a house is not a home unless everyone contributes to its upkeep.

Your home decor is always pleasing to the eye. You decorate with bright colors and luxurious fabrics and spare no expense for comfort. If you own any antiques or valuable items, you openly display them for all to enjoy. You do not hide things from view— you believe in enjoying all you have for as long as you can. You use your china, crystal, and silver every day instead of keeping them for special occasions.

For you, special occasions *are* every day as long as you are spending them with the special people in your life. Nothing you have is too good to use for their comfort and enjoyment. You believe in enjoying God's blessings while you can and focusing on things that are eternal. You do not believe in storing up earthly treasures for the moths and worms to eat. You savor each moment and every special person the Lord brings into your life. To you, these are the things that are really important.

> . . . We do not look at the things which are seen, but at the things which are not seen. For the things which are seen are temporary, but the things which are not seen are eternal.
>
> II CORINTHIANS 4:18

Sensual Exotic Strengths in the Body of Christ

Intercessor
Usher Ministry
Hospitality

Sensual Exotic and Family Life

As a mother, you do not worry about your material things being broken. If something is broken, then it's broken. If it can be repaired, then you have it repaired. The feelings of the person who broke the item are your chief concern. When someone breaks or destroys something, it is usually an accident. If one of your children is the cause, you view the situation as an opportunity to teach a lesson. Rather than getting visibly angry, you try to remain calm so you can discuss the matter. If the piece was valuable, you express your disappointment and calmly explain your feelings. You feel it is important for your little ones to know your true feelings. It is also important that they understand that even negative feelings can be expressed appropriately. Their Sensual Exotic mother is just the one to teach that lesson. You choose not to "sweat the small stuff." You immediately look into having the broken piece replaced or repaired so you can move on to important things, such as teaching your child one of life's lessons.

You involve your little ones in the replacement process. You let them know that they are still responsible for the incident until it is resolved. They are encouraged to help by using their allowance to help pay for the broken piece. This helps your children feel important. They are also learning the valuable lesson of being responsible for their actions. Through this process, you orchestrate restoration and renewal in your child. Restoration of the broken item and the dignity of your child and renewal of your relationship are the ingredients of joyful parenting.

You carefully screen all entertainment activities. Any movie or book that you feel may defile their precious spirits cannot stay in your home. You discuss your decisions with them and let them know your position. It is critical that they be educated not only in the natural, but in the spiritual things as well. You assist them in cleaning out their rooms regularly so that the enemy will not find openings into your home. You never throw out anything without first discussing it. You also give them the opportunity to voice their opinions openly. You feel this promotes healthy communication and an openness that is sure to carry over into their teens. You let them know that the Lord established the home as a safe haven, and Mother Sensual Exotic seeks only to do His will in keeping it that way. After establishing the ground rules, your children learn to keep their own rooms clean without you. Your only job, at that point, is maintenance.

Your home is the neighborhood teen hangout. Your children's friends enjoy calling you their "second mother." If they are having problems, they often come to you for a practice discussion before going to their parents. You realize that although you are honored with this role, you must keep yourself thoroughly rooted and grounded in God's word, since you sometimes hear things that cause your hair to stand on end. You must always be in a position to give godly advice and direction. Your goal is to always lead them back into the arms of Jesus and their parents. You never go against the authority of their parents, but try to help them see both sides of every situation. Your best friend during these times is Jehovah Jirah, your Provider, who is always just a prayer away, and who has given you uncommon wisdom, like your biblical sister Bathsheba.

You minister to your children's needs by giving them your best, including your love and acceptance. You are the mother in the silk dress whose three-year-old feels free to hug her, even with jelly hands. An uninterrupted hug means more to you than a dress you can have cleaned. You want those hugs as long as you can get them. You are wise to know that the time will come when they will not be given so freely. Love is the answer, and you want your children to feel free to come to you for anything. You never want them to doubt that they are one of your top priorities. Silk dresses can be replaced, but the love of a child cannot.

You decided long ago that a *could have, should have, would have* attitude does not work for you. There are too many parents with regrets because they did not show their children that they accepted and loved them when they had the chance. You do not plan to join this sad group. You do not want to be a mother who doesn't feel welcome visiting her children or whose children do not want to visit her. Your door will always be open to them. The Lord has given you a great capacity for love, and when it comes to your children, you pull out all the stops.

You are a risk taker in matters of the heart. If there is a disagreement, you are the first to try to resolve the matter. You mediate between the parties, whether you are directly involved or not. Even if it takes years, you work until things are settled. If you are directly involved, you quickly try to talk things out and ask for forgiveness. You know most disagreements come about through misunderstanding the actions or words of another person. Knowing this, you work hard to find the core of the issue so you all can move on to bigger and better things.

You believe life is too short to waste energy on anger and envy. When people refuse to communicate, they are just holding on to bitterness. That bitterness easily starts to resemble a cancer that eats away at the mind, body, and spirit. You believe in following Christ's honorable example of love and forgiveness. You know that bitterness and anger can be washed away by the precious blood of the Lamb. Encouraging your children to do the same, you set a gracious standard for all.

> The children of Your servants will continue,
> And their descendants will be established before You.
>
> PSALMS 102:28

Bathsheba

THE MOTHER OF WISDOM

> Then it happened one evening that David arose from his
> bed and walked on the roof of the king's house. And from
> the roof he saw a woman bathing, and the woman was
> very beautiful to behold.
>
> II SAMUEL 11:2

It was a hot evening. The night air felt delicious as it gently danced across her golden skin. She threw back her head and closed her eyes as the breeze ran its cool fingers through her hair. Tonight things seemed different. There was a stillness that disturbed her. On most nights, when she bathed on her rooftop, she felt safe. She decided to ignore her uneasiness. After all, she was far above the city where no one could see her. Pushing aside the veil of anxiety, she continued with her nightly routine.

But tonight, as she eased into her bath, she had an unseen visitor. Tonight, as she delicately coiled her long hair into a knot and secured it with her comb, her unseen visitor watched. Tonight, as she gently took her cloth and swiped away the day's perspiration, her unseen visitor looked on. He watched as she poured the water over her body and gently dried herself. He watched as she stepped from her bath and as her dazzling shadow followed her in the moonlight. He watched from a place where only royalty could watch. He watched from the roof of the royal palace. Tonight her unseen visitor was Israel's monarch, the mighty King David.

After David became king over Israel, the Lord continued to bless him and his nation. The Lord granted his every petition. All of Israel was at his command. David had seen Bathsheba, and he wanted her. He sent word for her to visit him at the palace, but discovered that she was the wife of Uriah, the Hittite, one of his most trusted warriors. This discovery was insignificant to the monarch. He took whatever he wanted, and he wanted Bathsheba.

Somehow, the thought of sin never entered his mind as he watched her enter the palace. As they sat and talked, he could only think back on how beautiful she had looked during her moonlight bath. He sat and watched as she delicately pushed a wisp of hair from her face. He became intoxicated with the way she gently tilted her head as she spoke. It only made it more difficult for him to control his passion.

As he led her down the palace corridors, he never gave a second thought to the fact that she was the wife of another man. He was king, and his word was law. He now held her captive and there was no turning back. The thought of displeasing the Lord was a fading, distant drumbeat, drowned out by the flood of his selfish desire for a beautiful, Sensual Exotic woman.

We can imagine that Bathsheba was a golden-skinned beauty with deep brown hair with lovely golden highlights. The color combination of her skin and hair, accented by her deep hazel eyes, excited the senses. The Lord did some of His best work when He created her. Her figure was flawless. In her dresses of coral, teal, and purple, she was a vision of loveliness. On her head, she wore golden hairnets to secure her tresses and deep-colored headdresses to match her dresses. On many occasions, she simply held her long hair in place with an ivory comb encrusted with jewels. A linen sash gently encircled her waist. On her delicate feet, she wore soft sandals of badger skin.

Bathsheba was honored to be called into the king's presence and went willingly. What she probably did not expect was the sequence of events that followed. The Bible tells us, in II Samuel 11:4, that King David sent messengers and took her; and she came to him, and he lay with her. David was a powerful man, both in physical stature and in position. He was the lord and master of Israel and everyone, including your sister Bathsheba, was at his command. She entered the palace at the request of the king and submitted to his will.

After her palace visit, Bathsheba discovered that she was pregnant with the king's child. When David received this news, he immediately tried to hide his sin. He sent for Uriah from the battlefield. When he arrived, David told him to go home to his wife. Uriah was a warrior, consecrated for battle, and he refused to go home. He slept instead at the door of the king's house with all the servants. After his attempts to persuade Uriah to go to Bathsheba failed, David devised a murderous plan.

In II Samuel 11:14–15, he sent a message to Joab, his general, to set Uriah in the forefront of the hottest battle. Joab was to then retreat from him so Uriah would be struck down and killed. Uriah hand-carried his own death sentence when he delivered this message upon his return to the battlefield. David, deep in the clutches of sin, had Uriah deliver his own death warrant. Sometime later, Joab sent word to David that Uriah had died during the battle.

After her time of mourning was over, David brought Bathsheba to the palace, and she became his wife. Bathsheba gave birth to a son. To punish David for his sin, the Lord took the life of this son. The Bible does not mention Bathsheba's grief for the loss of her husband or her child, but in II Samuel 12:24, it says David comforted her. Sometime later they married and she again became pregnant. This time she gave birth to a second son. David named him Solomon, which means "peaceful." After he repented from his sin, he was again at peace with the Lord. At this time in history, Israel was also at peace.

Bathsheba was a woman of great physical and spiritual beauty. She was bound by duty to obey and honor the royal monarch. Her will was but the will of a single woman against the throne of Israel. She had no choice but to obey. She was in a no-win situation and submitted. This is not to say that she did not love David. It is easy to imagine that she did eventually fall in love with her new husband and joyfully gave him a new son. Although David had many wives, it is evident that Bathsheba was the most influential. After coming to the royal court, it is clear that Bathsheba affected what happened in the palace. In later years, there was a display of this influence.

Nathan, the prophet, who in earlier years had confronted David with his adulterous liaison with Bathsheba, worked with her to ensure that their son Solomon succeeded David as king. Nathan, a man of God, would never have gone to her if she were not a wise, godly woman. Bathsheba's plea to the elderly David showed that she still had his attention and had great influence with him. David, after hearing her stirring appeal, assured her that Solomon would become Israel's next leader.

The Lord used her physical and spiritual beauty to usher in a new era. Bathsheba, your Sensual Exotic sister, gave birth to awesome wisdom, the likes of which the world had never known before—or since. Her beauty was not just physical, for she influenced the world's wisest king. Her son Solomon asked the Lord not for gold and silver, not for jewels, but for wisdom to rule the Lord's people.

Only a godly mother could have instilled such humility in the heart of her son. There has been no man before or since whose wisdom could stand against that of Solomon. There was something different about Bathsheba; something special, something exquisitely beautiful. Like you, her Sensual Exotic sister, she stood fair as the moon and clear as the sun. She was Sensual Exotic, awesome as an army with banners!

The Sensual Exotic Spouse

In your home, your husband is king. You wait on him hand and foot and always make sure he is comfortable. Some would call it spoiling him, but you call it wisdom. He fully appreciates your generosity, love, and acceptance. You get back what you put into the relationship triplefold. He adores you and treats you like his queen. You pull out all the stops when it comes to him and are not afraid to fully express your womanhood. He never knows what to expect when he spends an evening alone with you. Like your sister Creative Poetic, you are an expert at spontaneity, and his enjoyment is your delight. You never let him forget that on these nights, he is the center of your attention.

You never harshly judge him when he comes home and tells you about an incident at work where it is fully obvious that he is at fault. You listen, and after he has had time to think and you take time to pray, you go back and offer suggestions to help him. Because of your gentle approach, he willingly listens. He is relieved to have a spouse who takes the time to listen without judging. After your conversation, he feels refreshed and ready to go back out into the world with a new perspective.

He is fully aware that you help him find solutions to his problems. Although he may not admit it right away, he will express his gratitude in other ways. You know your man better than anyone, and you know when he is expressing his gratitude, even if he does not use words. He thanks the Lord for giving him such a gracious mate. He also does not forget to come to you when he faces problems at work. Isn't that what you want? You want to ensure that he comes home to you and only you. Where do you get your strength and wisdom? You know the answer: Jehovah Jirah, your Provider!

One of your top priorities is to make your spouse as comfortable as possible. You want him to be happy in his home. If he is happy, then your home life is happier. If your home life is full, then you are satisfied. You use the Holy Spirit as the quality-assurance Controller to ensure that your household is on track. You want your spouse's input so you can make sure he is always comfortable at home. Whether it is keeping his favorite snack or wearing his favorite perfume, you cover every detail. What is the reason for your attitude? You are one flesh and inseparable, just as the Lord intended.

Because of your need for comfort, you know exactly what it takes to pamper your spouse. Warm bubble baths by candlelight and delightful afternoon naps, complete with satin sheets, are events sure to stay on his mind for months. The touch of your hand on his arm and your fingers running through his hair make him smile. He savors these special moments. His co-workers watch his distant stares with bewilderment and wonder about the source. They question his ability to rise above the circumstances of a stressful day with apparent joy. You and your spouse both know the source of those joyful moments and happiness. For the Lord blessed you with your Sensual Exotic spirit, and your husband continuously praises Him for it! Like King Ahasuerus, husband of your Sensual Exotic sister Esther, he knows he can rely on your good judgment and spirit.

You always strive for excellence in your marriage. Your husband sees you as a gift from the Lord. As the Bible says, he knows he has found a good thing. Because you choose to honor him, you find favor from him and he finds favor from the Lord. You give him the seat of honor, making him head of his household as the Lord fully intended. What else could he ask for? He has favor from the Lord and a lovely Sensual Exotic wife!

> *H*e who finds a wife finds a good thing, and obtains favor from the Lord.
>
> PROVERBS 18:22

Queen Esther

BEAUTY THAT SAVED A NATION

> The king loved Esther more than all the other women
> and she obtained grace and favor in his sight more than
> all the virgins; so he set the royal crown upon her head
> and made her queen instead of Vashti.
>
> ESTHER 2:17

As she bathed in the perfumed waters, thoughts of recent events raced through her mind. This environment was strange. She had handmaidens bathing her. They dried her and massaged warm oils into her skin and dressed her in attire so lavish that her mind could barely comprehend what was happening to her.

As she felt the silk touch her skin, she thought about how she had come to this place and how her life had suddenly changed. The feel of the comb and smell of the rich, sweet ointments permeating her long dark hair brought her back to reality. Pangs of guilt crept into her heart and stung like icy needles. She felt uneasy in this place. Who was she that the Lord would allow her to be in extreme opulence? In what seemed like an instant, she was transported into another world; the world of royalty.

She was Jewish and her people were subjects of the Persian empire. They were now a conquered people and served a foreign monarch. Her cousin instructed her not to reveal her race. He had always been right in the past, so she listened and acted in obedience. As she looked around at all the extravagance, she could hardly believe she was in the royal palace. The beauty literally took her breath away. There had to be a special purpose for her selection, but she had no idea what it could be. Why was she here? She knew that they would soon escort her before the king. The loud voices of the eunuchs giving directions to the servants who attended this large group of young women interrupted her thoughts. From this group, the king would select a new queen.

As she listened to the instructions, she decided that she would listen and do only as she was told. She soon put all other questions out of her mind. As she was dressed, pampered, and perfumed, she watched all the activities around her with wonder. She was now a part of the royal harem, and her only job was to be beautiful and appealing.

She was very different from all the other young women. She was not an idol worshiper and believed in the one true Lord. She worshiped El Roi, the God Who sees all, and His eyes were on her. He ensured that she found favor in the eyes of all who saw her. She possessed an inner beauty that cut through the senses. All who saw her knew she had something special—something more than physical beauty. That special something she possessed was her Sensual Exotic spirit. The Lord placed her in this place and would soon reveal His purpose. This lovely young woman, destined for greatness, was your Sensual Exotic sister, the beautiful Esther.

We can imagine that Esther was a statuesque beauty with chiseled facial features. Her olive skin was flawless, its texture resembling spun silk. Her eyes, framed with long, gentle lashes, were a deep, rich brown. They were accented with golden highlights and danced with each ray of light that entered their sphere. High cheekbones made her face look like a portrait, elegantly framed and ready to be hung in one of the finest museums. Her lips, hand-painted by her Creator, had no need of the royal makeup artist's touch.

She wore her long, dark hair braided and coiled in a crown-like style on top of her lovely head. A radiant web of spun gold, whose glow was matched only by her dazzling smile, covered her head. She dressed in shades of deep turquoise and crimson silk. On her ears were heavy gold earrings, kissed with precious jewels. Around her delicate neck was a golden necklace with jewels. On one wrist, she wore a bracelet with a small stone; rings of gold adorned one finger of each hand. Her beauty and appeal stood as an awesome banner above all the other young women in her company. She was, like you, the Lord's beautiful example of His Sensual Exotic handiwork.

The king was hosting a great celebration. Princes and nobles from all the royal provinces were in the palace, eating and drinking and celebrating the greatness of the king. All the royal women were also at the palace, attending a gathering hosted by Queen Vashti. Vashti was a woman known far and wide for her great beauty. Time would show that she was not only beautiful, but also vain. This vanity would prove to be her downfall.

After he had consumed quite a bit of wine, the king wanted to show off the beauty of his queen. He sent for Vashti and asked her to attend him and his guests. He requested that she be dressed in her finest attire and wear her royal crown. Vashti, busy with her own activities, refused. How dare he request her presence when he knew she was busy with her guests? Did he really expect her to jump each time he spoke? After all, she was queen. Vashti decided to show the king how she felt. She denied his request.

King Ahasuerus went into counsel with his advisers, and they decided that her act of defiance would cause a great ripple of confusion in the realm. They advised the king to remove Vashti from the throne. She no longer deserved to be queen. Vashti's vanity had finally proven to be a liability. She was stripped of her royal crown and position. Word went out to all the provinces that young virgins would be sent to the king so that he could select a new queen. Your sister Esther was among those selected.

As she prepared to go in to the king, she listened intently to the eunuchs and followed their instructions to the letter. Because of her humbleness and beauty of body and spirit, she found favor with the custodian of the women, Hegai. He gave her a larger portion of beauty treatments and everything else necessary for royal preparation. Seven choice handmaidens were selected to attend her. Hegai also gave Esther and her handmaidens the best place in the house of the women.

She was going through her twelve months of preparation. During the first six months, she was bathed and massaged with oil of myrrh. Now in her second six months, she was being treated with perfumes and other beautifying preparations. After this long process, she would go in to see the king. After this visit, she would go to the house of concubines and be attended by the chief eunuch. She would then not return to the king unless he specifically called for her.

When Esther went in to see the king, she immediately found favor with him. The Bible tells us, in Esther 2:17, that he loved her more than all the other women, and King Ahasuerus placed the royal crown on her head and made her the queen to replace Vashti. He then held a great feast and called the event the Feast of Esther. Esther, acting on the instructions of her cousin Mordecai, had still not revealed that she was a Jew, not even to her new husband.

During the feast, Mordecai was sitting inside the palace gates and overheard two eunuchs plotting to kill the king. He passed on the information to Esther, who informed her new husband. The plot was uncovered, and the two men were hanged on the gallows. This incident would not go unnoticed.

Also during this time, the king promoted the prince Haman and placed him over all the princes and nobles in the kingdom. All the servants inside the palace gates bowed and paid homage to Haman; all except Mordecai. Mordecai knew that Haman was a vain and proud man with an evil heart. He refused to bow before him. This angered Haman so much that he could barely stand the sight of Mordecai. The very mention of Mordecai's name made him burn with anger. It consumed his every thought and action. Haman was no fool. He knew he could not afford to single out Mordecai, so he decided to plot against all the Jews.

Haman went to the king and told him the Jews were not

keeping the laws of the land. He further asked the king to allow him to rid the kingdom of these dissenters. Haman promised to pay into the royal treasury the sum of ten thousand talents of silver ($218,400,000) to ensure that the decree was carried out. He told the king that he would handle the entire matter and requested a royal decree be given to make it legal. The king, trusting Haman's judgment and unaware of his plot, gave him permission to carry out the order.

When the order was posted in the provinces, all the Jews began fasting and praying. Mordecai tore his clothes and put on sackcloth and ashes. He went through the streets letting out loud, bitter cries. He then sat near the palace gates. When Esther heard, she sent Mordecai clothes, but he would not take them. When she discovered the reason for his sorrow, she was deeply distressed. She sent word to Mordecai that anyone who went before the king without being summoned would be put to death. If the king found favor with the person, he would hold out his golden scepter, and the person's life would be spared. This law even applied to her. Even though she was queen, she had not been summoned within the last thirty days.

Mordecai responded by sending Esther a reminder that she, too, was a Jew, and that the edict applied to her as well as her people. He also sent a question that still stands as one of the most memorable in the Bible. In Esther 4:14, Mordecai asked Esther, "Yet who knows whether you have come to the kingdom for such a time as this?" After receiving this message, Esther responded by telling Mordecai to gather all her people and fast with her and her handmaidens for three days and nights. In Esther 4:16, she displayed her resolve by saying, "And so I will go to the king, which is against the law; and if I perish, I perish!"

After the three days were over, Esther put on her royal robes and stood in the inner court of the king's palace. Esther's beauty so overwhelmed the king that he held out his golden scepter. In her royal robes with her Sensual Exotic beauty, your sister Esther was radiant. The king was so awestruck that he not only wanted to know the reason for her visit but also offered her anything she wished. The king was so mesmerized by her Sensual Exotic perfume that he offered your sister half his kingdom.

The Lord not only answered Esther's prayer by saving her life, but used her Sensual Exotic beauty to melt the king's heart and overpower his senses as well. Her courage and beauty moved a royal mountain. The king knew that Esther would never have jeopardized her life unless her need was urgent. He was so moved by her bravery and her Sensual Exotic spirit that he gladly welcomed his queen into the throne room.

Soon after this event, Haman's plot to annihilate the Jewish people was uncovered and he was hanged on the very gallows he had built to hang Mordecai. Mordecai was given a high position in the kingdom. Esther's actions had saved her people.

The Lord had placed her in the kingdom for a very special event only He knew would occur. Being a woman of faith, Esther knew she had to act. She knew that her life and the lives of her people were at stake. With Haman's treachery, Esther finally understood and realized the Lord's purpose for placing her in the royal palace. El Roi created her to become queen of Persia and to save His people. The Lord used your sister Esther, His beautiful Sensual Exotic vessel, to save the apple of His eye, the nation of Israel. Who knows whether you, with your Sensual Exotic beauty, have come to the kingdom for such a time as this!

Sensual Exotic Working Style

Your working style stands out in a crowd. The comfort and well-being of your staff is your biggest concern. Temperature and aesthetics are Sensual Exotic necessities. Your office environment must be pleasant. You realize that people spend the bulk of their time at work and feel the workplace should be an extension of home. If there is no budget, you take it on as a personal project and persuade someone to donate the needed items. If necessary, you bring items from home to make the office more pleasant.

For you, sitting in a corner without proper lighting is a nightmare on Working Avenue. You need not only light, but also stimulating interaction with other people. If you are a supervisor, you want everyone to be comfortable. In many cases, you allow subordinates to bend the dress code rules if management does not do its part in keeping the heat and air-conditioning going. Your subordinates appreciate your concern for their well-being and work twice as hard as their counterparts in other departments. They want to make you look good because you take care of them.

Other managers come to you for advice on developing employee loyalty and motivation, because you seem to have more than your share. What they do not realize is that your relationship with your subordinates didn't just happen. It takes commitment, sacrifice, and prayer. Using wisdom, and knowing when to keep silence and when to speak, has paved the road to successfully gaining the trust and respect of your subordinates.

> *T*o everything there is a season, a time for every purpose under heaven. . . . A time to keep silence, and a time to speak. . . .
>
> ECCLESIASTES 3:1, 7

You have brilliant people and organizational skills. Like the Elegant Flamboyant, you are able to get into doors no one else can. If door guards are men, then you especially have no problems. If not, you get to know the gatekeepers. If the gatekeepers cannot help, then you use your keen eye for observation. You watch to see where the people of power congregate. You get to know schedules and find a way to meet them informally to get things done formally.

Before anyone knows what has happened, your suggestion comes down from upper-level management as a new company policy. Others wonder how management even heard about your idea. For you, it is no secret. You used wisdom, networked outside formal channels, and produced Sensual Exotic results.

You do seem to have better success with men than with women. Your sensuous appeal makes a man feel more masculine when he is around you. Sometimes that very asset is what makes other women feel uncomfortable. Women sometimes misinterpret your actions as provocative, when this is usually not the case. Many times, these women feel discomfort because they have an identity crisis. When people do not know who they are, they are easily intimidated.

Watch and pray when you sense this happening. Because you are in tune with the senses, you will be able to discern how others perceive you. There is little you can do on your own to make others feel comfortable. You cannot change the way you were created. The most effective weapon you have is prayer. Pray and ask the Holy Spirit to intervene for you. Since He can open the ears of the deaf, open the eyes of the blind, and cause the dumb to speak, then changing hearts is certainly within the realm of His power.

> Then the eyes of the blind shall be opened, and the ears of the deaf shall be unstopped. Then the lame shall leap like a deer, and the tongue of the dumb shall sing. For the waters shall burst forth in the wilderness, and streams in the desert.
>
> ISAIAH 35:5–6

You are great at handling unexpected deadlines and situations. Since you have a deep sense of people, you strategically surround yourself with others who strengthen your circle of influence.

Your unique management style gives others a sense of comfort and ease, making them more responsive to change. Your team members willingly work endless hours to complete all projects before a deadline. When your department receives a last-minute assignment, you can always depend on them to pitch in and get the job done. With your enthusiastic leadership style, you inspire all team members to strive for their personal best in the professional arena.

You help others see their strengths and use them. Feeling comfortable with your God-given strengths, you pass on His goodness to your fellow workers. Creating projects and being able to see how they can best serve the organization helps everyone stay focused and productive. You know that if people are productive, then they are happier at work. There is nothing like being able to use your God-given gifts and the feeling of accomplishment that goes along with using them. It is an experience only the Lord can give.

> *A* man's [woman's] gift makes room for him [her], and brings him [her] before great men [women].
>
> PROVERBS 18:16

You work hard to keep your team informed of all new policies and procedures, especially those that will directly affect your department. You are always honest, never sugarcoating the truth, and they appreciate your candor. Loyalty and respect are your badges of honor because you also stand by them in hard times. They remember all you do and reward you by working hard to make you look good. Even team members who do not like you personally seem to fall in line when they see your true fiber. You are the consummate professional. You know that to gain respect, you must earn it and be able to give it to others. You let others know the Lord Jesus is your example—and He made you a competent, talented Sensual Exotic.

Great Career Choices for the Sensual Exotic

Entertainer
Actress
Teacher
Attorney
Public Relations Executive
Entrepreneur

The Outer You

SENSUAL EXOTIC CLOTHING CHOICES

The two G's, Glamour and Glitter, are the focal points of your clothing choices. You like formfitting clothing and use fabrics that accent your femininity to the fullest. If you wear silk, you choose fluid silk over raw. You love the touch and feel as it glides over your skin and dances with your body movements. Knits that cling softly to your feminine curves are also Sensual Exotic favorites. Off-the-shoulder sweaters, belted at the waist or hips to enhance your figure, speak the Sensual Exotic language. Accented with beading and glitter, and worn with your favorite straight skirt, these sweaters sing your favorite song.

When you wear long skirts, they are straight with a side or back split that gently opens and shows a glimpse of your lovely legs as you walk. The car wash skirt was designed for you and your

Sensual Exotic sisters. A straight underskirt with multisplit over-skirt proves a Sensual Exotic wardrobe staple. The underskirt is body hugging, and the overskirt is flirty and a protective layer to keep it from being too revealing. Your flared skirts are ankle length and dance in rhythm with your footsteps. With these won-derful skirts, you wear belts with large, exotic buckles. They adorn your waist beautifully and support your image credibility.

Sensual Exotic tops range from one-shoulder creations to ex-otic prints with necklines that show your beautiful shoulders and natural curves. You also love wrap styles that accentuate your waistline. These are what your heart longs to wear. Notice, I said what your heart *longs* to wear, not what you actually do wear. Be-cause you are often misjudged by your true clothing choices, you have successfully learned the art of role camouflage. If you need to wear a suit with Harmonic Refined styling in the workplace, underneath you will wear not a standard blouse, but a favorite camisole in a vibrant jewel tone. You button your suit except for the top button so a splash of color peeks through and whispers the beauty of your image type. This look is the wonder of Sensual Ex-otic. You are the essence of femininity that stirs the senses. You are just as the Lord created you, a wondrous creation, filled with His glory.

A Chantilly Graceful would wear the brilliant camisole as an undergarment because wearing it out in the open would be a bit too dramatic for her. She would be satisfied in knowing her beau-tiful lace camisole was safe and hidden under her clothing. If she wore it as a blouse, it would be in a soft, safe, neutral color that would hardly be noticeable. Her style signature is softness. You, on the other hand, are more bold and love the brilliance of exotic coloring. The touch of satin and lace against your skin makes you feel glamorous. The suit keeps you safe because of its structure, and it keeps you within the appropriate guidelines for the work environment. The satin and lace whisper your name for all the world to hear.

As a Sensual Exotic in the body of Christ, many times you are misjudged. You have learned to survive by hiding your true spirit. You and your sisters have been hurt so many times after revealing your true spirit that you have built a protective wall, especially in the clothing department. Stay with me now and do not press the panic button. This is a touchy subject, but the Lord has instructed me to be honest and tell it like it is. Many times you may want to show a little more leg than your fellow church members can handle. You may feel fine with your dress an inch or two above your knees with your ankle-strap high heels and textured hose. While you may feel comfortable and look beautiful in this outfit, remember that you are dealing with other people who think and interpret actions differently than you.

Analyze your audience and, above all else, pray before you get dressed. People can be so judgmental. This judgment can quickly become condemnation. Such condemnation can give the enemy the rope to set a trap for you as well. When that happens, both sides lose. Your fellow church members lose because they have misjudged you. They become blind to your beautiful spirit. This judging has caused many a Sensual Exotic to leave a church. That is not a response from the Lord! You lose because you strike out in the flesh because of your pain.

Above all else, pray! There should be no condemnation in the body of Christ, but because we are dealing with men (and women), it exists. Do not hold it against them. Forgive and love as your Lord Jesus continuously does for you. His love can melt an iceberg of condemnation. His Holy Spirit will do battle for you.

There is therefore now no condemnation for those who are in Christ Jesus, who do not walk according to the flesh, but according to the Spirit.

ROMANS 8:1

If the Holy Spirit has not convicted you about wearing your dresses at your knees, then wear them at your knees. You should answer to God and God alone. Here is a word of caution. The Lord still wants you to use wisdom. He wants you to be wise as a serpent and harmless as a dove in your dealings. If people speak to you regarding your dress, please be open. Make sure they are coming in the name of the Lord and are using the Bible. If they cannot show you in God's word, then question the source. Do this especially if the Holy Spirit has not convicted you. Remember, God is a God of order, and He will have already shown you where and how to change before someone else talks to you. He will only send someone to you to confirm what He has whispered to your spirit.

Here is another word of caution. If it is in your church policy that women should not wear dresses above or touching the knees, then you have chosen to belong to this church and must abide by its rules. If your church policy states that you are not to wear certain items while at church, then do not wear them to church. You made a choice to be a part of that body, and in doing so made a choice to abide by its rules. Do not resort to rebellion and wear something obviously provocative or out of line with the church government because of hurt feelings. That is not what the Lord wants. He does not want us or our actions creating conflict in the body. Do not give the enemy an opening!

> *B*ehold rebellion is as the sin of witchcraft, stubbornness is as iniquity and idolatry.
>
> I Samuel 15:23

If you feel that you can no longer follow the rules established by your church, pray and ask the Lord for guidance before leaving. If it is truly His will that you leave, He will provide a new church home for you. He will also guide you through a smooth transition so you can leave without hard feelings. Stand still, and He will fight your battles. You are to be a godly example at all times. Remember, you are influential. You have younger Sensual Exotic sisters watching your every move.

Your job is to be a sweet fragrance to your heavenly Father. You can still wear your shorter dresses. Just leave them for another time and place. Remember, you are Sensual Exotic, even with a longer, elegant hemline. After you have done all you can to remedy a situation, release it to the Lord. You do all you can do within your reach, and He will definitely do the rest. He is the great Physician, and He can do anything but fail. Remember, the Lord sees all. There is nothing hidden from Him, including a person's motives. Man sees the outside and makes judgments. The Lord looks upon your heart and gives blessings. Hallelujah!

> *F*or the Lord does not see as man sees; for man looks at the outward appearance, but the Lord looks at the heart.
>
> I Samuel 16:7

There are times when you want to be totally free in your dressing. Always use wisdom and prayer and you will never go wrong. When led by the Holy Spirit, you can be free and need not hide who you are. He will expertly guide you in displaying your beautiful Sensual Exotic spirit. You can wear your skirts, leggings, and jeweled sweaters without fear. When He leads the way, your image always gives Him glory.

Sensual Exotic Full-Figured Clothing Choices

Being full-figured does not change your image type. You wear the same clothing styles as your smaller sister. The only difference is the size. Do not be concerned about size as long as the piece of clothing fits well. Wearing different clothing lines may mean you wear one size in one line and a different size in another line. Size is unimportant if the garment fits. Let go of the label mentality. Your main concern should be how you look and feel. If you look and feel good, you will definitely shine fair as the moon and clear as the sun in your Sensual Exotic glory.

The dazzle and excitement of Sensual Exotic clothing were made for you. Large animal prints accented with feathers and electric patterns with oversized faux jewels adorn your frame with magnificence. One of your favorite outfits is a black knit dress with a side split that gently caresses your curves. You drape an oversized animal-print shawl around your shoulders. It is large enough to sweep around your waist and camouflage your stomach and hips with Sensual Exotic style. Your oversized feather earrings blend with the colors of your shawl and shout your image type for all to see.

Choose pullover blouses over front-button styles. Pullovers give you more flexibility and freedom of movement. You do not need to worry about buttons coming open. Silky T-shirt-styled tops suit you because you use your accessories to make them all Sensual Exotic. A plain black silk tee top instantly becomes yours when you add your favorite oversized animal-print belt and matching shawl. If you find a plain top that suits you, you redesign it with faux jewels and your hot-glue gun. You make it exotically different, and others wonder where you found it. All it took was a little time, some hot glue, and you to make an original.

Your favorite tops are oversized sweaters that fall just off your shoulders and below your hip line. Covered with large faux jewels and sequins, they speak the Sensual Exotic language. You have several because when you find something you really like, you buy the same style in every available color. Under these wonderful discoveries, you wear a sweater-knit skirt or leggings. When buying all your clothing, use the Fingertip Rule. This simple technique will enable you to wear just about any skirt and pair of leggings as long as they fit properly. Remember, let go of the label mentality and you will be free and clear to navigate in Sensual Exotic style.

To use the Fingertip Rule, your jacket or top should fall approximately a hand length below the fullest part of your hips. Stand with your arms relaxed at your sides. Notice where your fingertips fall. This should be the perfect length for your jackets and tops. If your arms are short, add two inches. This will enable you to wear those wonderful straight skirts or those clinging leggings if you choose to do so. It helps you camouflage full hips and thighs and still maintain image credibility. You have quite a bit of flexibility as long as you make wise clothing choices.

Do not fall into the trap of trying to get revenge when someone says or does something against you because of your image type. People talk negatively about the Lord—and He is perfect. So what else can you expect? You know if they talk about Him, you are an easy target. Remember, the Lord of hosts will do battle for you. He created you as awesome as an army with banners. You are a full-figured beauty, totally Sensual, totally Exotic.

> *D*o not say, "I will recompense evil," wait for the Lord, and He will save you.
>
> PROVERBS 20:22

KEY WORDS FOR THE SENSUAL EXOTIC DRESS CODE

Appealing
Dazzling
Glamorous
Exciting

SENSUAL EXOTIC COLOR SCHEMES

You choose colors that make you feel alive. Jeweled purples and radiant reds delight your Sensual Exotic spirit. Deep, rich, vibrant colors that are similar to those chosen by your Elegant Flamboyant sister also enjoy a high standing on your color listing. You love taking risks with colors and textures. It is not unusual for you to wear radiantly colored sequins even during the day. Those angora sweaters accented by brilliant beading and sequins were made for the Sensual Exotic daytime fashion taste buds. They catch the sun's rays and sing your Sensual Exotic daytime song.

Many times you use black as your core color. A formfitting black sweater dress that enhances your feminine spirit is key in your image vocabulary. If this is your fashion statement choice, you use dramatic animal prints as accents. You wear any pattern that is reminiscent of the jungle. Electric zebra, daring cougar, dazzling tiger, and jungle giraffe prints dance with your every movement. Exotic beading and feathers with hammered-brass, silver, and gold accessories hold the animal prints captive as your Sensual Exotic spirit does an uninhibited dance of freedom.

Your color dress code is exciting and always stimulating to the senses. You love glitter, glamour, and sequins. Your sultry evening dresses with sequins and beading catch the light and accent your Sensual Exotic style. A formfitting black gown with a high neckline becomes a Sensual Exotic classic. It is glamour at its best in black. As you walk away, a V-cut reveals a glimpse of your beautiful back. The V is trimmed with tiny hand-knotted pearls or exotic multicolored beading for just the right touch of evening fire. The high neckline spreads your glamorous message, and the lowered back whispers *Sensual Exotic*.

You also like crystalline white or icy pastels—colors so icy you can hardly see the color. Transparent color that softly shouts feminine appeal suits you. An opulent white outfit looks as if it has been kissed by color. Sharp contrasts in color are also in your palette. You dress in all navy and add a lightning bolt of white for effect. With a white suit, your white shoes with a slash of red dance as you walk. You add vivid stripes of red and white with your black suit. You then add your ankle-strap stiletto-heeled red pumps. You stand out in your regal best as a beautiful Sensual Exotic.

You always add your exciting touch to any ensemble, no matter how conservative. Your true spirit will always be the compass for your colorful rainbow. Dressed in bright, bold colors or sultry black with an added dash of animal print, you naturally choose just the right combination for your image. In silk, satin, linen, or velvet, with brilliant sequins and beading, you glorify your Lord. You are beautiful, His handiwork, and true loveliness revealed in your Sensual Exotic color palette.

> *I* clothed you in embroidered cloth and gave you sandals of badger skin; I clothed you with fine linen and covered you with silk.
>
> EZEKIEL 16:10

SENSUAL EXOTIC JEWELRY

Sensual Exotic loves large, intricate jewelry. You have lots and lots of faux, oversized jewels. Dangling earrings with feathers and animal prints dominate your jewelry box. Your jewelry style may be what others call excessive, but on you it looks fabulous. Ankle bracelets with your initials and dazzling rings are your signature pieces. Like your Elegant Flamboyant sister, you love oversized hammered brass, silver, and gold. The main difference is in the movement of the jewelry. There are times your Elegant Flamboyant sister prefers a more controlled look, choosing large earrings that stay put on her ears. You, on the other hand, like large dangling, moving jewelry. It is not unusual for you to wear large dangling earrings with bells that actually ring! Movement in your jewelry excites you. Although you wear metals well, you also love large, colorful plastic pieces.

You are known for highlighting your winters with accessories from the traditional summer. Although many consider shell jewelry just right for summer, you wear it even in winter, simply because you choose to. If it looks good with one of your outfits, then even in freezing weather, you wear it. Other image types are amazed at your boldness with accessories and may even be a little envious. Do not let this bother you. Pray for them and keep listening to the Lord. He created you just the way you are, and He knows you are His original. You can wear things that express your individual style and spirit like no other.

You love rings and may wear them on all your fingers. Each one has a story and a message. You collect them the way other image types collect stamps. Each one tells of your Sensual Exotic life in jeweled style. The large gold-and-diamond ring has sentimental value. It is an heirloom from your great-grandmother. The silver-and-onyx ring is a special gift from your mother. The silver-and-turquoise ring with matching bracelet is from your dear friend from the Southwest. Each piece fits in your life's puzzle and has special meaning. When you feel like it, you do not hold to convention and wear one piece. You wear them all.

You enjoy mixing metals and stones. It does not matter if society says they do not match. For example, you wear your two-carat diamond stud earrings with your favorite dangling beaded earrings, not giving convention a second thought. All that matters to you is that you like both pieces and want to wear both pieces with a particular outfit. That is the only reason you need, and that settles it. You mix faux and cultured pearls with your oversized faux emeralds to create your own dazzling, Sensual Exotic fashion. You know man-made jewels did not make you awesome as an army with banners. This was and is a gift from the Lord God Almighty, your Master Jeweler.

> *I* put a jewel in your nose, earrings in your ears and a beautiful crown on your head.
>
> EZEKIEL 16:12

SENSUAL EXOTIC HAIR

Your Sensual Exotic identity is expressed through your hairstyle. Whether curled or straight, you show other image types the true meaning of "crowning glory." If you wear it long, you drape it over one shoulder, leaving one ear exposed. On the exposed side, you have a single curl that falls gently on your shoulder. If you wear it short, one side is longer than the other. The longer side playfully hangs slightly over one side of your face for a wondrous Sensual Exotic portrait.

You spray your hair with temporary coloring that catches the light for an electric Sensual Exotic entrance. Like your Creative Poetic sister, you do not think about how others will react because you do not style your hair for them. Your styling is for appeal. If the style is appealing to you or your spouse, then it's the style for you—and the case is closed. You take care not to use an excessive amount of spray to keep your hair in top condition. You want it soft to the touch so that it flows as you walk. This is the hairstyle trademark of the Sensual Exotic.

Sensual Exotic women of color, beware on this note: Make sure your hair blends with your natural skin tone. Remember, you want appeal, not harshness. Try blending as opposed to contrasting your hair coloring. A deep rich auburn, a cocoa, or a chestnut brown will look wonderful. There are also some wonderful burgundies on the market that give your hair brilliance and luster in any type of lighting. They also look great with any skin tone. Choose your coloring wisely to complement your honey-gold, caramel-brown, walnut, cocoa-brown, or ebony skin coloring. If you must experiment with blond and you are not a natural blond, use temporary coloring. Remember, the Lord presented you with the natural gift of awesome coloring, so do not distort it.

This word goes out also for women of Latina, Asian, and Native American descent. Please try to leave your magnificent dark hair the way it is. Nothing man has created can compare with your rich, lovely tresses. If you just have to experiment, try some of the burgundies described above. They will add sensual highlights without detracting from your God-given beauty. Burgundy also blends with your natural skin coloring. Remember, the Lord presented you with the natural gift of awesome skin coloring; remember that when coloring your hair.

You seldom wear your hair in a simple straight style. That would be a little too subdued for you. Finger waves send the independent, Sensual Exotic message that you have arrived. Fluff and curls are also some of your taste delights. Your short hair is always accompanied with crimps and curls. Curls with an extra bounce are exciting and add to your obvious appeal. You even tease them for the appearance of extra body. If your hair is long, fluid curls seem to flow endlessly down your back and glide with your body movements, dancing in the air. One side can easily be pulled back with one your beautiful, exotic hair combs.

Perms that seem to go wrong for others do not bother you because you have a supply of wigs and hairpieces. You use them to frequently change your look. If your hair is short and you want it long, you already have the wig in the right length and color—or you have your stylist weave in extra hair for added effect. Missing a beauty shop appointment is never a problem. You have even been known to wear a wig to bed so your husband will not see your hair unkempt. Getting up an hour early to style your hair or wig is not unusual. It keeps him wondering how you manage to stay so beautiful. If he only knew all that you go through to keep your look.

You always want to look beautiful for him and you work hard at keeping things in that department in order. You know you represent the King of kings and the Lord of lords, even in the way you wear your hair. To you, appearance is a very serious and personal matter. You seek advice from the Expert. The Lord, who made the heavens and earth, serves as your Beautician, and with Him nothing is too difficult.

> *A*h, Lord God! Behold, You have made the heavens and earth by Your great power and outstretched arm. There is nothing too hard for You.
>
> JEREMIAH 32:17

SENSUAL EXOTIC MAKEUP

Electrifying glamour is your trademark. Bright, vivid coloring with extra sizzle sends up Sensual Exotic fireworks. If you wear fuchsia, it will be brilliant fuchsia. If you wear red, it will be dazzling red. All your colors sing your glamorous song and blend with your Sensual Exotic spirit. You are the ultimate glamour girl. You do not like to be seen without your makeup. It is not unusual for you to get up an hour earlier than your spouse so he will not see you without your face on.

Once you have found a look that works, it is hard for you to change. Many times your makeup will be what some consider outdated. Your well-meaning friends have tried to get you to stop wearing your false eyelashes and iridescent lipstick, to no avail. You do not seek the opinion of others and secretly pray they would not offer any unsolicited advice. After all, you do not offer advice to your ultraconservative Harmonic Refined friend. Her safe, sedate plum lipstick suits her. You do not try to stop your Jaunty Esprit friend from wearing her clear lip gloss, and wish she would stop trying to give you advice. Her "natural look" is well suited to her but just too plain for your tastes. Your glamorous tastes suit you just fine. You are perfectly content and confident in your own ability to choose what works best for you. The only other earthly opinion you value is that of your husband, and he loves the way you look.

You do not spend a great deal of money on your colors, since they are usually on sale. No other image type, except perhaps the Creative Poetic, would dare compete with you in this area. That shimmering pink and frosted orange still remain your makeup staples. As long as they are sold, you will continue to wear them. You do not have a loyalty to any one brand. Whoever sells what you like gets your money. You are also smart enough to establish relationships with cosmetics salespeople. They save your unique color preferences and call you for pickup or delivery. When you get them, you find a whole array of Sensual Exotic colors ready to help you create a wondrous look just right for you.

Like your Creative Poetic sister, you use makeup to express your moods. If you are in an exceptionally good mood, you wear your most daring reds. Your cheeks, lips, and even your eyes will send a fiery message. If you are in a more mellow mood, you use smoky plums and misty blues to make your style statement. There are times when your makeup can be considered a little excessive. Analyze your audience before adding your finishing touches. If you are going on a job interview, remember that the person interviewing you may not be a Sensual Exotic and will judge you accordingly. You may want to tone down your usual look.

If you are medium- to dark-skinned, you see your skin as a canvas for your exotic picture. You use brilliant reds, plums, and shining coppers to enhance your radiant dark beauty. Expertly highlighting your ebony, bronze, or olive skin with rich, vibrant coloring is your exotic trademark. Your lips, cheeks, and eyes will be color-brushed with your sensational flair. Deep navy, paradise purple, electric blue, and bronze copper sing your Sensual Exotic song. Fiery colors dance through your palette, and the beauty of your countenance—from café au lait to deepest ebony—shines for all the world to see. You are as beautiful as Queen Esther as she entered the throne room to seek the king's favor in all her Sensual Exotic beauty.

Whether your ethnic heritage is that of the European queen, the Asian empress, the Latina *condesa*, the Native American or Nubian princess, you are an exotic creation of the Most High God. You are ready to speak your language without saying a word. Pray and ask the Lord for guidance with your makeup. He will never steer you in the wrong direction. Listening to Him, you discover what is in store for you around the next corner. In doing so, you are prepared for any situation. He will not desert you. You have His promise.

I will not leave you nor forsake you.
JOSHUA 1:5

I am the rose of Sharon, and the lily of the valleys. Like the lily among thorns, so is my love among the daughters.

Song of Solomon 2:1–2

8. Accepting Who You Are

I will greatly rejoice in the Lord, my soul shall be joyful
in my God; for He has clothed me with the garments
of salvation, He has covered me with the robe of
righteousness, as the bridegroom decks himself with
ornaments, and as a bride adorns herself with her
jewels.

ISAIAH 61:10

I sincerely hope and pray you enjoyed your journey. But wait! It is definitely not over. This is just the beginning. Now that you've discovered the beauty of your image type and your Bible sisters', you are ready to share those discoveries with other women. Now that you have the information, you have a responsibility to use it. God has given you a great gift. This gift will put your life on a new course and set you free, if you allow it to do so. It will open the bolted doors of your life and air out the cobwebs of depression, oppression, and strife. Now that you know who you are, you no longer have an identity crisis.

An identity crisis is a dangerous thing. It robs you of your self-respect and vision. It keeps you in bondage because you do not know who you are or where you are going. As a wife, mother, or even as a friend, other people look to you for guidance and advice. When you do not have a clue about your own whereabouts, how can you help someone else? It is like the blind leading the blind. The enemy loves it when you cannot see. He loves it when you stumble and bump into the walls of sin. He laughs when you cannot see the way of escape the Lord provided.

What you have just read is a way of escape. The Lord has not only given you a way of escape, but reaffirmed your identity as well. You are His lovely daughter, and nothing can change that. You now have confirmation that you belong to Him. This makes you a free woman, and you are dangerous to your enemy because you are free. You are now free to share with your sisters and free to be the woman God created you to be. You now have an obligation to use the information contained in these pages to enhance your life and the lives of those around you. By sharing, you become stronger in the knowledge just presented to you. Use this knowledge to restore everything stolen from you by accepting who you are. Use it to educate other women so they, too, can experience the joy of knowing they are daughters of the King.

Knowing that it is wonderful for you to wear sweats and be comfortable is Jaunty Esprit freedom. Accepting your tailored slacks and jacket as appropriate to grocery shop is beautifully Harmonic Refined. Entering a room wearing a dramatic shawl and matching hat is not showing off, but is Elegant Flamboyant and dramatically all you. Being and doing the unexpected according to your moods is Creative Poetic freedom and wonderfully you. Wearing floral-print, antique lace dresses is softly Chantilly Graceful and romantically all you. Your angora sweater with swags of sequins and beading, and a leather skirt with a side-seam zipper, lets everyone know you are beautifully Sensual Exotic. God made every woman in His image and beautiful to behold.

Always ask yourself if you are walking in the freedom of the image type God provided in the pages of His word and in this book. If you can say yes without hesitation, then you have your answer. If there is any hint of doubt or question in your mind, then seek the Father about your choice. You should never have to struggle over an outfit to make it work. Be led by the Holy Spirit when selecting your clothing and you will never go wrong. You will be as a pleasing, sweet fragrance to your heavenly Father.

> *A*ll Your garments are scented with myrrh and aloes and cassia, out of the ivory palaces, by which they have made You glad.
>
> Psalms 45:8

As women, we must educate ourselves to stay ready for the unexpected. The Lord does not want us to be ignorant. Ignorance breeds envy, strife, and fear. These things eat away at our spirits like unrestrained cancers. They leave gaping holes in our walls of defense and give the enemy openings. We experience these openings when we decide to leave jobs, churches, and friends because we feel unwelcome or someone offended us. Without letting others know how we feel, we exit stage left and move on to the next play. We do not realize that the Lord will allow us to experience the same thing again until we learn to deal with these situations His way. He will allow us to pick up a script for the next play and be chosen for the same part again until we learn His lesson. His lesson is that we must learn to walk in who we are and be bold enough to confront life's situations. We leave gaping holes in our life's walls when we respond in ways that hurt.

The holes are there when we stop speaking to people because they said something to offend us. We do not let them know they offended us. We leave and discuss the situation with others, creating more conflict, depositing more trash in someone else's life. We never stop to think that they, too, are experiencing difficulties. We never stop to think because of our own selfishness. When others make decisions that do not suit us or even when we do not get our way in a situation, the enemy is smiling when our responses cause further discord and strife.

He knows that if he can keep our focus on our own selfish desires, he has won. He knows that if he can keep our eyes on the problem, then we make his job easier. Our focus must be on how the Lord handles things and not on the actions of others. What did Jesus do when He saw things that displeased Him? He prayed to the Father. Then, being led by the Holy Spirit to act, He acted. That is what you and I must do. We must ask ourselves, in every situation, what Jesus would do or say. The Lord knew this would not be easy for us, so He promised to help. He will not leave or forsake us. Remember, He bought us with a price. We are not our own.

> *F*or you were bought with a price, therefore glorify God in your body and in your spirit which are God's.
>
> I CORINTHIANS 6:20

His help also extends to your appearance. What is the Father saying you should wear today? He is faithful and will guide you to wisely choose acceptable clothing that fits your image type and any given situation, if you call on Him. He wants you to be comfortable with your image type. He wants you to be free. When He helps you choose your clothing, you will not only like what you wear, but also feel wonderful. Do you know why? He knows you and your image type like no one else. He is the Creator of all things, including image types. He loves His Jaunty Esprit, Harmonic Refined, Elegant Flamboyant, Creative Poetic, Chantilly Graceful, and Sensual Exotic daughters with a passion that cannot be defined in finite human terms.

Have you ever noticed that when trouble comes, it becomes the focal point of our lives? No matter how hard we try to fix things, the worse they seem to get. Trouble becomes an obsession and takes on a life of its own. As we lie down to sleep, it taps us on the shoulder and reminds us to include it in our dreams. When we get up in the morning, trouble is sitting on the foot of the bed waiting to greet us as we begin our day. It drools out the day's instructions and wets our spirits with its ugliness. As we go to our closet, it taunts us and tells us lies about how we look and how we feel. We allow trouble to permeate every second, minute, and hour of our lives. It is as if we embrace the darkness and let it have its way. We allow oppression to take control of our lives. Once it takes over in one area, it is easy for the rest to follow. These focal points then become stumbling blocks that keep us from discovering our real purpose.

A distorted self-image can easily become a stumbling block. It hinders us from having a closer walk with the Lord. These blocks also cause blurred spiritual vision. Just as a physical cataract overtakes the eye, so these blocks or spiritual cataracts overtake our spiritual vision. When you depend on your own abilities, the harder you try to see, the worse your vision becomes. As your vision becomes more blurred, the enemy applies more pressure. Your response to this pressure will determine your end.

When you allow the Lord to surgically remove the spiritual cataracts, you begin to see yourself as an honorable woman with clear vision. After your surgery, you heal and get on with the business of doing the Lord's will. When you accept yourself, you experience something wonderful called freedom. Your focus automatically changes so you can take your place in His royal court. You then stand before Him in the beauty of your image type. Your focus will be on the One who came to set you free, the Lord Jesus. When He becomes the center of your life, you experience a deep peace that anoints your hurts like a healing balm. Suddenly, the things of this world, including those stumbling blocks, become distant and not as important as you once thought. You are then able to leave them in His capable hands, knowing that nothing is too complicated for your Lord. You are able to stand boldly before the King and take your rightful place of honor—the place of honor bought and paid for at Calvary.

> **K**ing's daughters are among Your honorable women. At your right hand stands the queen in gold from Ophir.
>
> PSALMS 45:9

He created you for such a time as this. In your home, work-place, church, and school, you can make a difference for the Lord. That is the reason the enemy loves it when you embrace a dis-torted self-image. You must extend your hand to your sister Jaunty Esprit, Harmonic Refined, Elegant Flamboyant, Creative Poetic, Chantilly Graceful, and Sensual Exotic. If you do not, who will? He created you to draw others to Him. You are a beauti-ful instrument, who in His hands becomes fine-tuned for the Master's purpose. His purpose is that every woman should come to know who she is. Your sisters will be lost if you do not speak up and extend your hand.

Do you remember the pain and emptiness of your life before coming to the Lord? Stop right now and think back for just a mo-ment. Where would you be today if someone had not stopped and shared the news of the kingdom with you? Do you remember the feeling of release you experienced when you first heard that Jesus came to set you free so you could spend eternity with Him in His kingdom? If you can remember, then you will also realize that you have an obligation to share this freedom with others. You are under royal authority to do so.

Just like the Syro-Phoenician woman who astounded Jesus with her humility and wisdom, you make the choice to accept who you are. Just like the woman with the issue of blood, healing is yours by believing what God's word says about you. You have access not only to the hem of His garment, but to His blood, to His power, and to His ear that is ever open to your prayers. He loves you so much that He now sits at the right hand of the Fa-ther making intercession for you.

Like Mary, one of the most spiritually sensitive women of the New Testament, you, too, can honor the Lord. She anointed the Master's feet, gaining full access to Him. She recognized that He and He alone could heal, by just speaking a word. You, too, can anoint Him with your praises just as He anointed you with

His precious first gift. He longs to heal and purge your life and prepare you for the task at hand. You have His promise.

> *L*isten, O daughter, consider and incline your ear; forget your own people also and your father's house; so the King will greatly desire your beauty; because He is your Lord, worship Him.
>
> PSALMS 45:10–11

It is now time to tear down the strong holds of miscommunication. By accepting your inheritance, you honor the Lord. When you begin to see yourself as something other than His daughter, you deny His supreme sacrifice. By accepting and using your gifts, and by allowing others to do the same, you magnify the Lord.

It is time to tear down the walls of racism, envy, strife, oppression, and depression. It is time to forgive others for the pain they have caused in your life. Forgive them and your healing begins. The Lord is calling us to unity, and this unity begins with you. He will wash away your pain and make you whole. Only He can renew your spirit and heal the wounds no one else can see, but you feel. All you have to do is allow Him into your heart. All you have to do is believe and receive your healing. All you have to do is accept His gift. Once you forgive, you can truly experience freedom. You experience a freedom only Jesus can bring. He waits patiently for you to receive Him. He is your Lord, and He waits patiently for you to enter into His presence. He waits for you to hear His voice as He gently whispers your name.

It is my hope and prayer that you have read this book and become free. Free from the bondage of not accepting yourself as beautifully and wonderfully made. Free from the captivity of not accepting others who are beautifully and wonderfully different from you. Without this freedom, your life will be a life of struggle. God wants you to live victoriously. He already won the battle for you. I pray that you have discovered how He longs to use you and your individual image type to glorify Him. I pray that you are now free to be who He intended you to be.

This is the reason for your existence. He gave you His precious first gift, His magnificent image. He created you to intimately fellowship with Him and to serve in His royal court. He created you to be a daughter of the King!

Afterword

If you read this book and now realize that you need a change in your life, you will find the answer in the following prayer and verses of Scripture. All the people who live now, all those who lived in the past, and all who will ever live in the future are in need of a Savior. The Lord Jesus came to earth so that we could have life and have that life more abundantly. Pray this prayer and you have His promise that He will become Lord of your life and give you the gift of eternal life.

> Lord Jesus, I confess that I am a sinner and I need a Savior. Please, Lord, forgive me for my sins. I believe that You died on the cross at Calvary, where You shed Your precious blood. I believe that on the third day, You rose from the dead and You are now seated on the right hand of God the Father, making intercession for me. Lord Jesus, please take control and become Lord of my life, so that I can live with You for all eternity. I thank You for the precious gift of salvation according to Your Holy Word.

> That if you confess with your mouth the Lord Jesus and believe in your heart that God has raised Him from the dead, you will be saved.
>
> ROMANS 10:9

If you prayed that prayer, the angels in heaven are celebrating. Yes, they are throwing a heavenly party. Jesus said:

> *L*ikewise, I say to you, there is joy in the presence of the angels of God over one sinner who repents.
>
> LUKE 15:10

Please write and let us share in your joy of this newfound life in Christ Jesus.

Daughters of the King Ministries, Inc.
PO Box 71017
Durham, NC 27722-1017
E-mail: info@daughtersoftheking.org
Web site: http://www.daughtersoftheking.org

Bibliography

All of the Women of the Bible, by Edith Deen. Harper and Row Publishers, 1988.

Illustrated Dictionary of Bible Manners and Customs, edited by A. Van Deursen. Bell Publishing, 1967.

The Lion Encyclopedia of the Bible, edited by Pat Alexander. Readers Digest Association, with permission of Lion Publishing Corp., 1987.

The Open Bible, Expanded Edition; The New King James Version. Thomas Nelson Publishers, 1983.

The Compact Bible Dictionary, edited by T. Alston Bryant. Regency Library, Zondervan Publishers, 1967.

Webster's Third International Dictionary of the English Language with Seven Language Dictionary, volumes 1–3. Encyclopedia Britannica, Inc.

The New Strong's Exhaustive Concordance of the Bible, by James Strong, LLD, STD. Thomas Nelson Publishers, 1990.

Lord, I Want to Know You, by Kay Arthur. Multnomah Press, 1992.

About the Author

*I*dentity! Purpose! Destiny! When you hear Dr. Gail Hayes speak or read her writings, you will discover your identity, grasp your purpose, and fulfill your destiny!

When looking for a speaker or writer who ignites your spirit and creates an atmosphere of inspiration, motivation, and contagious enthusiasm, you have but to look directly at Dr. Gail Hayes—or Dr. Gail, as others affectionately call her. Her up-front, in-your-face, in-your-heart style of delivery leaves audiences panting for more and challenged to act on goals and dreams unfulfilled.

A gifted and much-sought-after communicator, Dr. Gail delivers messages that provoke others to action. She is bold, creative, amusing, serious, compassionate, and wise, all within the first ten minutes of her presentations. During her sessions, audiences laugh, cry, and come to a deeper understanding of God's purpose for their lives. She believes that once people discover their identity and walk in their purpose, they obtain joy unspeakable for their life's journey.

As the daughter and wife of US military veterans, Dr. Gail lived in the Far East for five years and in Europe for more than ten years. These experiences allow her to relate to diverse audiences. While in Europe, she founded and served as the director of the European Executive Women's Forum, the first active European network of the National Association for Female Executives (NAFE). She also served on the board of directors and executive councils of various organizations in Europe and in the United States.

Dr. Gail is an ordained minister, an accomplished vocalist, and the author of several books, including *Daughters of the King* and *My Vision Journal*. She is a columnist for several publications and also serves as the editor of *The Crown*, an online newsletter read by women around the world. Her writing appears in the anthology *God Allows U-Turns: A Woman's Journey* from Barbour Publishing.

Dr. Gail has appeared on the national television networks QVC, Total Christian Television (TCT), and the Christian Television Network (CTN). She also produced and hosted "Daughters of the King" television and radio programs. Dr. Gail holds a BS in criminal justice, an MA in public relations, and a PhD in counseling from Canterbury University.

She and her family currently live in Durham, North Carolina. To schedule Dr. Gail to speak to your group, contact:

Dr. Gail M. Hayes
PO Box 71017
Durham, NC 27722-1017
E-mail: gmhayes@mindspring.com
Web site: http://www.daughtersoftheking.org

Reading Group
Guide

Reading Group Guide

1. Have you ever done a personality profile before (e.g., Meyers-Briggs, Personality Plus, birth order, etc.)? In general, what do you think about such assessment tools? Do you find them useful and accurate? Fascinating or annoying? Why?

2. Take the inventory. Were your responses uniformly one type, or did you have a mix across the types? If your inventory shows mixed results, which is your dominant type? What other type or types comprises your personality?

3. In what contexts or environments do you "code-switch" between image types or styles? At home, at work, at church? Do you shift based on your mood or your comfort level with the people around you? Do the shifts feel natural ("heart choice") or forced ("head choice," based on others' expectations or requirements)?

4. How closely do you identify with the opening questions characterizing your type? How strongly do you resonate with the name of your dominant image type (e.g., Jaunty Esprit, Harmonic Refined, Elegant Flamboyant, etc.)?

5. The first area explored for each image type is "The Inner You," which describes some of the foundational strengths and weaknesses of each type. As with the specifics noted in the Image Indicator questions, consider the essential tendencies (more than the specific details) that give rise to the choices, reactions, or responses described for your dominant type. To what extent do you recognize the qualities of your dominant type in yourself?

6. Can you see yourself filling the roles in the church (or in the workplace) that the author identifies for your dominant image type? Why or why not? (Maybe you are already filling such a role! If so, how do you see your strengths maximized by your position or vocation?)

7. The second area explored is "Family Life." The author focuses primarily on relationships with children and spouse. What about relationships with parents, close friends, and extended family? How do you see your image type manifested in those relationships? What insights do you glean for improving your relationships through a better understanding of your own type?

8. The author only briefly mentions the interpersonal dynamics of one image type relating to another image type in the family circle (e.g., a Chantilly Graceful mother relating to a Jaunty Esprit daughter). How might better understanding of your spouse, child, or friend's image type benefit your relationship with that loved one? What current relational challenges have been illuminated by discovering your own image type?

9. In the section on each image type's spousal relationship, the author focuses only on the woman's style and expectations—not on the man's individual responses that arise out of his own personality. To what extent does such an approach offer helpful assessment? How accurately does this perspective reflect your own marriage/relationship experience?

10. The author explores each image type's working style. Were you able to recognize the different image types in your employer, staff, or co-workers? How might a better understanding of your own brand of professionalism benefit you (and your organization) in the workplace?

11. In each chapter's section titled "The Outer You," the author considers clothing, hairstyles and coloring, makeup, and jewelry. How accurate were her descriptions of your current fashion preferences? How helpful were her suggestions for change, whether to add more drama or color or to tone down an already flamboyant or exotic style to accommodate more conservative contexts?

12. The author talks about the "art of camouflage," especially for the more dramatic image types. She offers assurance that such camouflage is not deceitful but discerning, recognizing the need to accommodate others (e.g., in the workplace or in the church), lest we become stumbling blocks—to ourselves and to other people. Do you agree or disagree? Why and to what extent?

13. Consider the three biblical case studies offered by the author for each image type. Do you recognize the qualities of that type in each woman? Why or why not? To what extent do you identify with the biblical women associated with your dominant type?

14. Overall, with which traits in your dominant image type did you strongly identify? With which traits did you "part company"? Why?

15. Whom do you know who fits each image type? What insights about her character and style have you gleaned from this book?

16. "When you accept yourself, you experience something wonderful called freedom," Dr. Hayes exhorts. What do you think she means by that? What kind of freedom?

17. In what way might identifying our image type or types boost our self-image and contribute positively to who we are in the world?

18. How can personal self-assessments influence our relationships with other people—with God, with other women, with our family members, with co-workers or employers? (What light does a Scripture such as Matthew 22:39 shed on this question—to love your neighbor *as yourself?*)